goin' back to memphis

goin' back to

memphis

A

Century

of

Blues,

Rock 'n' Roll,

and

Glorious

Soul

James Dickerson

Schirmer Books
An Imprint of Simon & Schuster Macmillan
New York

Prentice Hall International
London Mexico City New Delhi Singapore Sydney Toronto

Schirmer Books
An Imprint of Simon & Schuster Macmillan
1633 Broadway
New York, New York 10019

Book Design: Rob Carangelo

Library of Congress Catalog Card Number: 96-6336

Printed in the United States of America

Printing Number
1 2 3 4 5 6 7 8 9 10

Library of Congress Cataloging-in-Publication Data

Dickerson, James.
    Goin' back to Memphis : a century of blues, rock 'n' roll, and glorious soul / James Dickerson.
        p.   cm.
    Includes bibliographical references and index.
    ISBN 0-02-864506-5 (alk. paper)
    1. Rock music—History and criticism. 2. Blues (Music)—History and criticism. 3. Soul Music—History and criticism. I. Title:
Going back to Memphis
ML3470.D52 1996
781.64'0973'0904—dc20   96-6336
                                                                CIP
                                                                MN

This paper meets the requirements of ANSI/NISO Z.39.48-1992 (Permanence of Paper).

For My Mother

contents

acknowledgments

I would like to thank the following for helping in big (and small) ways during the ten years it took to research this book and, in some instances, for offering encouragement and friendship along the way: my editor, Richard Carlin, and my publisher, Paul Boger, Rachel E. Dwyer, Bill Laing, Dr. Berkley Kalin (University of Memphis), Susan McCaskill, Janet McCaskill, Jennifer McCaskill, Jeff McAdory, Steve Gardner, Dawn Baldwin, Kim Spangler, Dave Darnell, Nancy Randall, Scotty Moore, Jim Stewart, Bobby Manuel, Johnny Cash, Jack Clement, T. G. Sheppard, Jerry Lee Lewis, Carl Perkins, Sam Phillips, Vicki Hein, David Vincent, Emmo Hein, Jim Dickinson, Chips Moman, Toni Moman, Casey Moman, Jim Howe, Andrea Kruse, B. B. King, Polly Walker, Willie Mitchell, Henry Nelson, Ron Olsen, Rufus Thomas, Carla Thomas, Bobby Bland, Estelle Axton, Klaudia Kroboth, Becky Russell, Wayne Russell, Rick Blackburn, Sharon Gary, Kerrie Lewis, Dick Hackett, Stacey Lehman, Beth Dooley, Michelle Hargis, George Hays, Greg Campbell, Sunshine Sonny Payne, Monique Moman, Don Nix, Memphis/Shelby County Public Library, the Center for Southern Folklore, Ed Frank and Cathy Evans of the Mississippi Valley Collection at the University of Memphis, and Angus McEachran, editor of *The Commercial Appeal*, for permission to quote from stories I wrote while at the newspaper.

FOUR HORSEMEN IN SEARCH
OF AN APOCALYPSE

ohnny Cash, Jerry Lee Lewis, Roy Orbison, and Carl Perkins filed into the cramped trailer with the solemnity of pallbearers. Waiting for them at the soundboard with the quiet patience of a schoolmaster was record producer Chips Moman. In the dimly lit room the four music legends stood with their backs to the wall as engineer David Cherry pushed the button that sent the reels whirling.

"We Remember the King," goes the song, a gospel-blues ballad that celebrates Jesus—or Elvis Presley, depending on your point of reference. As it played, the four stood in stony silence. It had been thirty years since any of them had recorded in Memphis. When the song ended, they stood stock-still, paralyzed by the moment. Finally, Perkins spoke.

"Well, fellows, it has taken thirty years for me to look all three of you in the eyes and say this, but I've got to get it out of my soul," said Perkins, his voice low and resonant. "I love all three of you and you won't ever be without a true friend as long as I'm living."

All four men wept.

"If you outlive me," he continued, "I want you to sing a verse of this when I'm gone. If you do, I might just raise up out of the box and help you sing it."

The four men embraced, the tears flowing freely. The recording session had taken its toll, but then, rock 'n' roll had taken its toll on

Class of '55 session. L to r: Carl Perkins, Jerry Lee Lewis, Roy Orbison, and Johnny Cash at American Studios on the final day.
Photo by Dave Darnell

all four men over the years. Each had his share of problems. Each somehow had survived. No one could have known then that the clock was ticking for Orbison.

"We've got to pull ourselves together," said Moman, his cheeks streaked with tears.

Like smooching teenagers caught in the sudden glare of a porch light, the men broke apart. Cash, the most aloof of the four, returned to the hotel. Orbison, the shy one, sought refuge in his bus. Lewis sat on the steps of the trailer with Perkins standing over him.

"Jerry, you know and I know how it hurts to lose someone you love," said Perkins. "I want you to remember these words: when you're running from God, He's crying just like you are now."

Jerry looked up at Perkins, his face expressionless. "You really do love me, don't you?"

"You'd better believe it. I always have."

In the early years, when the King and the Four Horsemen reigned over American music, Memphis music was the life force of teenage rebellion. It influenced clothing styles, created movie idols, helped end a war in Vietnam, and eventually changed the politics of a nation unaccustomed to listening to the voices of youth. By 1985, three decades after that rebellion had been hatched in the tiny studio of Sam Phillips's Sun Records, popular music had gone through many cycles, as had the artists who invented it, but seldom had the music, or the artists who created it, ever returned to its birthplace.

The *Class of '55* session, which took place in September 1985, was unique for a number of reasons. First, Moman had arranged with Dick Clark Productions to videotape the session. Gene Weed, vice president of Dick Clark Productions, said it was the first time a recording session had ever been taped from start to finish: "We think the marriage of the two—recording and television—could not only be a revival for the music situation in Memphis, but a revival for music on television."

The second thing that made it unique was the mass of high-tech equipment brought to the session. Obviously, the equipment that remained in the old studio was outdated. Moman brought in an eighteen-wheeler with a trailer loaded with the latest digital equipment and parked it outside the studio. Microphones were set up inside the studio and the wires run outside to the trailer, where Moman sat at the recording board with the sound engineer. Moman communicated with the Four Horsemen by using a speaker-and-microphone system. Technically, the music would be created inside the studio, but recorded outside in the trailer. The television crew of seventeen had a second truck packed with video equipment.

On the first day, when the Four Horsemen walked into the 18-by-29-foot studio, they were surrounded by television and newspaper photographers. The air was electric. The four men bounced off one another like energized cartoon figures in a video game. When Cash entered with his wife, June Carter, he walked up to Lewis and kissed him on the forehead. Lewis, seated at a microphone, looked stunned. He isn't what you'd call a touch-feely kind of guy. He smiled, looking pleased but slightly embarrassed.

After a minimum amount of polite conversation the four men gathered at the piano and clowned around for the cameras as Lewis pounded the ivories with his customary flare. It was good public relations, and that evening CNN and the three major networks all carried footage of the reunion. But the television lights had raised the temperature of the room considerably, and by the time the media left, the four men were exhausted. Moman asked the quartet to rehearse one of the songs. After a few bars, Lewis screwed up and called out for the others to stop.

"What are you trying to do to me?" he said to Cash.

"What do you mean?" Cash asked, puzzled.

"I idolize you and you make me nervous," Lewis said, laughing.

Cash shook his head, embarrassed by the compliment.

Once the rehearsal was completed, Moman called it a day and sent everyone home. Moman and I retreated to a nearby pancake house. His eyes sparkled with excitement. What impressed him most that day was the respect the Four Horsemen had shown Sam Phillips. "All four of them still call him Mr. Phillips," he noted with amazement. "That says a lot for these guys."

■　●　■

Tuesday got off to a wobbly start. Cash abruptly left town because of a family illness, and Orbison stayed shut up in his hotel room all day. Perkins and Lewis returned to the studio, bursting with energy. Lewis began the session with "Keep My Motor Running." At age forty-nine, Lewis was trim and wiry. With Lewis and the band inside the studio and Moman outside in the truck, the session began. Several times Lewis made mistakes on the piano and the music had to be stopped. Lewis was concerned his playing would not be up to par for the band.

"The guitar is playing lead, but I'll be playing piano—and you know me, if I put a lick in, just call me down on it," Lewis said to Moman.

Moman told him not to worry about it, to just keep playing.

Toward the end of the day, Moman suggested Lewis sing a ballad, "Sixteen Candles." Lewis tried the song while wearing earphones, then complained they got in the way. "I can't cut with earphones," he said, laughing. "That's faking it." Without earphones, Lewis gave a flawless performance. One of the musicians later commented he had never heard Lewis sound better. A string of personal tragedies, including the deaths of two wives and a son—and a serious tear in the lining of his stomach in 1982—may have scarred his body and his spirit, but it had left no mark on his art. Lewis was still, well . . . the Killer.

After knocking down "Sixteen Candles," Moman called a break and everyone fled to the back parking lot for a breath of fresh air. After pacing the parking lot for a few minutes and throwing pulled punches at friends, the hyperactive Lewis said he thought "Sixteen Candles" had the best feel of any song he had recorded since "Whole Lotta Shakin'."

"I usually do my records in one cut, but Chips wanted three," Lewis said. "It was a blessing for this man to record me. Anything he says to me, Jerry Lee Lewis ain't going to argue with. Playing in there again gave me a great feeling. Nothing could ever hold me back in that studio."

I brought out a small tape recorder, one I had used many times to interview Lewis. Suddenly, Lewis snapped. His eyes glazed and fixed in place, resembling cat's eye marbles. He grabbed the tape recorder and tried to pull it out of my hand. The strap had looped around my finger and I could not have turned it loose if I had wanted to. For what seemed like an eternity, Lewis and I scuffled, elbow to elbow, our feet grating against the gravel of the parking lot as we went round and round. Lewis's manager ran across the parking lot, calling out Lewis's name.

Lewis never demanded the tape recorder. He never said a word. He just grappled for it, his eyes fierce with determination. Inexplicably, he began biting the tape recorder. Sparks flew from his demonic eyes. Abruptly, the strap broke and the battery cover pulled off, ending the altercation. I had the recorder; he had the cover. He tossed it to me and retreated to the other side of the parking lot with his manager, J. W. Whitten. They spoke for a few moments, then Whitten returned. "Jerry wants to apologize, " he says. "He'd like to buy you a new tape recorder."

"That's not necessary. It's not broken."

Whitten reported back to Lewis. After a few minutes of conversation, he returned. "Jerry really feels bad," he said. "He'd like to buy you a couple of new recorders. That way, you'll have a spare." I shook my head. Forget it.

Whitten went back to Lewis. After a few minutes, he came back with a new offer. "Jerry wants to buy you a hundred new recorders," he said. His eyes pleaded, as if screaming out, "Please, for God's sake!" Again, I shook my head. Whitten relayed that message to Lewis, who threw up his arms and paced. By then, it was time to return to the studio. Lewis came over and shook hands with me. "I'm sorry, man," he said.

"Don't worry about it," I told him, and then changed the subject. How did it feel to be back in Sun? "It beats playing in the rain," Lewis said, laughing. The joke was his way of getting back on track. "No, it gave me a great feeling. I knew I should have been back in that studio all the time. Chips Moman knew it. These fellows knew it. And you knew it."

Interestingly, a few weeks later I saw him do that "eye thing" again. I was seated at a table in the bar at the Peabody Hotel with a small group of people. Lewis entered the room and joined the party. He sat next to me. He was in a good mood and his conversation was animated. We talked a while, then after about thirty minutes he suddenly turned to me and looked me squarely in the face. His eyes fixated, giving off sparks.

"Who are you?" he asked, looking puzzled.

Earlier I had noticed the handle of a snub-nosed, .38-caliber pistol protruding from his back pocket. That information, along with the sudden return of his demonic eyes, convinced me it was time to go home. It wasn't the pistol that bothered me. It was the eyes.*

*Years later, I consulted a psychologist about Lewis's symptoms. He said it sounded like Lewis might have had an epileptic seizure. That was reasonable. Lewis had a history of drug abuse, but I saw no indication of it on that day (although a magazine journalist later reported she had seen pills spill from his shirt pocket).

Everyone in the music business carried a gun in those days. People felt a little more comfortable if they were packing a piece. Usually with good reason. Moman carried a palm-sized .25 automatic in his back pocket. Once Moman and I were sitting outside his downtown recording studio at midnight, enjoying the celestial fireworks of a summer sky. Moman was on his big Harley, reclining against the handlebars. I sat in a chair a few feet behind him. As we talked, a black youth crossed the street and walked in our direction. He pulled a razor from his pocket and flipped it into the air, eying us with a menacing stare. Moman's hand eased into his back pocket. Luckily, the youth stopped flipping the razor and walked on past.

I once asked Moman about his pistol.

"I'll take a whipping," he said. "I'm man enough to take a whipping. But I'm not gonna let anybody kill me. That's the only time I would use it—if somebody was gonna kill me."

■　●　■

Carl Perkins was next up in the studio. Like the others, the fifty-three-year-old had had his share of personal misfortunes. Drug abuse or the deaths of loved ones were common threads through the lives of all Four Horsemen. Like the others, Perkins's career was plagued by periods of public neglect. In 1955 he had been on his way to New York for an appearance on the *Perry Como Show*, where he was to receive a gold record for his hit "Blue Suede Shoes," when he was almost killed in a car accident near Wilmington, Delaware. After the accident his career languished, and by the early 1960s he was ready to quit show business. Following Perkins's European tour with Chuck Berry in the early '60s, the Beatles recorded three of his songs, which in turn led to a series of concerts and new albums for Perkins. Still, despite an active concert schedule, it had been a long time since he had had a hit record.

Back in Sun Studios again in 1985, he showed none of the scars of thirty years of hard living and neglect. As comfortable as a country preacher at a church picnic, he mixed well with the musicians and the others in the studio, glad-handing his way around the room. He had been born again, and he knew it, and he was damned grateful. Before the session began, he walked about the room, almost in a daze, looking at the pictures on the walls. He told me about the first time he had walked into the studio.

"I left my two brothers and a drummer sitting out in a 1940 Plymouth," he said. "We had a bass tied on top in a nine-foot cotton sack. When I walked in I guess Marion [the receptionist] could tell I was a hungry picker.

"She said, 'If you came to audition, I'm sorry. Mr. Phillips isn't listening to anyone. We've got this boy called Elvis and he's real hot.'

"I said, 'I know.'

"I looked around. There was a life-size cardboard likeness of him. I said, 'Is that Elvis?'

"She said it was.

"I said, 'God, he's pretty.' And he was. He was a handsome dude."

Perkins is soft-spoken in conversation, but when he picks up a guitar and sings, his language has a raw energy to it that is anything but soft. He sang two songs. The second, "Birth of Rock and Roll," used the same hot guitar licks that had mesmerized George Harrison two decades earlier. Of the Four Horsemen, Perkins was still the consummate rocker.

When time came for Orbison to arrive at the studio, the musicians set up, but Orbison did not show. Moman explained to reporters that Orbison had picked up a virus. Actually, Orbison had been traumatized the day before, not just by the camera lights and the media commotion, but by the presence of the other Horsemen. He felt out of place; he had never belonged to the same musical club, and he felt intimidated by the familiarity shared by the others. They were Southerners, bound by a common devotion to the gritty twang of the guitar; he was a Texan, a crooner who dreamed of sophisticated musical arrangements. Some of their best work had been done at Sun; his best work came after he left Sun.

Eventually, Orbison showed up, several hours late, looking pale and nervous. He sang the first few bars of a song he had co-written, "Coming Home," then he left for the hotel, complaining of a sore throat. He had spent less than fifteen minutes at the studio.

Johnny Cash returned to Memphis on Wednesday. Dressed in black, he arrived at the studio early, ambling into the room and engaging in playful banter with the musicians and technicians. He picked up an acoustic guitar and sang a song that mentioned Jack Clement, Sam Phillips's right-hand man in the old days. Like everyone else, Clement had moved to Nashville, where he had enjoyed a successful career as a producer and song publisher. At the precise moment Clement's name was uttered in the song, Clement himself walked into the studio. He had come to play rhythm guitar on Cash's session. Everyone in the studio grinned. Seeing the grins, Cash turned and stood face to face with Clement. He burst into laughter.

With his sleeves rolled up to his elbows, Cash hammered out the lyrics to a song he had written, "Home of the Blues." Beneath the music, the

Class of '55 session. L to r: Perkins, Cash, and Orbison (Lewis is in the background behind piano) at Sun Studios on the first day.
Photo by Dave Darnell

drumbeat shuffled, a night train without a whistle. As Cash sang, a distant look came over his eyes, as if he were singing the song to himself. Perhaps he was. When he felt he had the song nailed down, he stepped up to the microphone. The tape rolled. Suddenly, the room was quiet but for the acoustic licks of the pickers and the steady rolling beat of the drums. When the song ended, Moman's voice boomed from a speaker: "That sounds good, John."

"Well, let's put it on the radio," joked Cash.

Cash left the studio, which by that time had become unbearably hot from the camera lights, and walked outside to the truck. He shook hands with everyone inside the cramped space. In the dim light, the interior of the truck resembled a control center for NASA. There were enough blinking lights, dials, and levers to put a rocket into orbit. Moman played the song back for Cash. It was a take, but just to be certain the film crew had enough angles for the television special, he asked Cash to go through it once again.

Later, Perkins came in to sing a duet with Cash. The song, "Waymore's Blues," had been written out by Waylon Jennings in longhand on a sheet of notebook paper. Cash and Perkins tried to read the handwriting but kept stumbling over the words. Finally, Gene Weed volunteered to type the song so it would be easier for them to read. He put a typewriter on a cardboard box and pecked at the keyboard while the band stood around and waited impatiently in the hot studio.

Using the typewritten lyric sheet, Cash and Perkins went through the song again. At the end of the song, Moman's voice broke the silence: "That could use a little more fire in it. It seems to lack energy."

"We'll try it," Cash said.

With his guitar slung high up under his arm, Cash arched his back, then twisted at the waist and spun his face down to the microphone, his voice rumbling like a distant train on the tracks, sparks flying. "Early one morning it was drizzling rain," he sang. "Around the curve came a Memphis train." Perkins, hands on hips, twisted and swayed as he sang on background. Occasionally during the song, their eyes met and they smiled. Beneath their voices, the drum shuffled, steady and unrelenting. Moman got his fire and then some.

Playing rhythm guitar on the song was Marty Stuart. Later he would become a country music star in his own right, but at that time he was just another picker. Well, not exactly. Not only was he a member of Cash's touring band, he was married to his daughter.

"It's like watching two brothers work together," Stuart said, motioning toward Cash and Perkins. "Take the Everly Brothers. They can go fifteen years without singing together, then they can get together and sing like brothers again. John and Carl are the same way. They know each other's limitations and they know what each other is capable of doing."

During the session Perkins gave Stuart a surprise gift: a Fender Stratocaster guitar, the guitar he used in the session. On the back of the guitar he wrote, "There is a great song in this guitar and you're just the cat to get it out." Stuart was dumbfounded. Later I asked Perkins why he had given Stuart the guitar. Perkins smiled. "He just had that look in his eye and I wanted him to have it."

Orbison and Lewis stayed away from the studio the entire day, while Moman concentrated his efforts on Cash and Perkins. For most of the day, Cash was surprisingly low-keyed and kept to himself. By the time the session that day was completed, everyone was exhausted. Later that night, sitting in the Gridiron Restaurant, across the street from the Peabody, Moman and his studio musicians talked about the session over scrambled eggs and grits. Bacon sizzled in the background. At a nearby table, a man wearing a set of plastic eyes attached to ten-inch springs stared at Moman.

"This album is an extremely important part of history," said Moman. "Sun Studio is a monument to music. It's not just history. It's a monument. It's important to me personally because I looked up to these guys for years. Our lives ran parallel, but we never got involved. Then down at the crossroads we met."

The man with the plastic eyes dashed from the restaurant and returned moments later flashing a blackjack. Moman's bodyguard, a decorated Vietnam veteran named Frank, was already on edge after a full day of keeping the peace at the studio. When he spotted the man with the blackjack, he watched his every move, ready to pounce into action.

At the end of a full course of eggs and grits, Moman and the band rose to leave the restaurant. As they approached the cash register, the man with the plastic eyes leaped from his chair and hurried over to Moman's plate. There was a moment of uncertainty. Was he going to attack someone with the blackjack? With his eyes glued to Moman, the man with the plastic eyes scooped up the food left on Moman's plate, packing his face with the leftovers, his eyes black and hollow.

■　●　■

On Thursday the session moved to American Sound Studio, the former location of Moman's American Recording Studios. Dreary and in disrepair, the windowless studio looked old and tired. Nonetheless, it brought back warm memories to Moman and the band. "There's something magic about it," said guitarist Reggie Young. After listening to a practice session from the truck, Moman entered the studio. "That old sound is still here," he said, smiling.

For the Four Horsemen it was a new experience.

"I've never recorded here, but I think I'm going to like it," said Cash. "It has a mood more than anything else." If the walls could have talked, they would have done so with the voices of Elvis, Neil Diamond, Dionne Warwick, Dusty Springfield, the Box Tops, Wilson Pickett, Petula Clark, Brenda Lee, Joe Tex, B. J. Thomas, Paul Revere and the Raiders, the Gentrys, and countless others. Between January 1968 and January 1971, twenty-six gold singles and eleven gold LPs were cut in the studio. In all, eighty-three singles and twenty-five LPs made their way to the national charts.

Adjacent to the studio was a room filled with Elvis memorabilia. When Moman owned the studio, it contained a pool table. The new owners had converted the room into a shrine. Pictures by the hundreds lined the walls. In glass cabinets were Elvis spoons, Elvis cups, and Elvis ashtrays. In the corner was a four-foot-high cardboard likeness of Elvis.

When Lewis spotted the cardboard Elvis look-alike, he asked if he could take it home. As a joke, Elvis once put Lewis's picture on the toilet seat in Sun Studio. "I wish he hadn't done that," Lewis murmured, cracking an uneasy smile.

For Perkins, Elvis's larger-than-life persona was no myth. "No one has ever had the style Elvis had. I'm never expecting to meet anyone else who is as complete an entertainer as he was."

Perkins, never late for a session, was first to sing that day. The song was "Class of '55," a ballad written by Moman and keyboardist Bobby Emmons. Two nights earlier Moman had played it for the first time for Perkins in the privacy of his bus. "He's very shy," Perkins said of Moman. "He won't push his own material. Carl Perkins is a million miles from having a hit single, but there is a feel on that song that is convincing. It seems like something I wrote myself."

Seated on a stool, wearing jeans and white sneakers, Perkins twisted a pencil in his hand as he sang. "That sure is good," said Moman when Perkins finished. "It makes me feel good just hearing music of mine again in this old building."

For the first time since Monday, all four artists were in the studio together. As Cash sang his part on "We Remember the King," Perkins sat on the floor near the piano, his legs folded beneath him. More than once he gave Cash the high sign, showing his approval of the way he was doing the song. Later they all joined in on the chorus. Cash, responding to Orbison's obvious discomfort, put his arm around his shoulder as they sang.

By Thursday everyone but Orbison had recorded a single. Not until late that night did he venture from his bus into the studio. The room was cleared of all but essential personnel and the lights were dimmed. "Coming Home," the song he had co-written for the session, is a ballad that pulls at the heart. Whatever he felt that night, he poured himself into the song, living up to his reputation as one of the most durable vocalists in the history of rock 'n' roll.

Hardship was the common thread throughout the careers of all Four Horsemen. Orbison was never linked to drug abuse, but the tragedies in his life would have driven lesser men over the edge. His wife, Claudette, was killed in a motorcycle accident. No sooner had he recovered from that than a fire at his Nashville home killed two of his three children. Somehow he survived.

For most of the Memphis sessions, Orbison looked shaky. His hands shook and his voice trembled. On the first takes of "Coming Home" his voice was embarrassingly tenuous. He was a pitiful sight sitting in that darkened studio with a roomful of musicians. After several takes, Orbison and Moman, who had stayed in the studio to offer moral support, went out to the sound truck to listen. The technicians were unanimous in their verdict. They told him it was a smash. Orbison leaned against the wall and listened to the playback. Once or twice he smiled. Moman said he thought it was great. Orbison nodded, but said nothing. One can only guess at the emotions that flowed through him while he listened. He had come home to Memphis, but his wife and children, for whom the song seemed directed, had been tragically lost along the way.

For Perkins, the specter of Elvis loomed greater with each passing day. The more he looked to the future, the more he saw the past. "I had been playing that music all my life, but I sure never got a contract," he said. "I sent tapes to record companies, and I would get them back with notes that they didn't know what it was. That's when I set my sights on Sun Records. Nobody that I ever knew or met since then—the Beatles, the Stones—nobody has ever had the magic, the charisma, the style, and class Elvis had in his younger days. That's why he will never die. That's why you have to stand in line to get into Graceland. The more they compare him to anyone who comes along, the bigger he will get. Greatness just won't die."

■　●　■

By Friday everyone was exhausted. For the final song, Moman selected "Big Train (from Memphis)," written and previously recorded by John Fogerty. Shortly before they were to record the song, Fogerty walked into the studio and introduced himself to the Four Horsemen. He had flown in that day from Los Angeles. When Fogerty arrived at the airport, he realized he didn't know where the studio was located. He phoned Duck Dunn, formerly of Booker T. & the MGs and more recently the bassist with Eric Clapton's touring band, to get directions.

Fogerty was light-headed in the presence of his heroes. "I was trying to relate back to when I first heard the Sun sound," he said, talking about the genesis of "Big Train." "I was about ten and used to play on the tracks. You know the old game. You put pennies on the track and a freight train flattens them, all very innocent stuff. Yet that was the sound I loved, and I wanted to write a song about that, with my producer being Sam Phillips. Obviously, it is a tribute to Elvis, but it is more than that. It is a tribute to the whole era."

Also dropping in for the jam were Rick Nelson, who, like Fogerty, had made a special trip to Memphis, producer Dave Edmunds, saxophonist Ace Cannon, and the Judds. Edmunds wandered about the studio speechless. "I'm just overwhelmed by the whole thing," said the Englishman. "Memphis is the home of rock 'n' roll. I'm a bit in shell shock."

Nelson, dressed in black, moved quietly about the room, watching—shyly it seemed—the legends from a distance. I tried to strike up a conversation with him. He politely confessed a loss of words and faded into the background. Later we did talk. "I've always been such a big fan of all these guys," Nelson said, his eyes locked on the Four Horsemen. "I wouldn't have missed it for anything."

The next morning, while taking off from the Memphis airport, Nelson's forty-five-year-old DC-3 developed engine trouble and the takeoff was aborted. Nelson left the airplane in Memphis for repairs and returned to Los Angeles aboard a commercial flight. Marty Stuart, on board the plane when it attempted to take off from Memphis, said he and Nelson were talking about a mutual hero, Buddy Holly, when the plane started down the runway. "We were talking about Buddy Holly's glasses, about how some farmer found his glasses after the plane crash," says Stuart. "Rick was laughing, and he was talking about how the plane used to belong to Jerry Lee Lewis. But I was thinking about how rickety I felt on it." Three months later, on New Year's Eve, Nelson and his band perished in the DC-3 when it crashed under mysterious circumstances in Texas.

On the night of the jam session, tragedy was the furthest thing from anyone's mind. The mood was jubilant. Bassist Mike Leech said he felt like an autograph hound. "I'm taking pictures and getting autographs like people off the street, and I've worked with all these guys at one time or another," he said. "I'll be sitting there talking to someone like Carl Perkins, then I'm thinking, 'Gosh, I'm talking to a legend.' Then the next thing you know I have my camera out taking pictures."

Sam Phillips, who you think would be used to such things by now, said he had never seen a group of artists gather under such circumstances. "Invariably, everyone here I have talked to feels the same way," he said. "You can feel it in the air. It's not just, 'Oh, boy, we have us a hit record.' They see a future in a city they know started it all, and believe me, this cycle is going to make itself known again."

The jam itself gave everyone goosebumps. There were seven musicians, fourteen voices—all wailing the words to "Big Train." As the driving bass and guitar licks of the song walked the music downward, the spirits of the singers climbed upward, setting the stage for a collision that, when it occurred, filled the room with excitement. Even the sound and video technicians, frightfully mum throughout the session, erupted into spontaneous applause when it ended.

In the early hours of Saturday morning, there was a sudden hush, as if people were thinking you really *can* go home again, then the studio cleared quickly, the Four Horsemen of apocalyptic vision running fastest of all. As everyone filed from the studio, Moman sat on a stool in the center of the room. Tears streaked down his cheeks. "I can't believe this happened," he said, looking at me with eyes bursting with happiness. "I never thought I'd ever see anything like this."

The room emptied, technicians turning out lights as they exited. We stood beneath the only light remaining in the vast room. I didn't know what to say, so I said nothing. Moman was paralyzed by his emotions. Little did he—or I—know then, but storm clouds were forming over Memphis. Dark, ugly clouds that would rain on the *Class of '55* session and send Moman's high-flying career into a tailspin.

To understand why, you must go all the way back to the beginning.

IN THE BEGINNING, THE
BLUES WERE KING

n 1905 Memphis, Tennessee, had a national reputation.

It was the murder capital of the United States. Cocaine addiction was at epidemic proportions. And the city's booming sex industry was attracting ambitious young girls from all over the mid-South. With a population of 150,000, the city had over five hundred saloons, most of which had back rooms used for gambling and prostitution. Not surprisingly, the city was governed by underworld figures who forged an underground economy so entrenched in the social fabric of the city that it exists to this day. In fact, the crime syndicate based in Memphis today, an organization I will call the "Hoodoo cartel" because of its mysterious shroud of secrecy, is run by descendants of families who have dominated the underworld since shortly after the turn of the century.

For Memphis residents, 1905 began with a gruesome New Year's Eve murder. Readers of the city's morning newspaper, *The Commercial Appeal*, celebrated the new year with the following headline: NEGRO DEMON BEATS THE HEAD OF HIS VICTIM INTO UNRECOGNIZABLE MASS.

A black woman, Mattie Maben, was bludgeoned to death while her husband attended midnight church services. The killer was apprehended by neighbors and turned over to the authorities. As horrible as the murder was, it was just one of many that month. On January 28 *The Commercial Appeal* ran a story bemoaning the fact that there were five women in jail charged with killing their husbands. What was

Beale Street in the early days.
Photo courtesy of the Mississippi Valley Collection,
University of Memphis, University Libraries

the city coming to? It was the question on everyone's mind. A study done by the Prudential Insurance Company of America found that, for the decade ending in 1910, Memphis had the highest homicide rate of thirty-one major cities surveyed. The author of the study called Memphis the "murder town" of the nation. It was a distinction the city would have for over three decades. But murder was not the only problem facing the city.

Judge Moss, a county official who enjoyed the support of the newspaper, declared war on gambling. NO MERCY ON CRAP SHOOTERS, read one headline. JUDGE MOSS LAYS DOWN THE LAW, DECLARES CRAP SHOOTING MUST CEASE AND NEGROES WORK. "It seems to me the Negroes of Memphis have gone crazy on the subject of crap shooting," said Judge Moss, reflecting the institutionalized racism of the day. "You Negroes are needed in the cotton fields and should be there at work instead of gambling and shooting each other to pieces."

W. C. Handy (seated with horn and cane)on a visit to Memphis.
Photo courtesy of Memphis/Shelby County Public Library

Into this social maelstrom walked W. C. Handy. The son of slaves, he was born in Florence, Alabama, in 1873, only eight years after the end of the Civil War. As a child he displayed a knack for music. His father, a Methodist minister, let Handy know in no uncertain terms he would prefer having no son at all as to one who pursued a career in music. But Handy could not suppress his love of music. One day toward the end of his tenure at the Florence District School for Negroes, where he sang in the choral group, he met an alcoholic fiddle player from Memphis. The man, fleeing a love affair gone sour, stopped off in Florence long enough to organize an orchestra, befriending Handy and filling his head with stories about Beale Street.

Handy bought a cornet but didn't tell his father. He could hardly believe his good fortune when a circus was stranded in Florence. To make a living, the white bandleader gave music lessons in the barbershop.

Handy stopped by the barbershop every day after school. He peered through the windows and memorized the blackboard charts the bandleader made for his students. He applied that knowledge to the musical training he received in the choral group. By the time he left school, Handy played cornet well enough to join a traveling minstrel show.

After several years of traveling the back roads of the South, Handy got his first big break. He was booked to play at a society barbecue in Henderson, Kentucky. He met Carl Lindstrom there, cornet soloist in the Patrick Gilmore Band, a famous group that once counted John Philip Sousa among its members. Lindstrom urged Handy to stick with his musical career. Encouraged by his experiences in Henderson, Handy joined a band and stayed a while longer. He met Elizabeth Price there, the woman he would marry. Henderson had a German choir of several hundred members. Handy was so impressed by the quality of their music, he took a job as a janitor in their rehearsal hall to learn their techniques.

After several more years of performing around the South, Handy got a job with a minstrel show based in Chicago. That didn't please Elizabeth's parents, who felt such work was only for lower-class blacks. But the job paid well, and Handy soon was able to afford a new Conn gold-plated trumpet. More years on the road followed. In 1903 Handy settled in the Delta town of Clarksdale, Mississippi, where he formed a band. By then he was a seasoned musician. His band performed for the usual social functions and sometimes worked as a warm-up act for white politicians out on the stump. Typically, Handy played the music of the day, then sat quietly while the politicians baited their white audiences with promises to keep "the nigger" in his place. Handy pocketed the money, tolerated the racist talk, and followed his dream.

Handy was influenced by the folk blues he heard in Clarksdale. He heard it as hollers in the fields and as wails on shanty porches at day's end. Handy, moved by the music's emotionalism, felt a subterranean attraction to its rhythmic chants; but he was a classically trained musician, a trumpet player who felt an equal attraction to the European-based music he had enjoyed since childhood. What on earth could he do with field hollers and what he considered primitive folk music? The question gnawed at him.

In 1905, at the age of thirty-two, Handy moved to Memphis. His impressions of the city, as expressed in his autobiography, indicate he was dazzled, if not overwhelmed, by the bright lights and excitement that greeted him on Beale Street. He set up shop at Pee Wee's Saloon, as did many other musicians. "Through Pee Wee's swinging doors passed the heroic darktown figures of an age that is now becoming fabulous," Handy wrote many years later. "They ranged from cooks and waiters to professional gamblers, jockeys and racetrack men of the period. Glittering young devils in silk toppers and Prince Alberts drifted in and out with insolent self-assurance. Chocolate dandies with red roses embroidered on cream waistcoats loitered at the bar. Now and again a fancy gal with shadowed eyes and a wedding-ring waist glanced through the doorway or ventured inside to ask if anybody had set eyes on the sweet good man who had temporarily strayed away." Pee Wee's Saloon was popular with musicians because Pee Wee, whose real name was Vigello Maffei, would allow them to congregate there. Pee Wee, a diminutive Italian, and his son-in-law, Lorenzo Pacini, further endeared themselves to musicians by taking phone messages for them.

At this time, Beale Street was the most prominent gathering place for blacks in the nation. But unlike other entertainment districts of that era, Beale Street was not racially segregated. White-owned and black-owned businesses thrived side by side, as both white and black customers gathered to gamble, drink, whore, pawn valuables, shop, snort cocaine, and dance the night away. The street itself was several blocks in length and ended at the Mississippi River on a bluff that served as a natural levee to protect the city during times of high water.

One of the street's oldest bars was Hammitt Ashford's saloon at Beale and Fourth. Ashford, a light-skinned black who dressed fashionably and wore a diamond stickpin in his tie, presided over what was probably the most popular joint on the street. With a mahogany bar and marble tabletops, it had an air of decency about it. The classiest nightspot was probably the Monarch Club. It boasted mirrored walls, cushioned seats, and a brass-railed mahogany bar.

Also setting his sights on Beale Street was a transplanted Mississippian named E. H. Crump. A tall, gangly redhead with the gift of

E. H. (Boss) Crump, c. 1930s.
Photo courtesy of the Mississippi Valley Collection,
University of Memphis, University Libraries

gab, Crump married a Memphis socialite and invested in a buggy business. Before long, he got involved in politics, and he was not adverse
to using his fists to settle political differences of opinion. In 1905, at
the age of thirty-one, he won a seat on the city's lower legislative
council. As Handy settled into the music scene, Crump settled into
backwater politics. For Handy, that meant playing the music of the
era: polkas, waltzes, and one-steps. For Crump, it meant pursuing the
black vote. He had seen the future, and the future was black with
promise. It was the chance intersection of the lives of those two men—
Crump and Handy—that would alter American music history. As Handy
and Crump cemented their destinies, Beale Street flaunted its bare-
assed wildness for all to see.

The Commercial Appeal pleaded for someone to do something about
the Memphis crime problem. A murder was being committed almost

every day. Armed robberies occurred with even greater frequency. A black community leader, Professor Willie Councill, let it be known he had found the solution, and before an audience of twelve hundred at the Church Park auditorium, he summoned all the oratorical splendor at his command to denounce the influence of "coon songs." "Make the young negroes turn from coon songs and go to the songs of our mothers and fathers," the professor pleaded. "The coon songs . . . make sentiment against us."

Ever the romantic, Handy, who had played his share of "coon" music as a minstrel musician, saw only good things in the city. On the surface, Beale was a thriving entertainment district. Women often were well dressed: skirts were worn ankle-length, and hats were gaudy and adorned with handsome plumes. Furs were a common sight. A catalog for Ell Jay Garments advertised blue-gray Russian wolf wraps for $6.95 and tailored "imported Persian lamb cloth" coats for $22.75.

Crump led a campaign to reshape city government. He successfully lobbied the General Assembly in Nashville for the creation of a commission form of government for the city of Memphis. The new form combined the functions of the legislative and executive branches, creating a five-member commission that would be presided over by the mayor. In 1909 Crump ran for the office of mayor. The commission form of government went into effect in 1910. If he won, Crump would become the first mayor to serve as head of the commission.

Crump ran against a political machine that was ingrained in the white power structure. His only hope of victory lay with a combination of white and black votes. He ran on a reform ticket, which endeared him to many white voters, but his promises to clean up the gambling dens were not popular among black voters. To boost his popularity among blacks, one of Crump's political committees hired Handy to compose a campaign song for Crump.

Handy needed a song that would appeal to black voters without alienating white voters: a song that could be played on both sides of the street. Handy racked his brain. What kept coming to him was the music he had heard in Clarksdale. Once, at one of those Delta dances that had become a staple for his nine-piece band, he was asked if some local men could perform a few songs of their own. Handy was apprehensive when three raggedly dressed black men took the spotlight, but when the men performed, "a rain of silver dollars began to fall." Handy wrote in his autobiography: "The boys lay more money than my nine musicians were being paid for the entire engagement. Then I saw the beauty of primitive music."

Handy decided to write a campaign song for Crump that would combine the emotional appeal of the "primitive music" of the Delta with the classical familiarity of orchestra music. Up to that point, the blues had been confined to cheap guitars, washboards, and empty jugs. The standard measure for popular American music was the sixteen-bar strain. Handy based his campaign song, titled "Mister Crump," on the twelve-bar, three-line structure of the folk blues. He added a bass line in tango rhythm and a three-chord harmonic structure. Then he wrote parts for the instruments in his band. When he finished, he had a song with African rhythms and European instrumentation.

"Mister Crump," with lyrics promising nothing but good times ahead with a Crump victory, was popular with both blacks and whites. Handy later wrote lyrics that poked fun at Crump and his promises of reform. "Luckily for us, Mr. Crump himself didn't hear us sing these words. But we were hired to help out over his campaign, and since I knew that reform was about as palatable to Beale Street voters as castor oil, I was sure those reassuring words would do him more good than harm," Handy later wrote. Crump won the election by a mere seventy-nine votes and went on to establish a political dynasty that lasted more than four decades.

Encouraged by the positive reaction to "Mister Crump," Handy rewrote the lyrics and changed the name of the song to "The Memphis Blues." He offered it to the major music publishers in New York. They all turned him down. Three years later, dejected but confident of the song's worth, he turned to a local music store for help. The white store manager told Handy that if Handy would get the song sheets printed, he would sell them in the store. That sounded like a good deal to Handy. In 1912 Handy's self-published version of "The Memphis Blues" went on sale. Unfortunately, Handy was unable to get the other stores in town to sell the music. After a while, his partner told him the music had stopped selling. He offered to reimburse him for the printing costs in exchange for the copyright to the song. Thinking he had hit a dead-end with the song, Handy agreed. That was a mistake. The "Father of the Blues" was shut out of receiving any royalties from "The Memphis Blues" until the copyright expired and reverted back to him twenty-eight years later.

"The Memphis Blues" spread like wildfire, south to New Orleans and north to Chicago. Soon it was all the rage in New York. Handy wrote a number of hit songs: "The St. Louis Blues," "The Beale Street Blues," and "Joe Turner Blues," to name a few. He moved to Chicago in 1918 and then to New York, where he established a publishing house. He died in 1958 at the age of eighty-five. He lived to see Memphis honor his achievement when in 1931 the city named a park on Beale Street after him.

W. C. Handy didn't invent the blues. His accomplishment was to merge black folk blues with European instrumentation. That union created a new musical form, one that combined the raw energy of his African heritage with the stoic discipline of his European-influenced education. Handy defined the blues by being the first to compose sheet music for standard instruments of the day. Along the way, he launched a revolution in American music.

■　●　■

Apart from being the home of the blues, Memphis had another distinction at the turn of the century. Beale Street was the only entertainment district in the nation openly hospitable to women entertainers. They were provided a safe environment in which to perform and afforded equal status with men. That enlightened attitude was not the result of a premature flowering of feminism in the musky, bare-knuckled river town, but of the fact that black women, along with cocaine and whisky, were the currency of choice in that man's world. Because their economic value was so high, black women were protected from the rowdiness of male patrons and encouraged to work on the street as entertainers and prostitutes.

Three of the best-known blueswomen of the early years were Alberta Hunter, Memphis Minnie, and Lil Hardin, the second wife of Louis

Armstrong. Of the three, Hunter and Hardin fled Beale Street to escape what modern-day record producer Jim Dickinson, paraphrasing bluesman Sleepy John Estes, once called "the center of all evil in the known universe." Only Memphis Minnie, perhaps the most accomplished female guitarist who ever lived, succumbed to the temptations of the street and supplemented her earnings as a performer by working as a prostitute. But who can fault her for that? The times were tough; she did what it took to survive.

Alberta Hunter was born on Beale Street. Her father, Charles Hunter, worked as a Pullman porter, a job that gave him high social status in the black community. Her mother, Laura Peterson Hunter, worked as a chambermaid in one of the street's more elegant whorehouses. Alberta's father abandoned the family before she was old enough to remember him. Alberta's mother moved in with her mother for a number of years, and then rented a room at 170 Beale Street, where Alberta grew up in the heart of the district. The Handy Band, with its bright uniforms and glitzy instruments, grabbed her attention as they marched and strutted up and down the street outside her apartment. "We'd hear that ta-da, ta-da of the band, and Lord, we'd be out the door so fast," she told Frank Taylor, coauthor of *Alberta: A Celebration in Blues*.

Alberta began singing at an early age, and there is evidence that she performed as a teenager at Memphis's famous Palace Theater, which featured the top black entertainers of the day. In later years Duke Ellington, Count Basie, and Ella Fitzgerald would be frequent headliners at the theater. Special shows for whites would be offered once a week there, usually featuring girlie shows. Sometimes there were problems: men often rushed the stage to get at the dark-skinned women, and it was difficult for the management to maintain order. Because of the street's reputation, Alberta in later years always denied performing there. "I always wanted to stay away from anything that had a reputation of being bad," she told Taylor. If singing on Beale had been her only chance for success, she said, she would "rather not have the chance." Despite her denials, there is evidence she succumbed to the bright, naughty lights of Beale. In 1948, while visiting Memphis for a performance, she expressed regret to a newspaper reporter that she would not be able to visit Anselmo Barrasso, owner of the Palace Theater. The newspaper credited Barasso with discovering Alberta as a teenager and giving her the opportunity to appear on his stage.

Alberta's criticisms of the wicked lifestyle of Beale may have deeper psychological roots than would appear on the surface. Alberta was a lesbian and those complex, socially unacceptable feelings, when mixed with the normal surging hormones of a teenager, may have led her to project the "wickedness" of her own feelings onto the prostitutes. It also could explain why she fled Memphis at such an early age. If prostitutes were wicked for selling themselves to men, how much more wicked must she be, in her mind, for wanting to be with the prostitutes herself?

In 1911, at the age of sixteen, Alberta boarded a train for Chicago. She landed her first real job at Dago Frank's, a well-known hangout for prostitutes and pimps, where she sang for the johns who waited their turns with the prostitutes. Alberta thrived in Chicago. Her soulful soprano voice made her a favorite in nightclubs, where cash-heavy mobsters often sent her home with tips of four or five hundred dollars a night. In 1921 she went to New York to record for the Black Swan label, a short-lived, black-owned record company. The following year, Paramount Records kicked off its "race" series with her recordings, making Alberta one of the first women to record the blues. As composer of "Downhearted Blues," Bessie Smith's first big hit, Alberta attracted attention from other singers and composers, including her childhood idol W. C. Handy, who selected her to introduce his new work. By 1923 she had replaced Bessie Smith in the Broadway musical *How Come?* She continued to record for Paramount throughout the 1920s. In 1927, following an abortive marriage, she went to London on vacation. While there, Oscar Hammerstein and Jerome Kern asked her to audition for the London production of *Show Boat*. Competing against a white woman, she got the role and by the end of the decade her version of "Can't Help Lovin' Dat Man" had made her an international star.

After two decades of success, she retired in the early fifties to care for her ailing mother. When her mother died in 1954, she quit singing. "I didn't want to spoil what I had done," she told Chris Albertson. "I didn't want them to say, 'Is she still here?'" The day after her mother died, she enrolled in nursing school and worked as a hospital nurse for the next twenty years. "I've always been liberated," she told Sally Placksin, author of *American Women in Jazz*, "because I've always made my own, and you know, I've always been independent and never asked anybody for anything, and never wanted anybody to give me anything."

Alberta Hunter died in 1984, but not before staging a spectacular comeback in the 1970s. She appeared on television's *Today Show* on a regular basis, and wrote the musical score for Robert Altman's movie *Remember My Name*. The greatest moment of her life occurred in the 1970s, she said, when she sang for President Jimmy Carter at the White House.

■ ● ■

It was while performing at the Dreamland in Chicago in the early 1920s that Alberta first met fellow Memphian Lil Hardin and her husband, Louis Armstrong, who also were booked at the popular nightspot. Like Alberta, Lil had fled the wickedness of Memphis to find a better life. Unlike Alberta, Lil had enjoyed a black middle-class upbringing. Born in 1902 or 1898 (she gave conflicting dates), she was two years old when her father died. Raised by her mother and grandmother, both of whom hated the blues and banned it from their house, Lil was enrolled for piano lessons in the first grade. From the beginning she was nudged toward a career as a church organist. But Lil had other ideas. Once she was beaten with a broomstick by her mother after a copy of "The St. Louis Blues" was found in her possession.

The attitude of Lil's mother was not unusual in those days. Sex was inextricably linked with blues and jazz. It was not a prejudice: it was a fact of life. Once, in conversation with jazz legend Miles Davis, I made the mistake (in his eyes) of referring to his music as jazz. "Don't say that, man," he growled, in his trademark raspy voice. "It means Uncle Tom and stuff like that. To me it does. Know what I'm saying? What you call jazz is an old Negro thing. If the white man heard jazz, he didn't want his daughter to listen to it because it might want to

Lil Hardin Armstrong, c. 1950s.
Photo courtesy of the Institute of Jazz Studies

make her fuck black men with big dicks and shit like that—and smoke
marijuana. You understand what I'm saying? If a girl goes out with a
man, and the father asks what he does, and she says he plays jazz,
that girl will get locked up." In Davis's eyes jazz was linked with white
prejudice. In truth, black parents were also disapproving of blues and
jazz music, and often pulled out the broomstick when their daughters
showed an interest in the "devil's music."

Lil may have been rebellious, but she was no fool. To placate her
mother, she became the organist for her Sunday school. That worked
for a while. Then one day she played a jazzy version of "Onward Christian Soldiers" in church, drawing a disapproving look from the pastor.
Determined to shield her from the evils of Beale Street—and ever hope-

ful of making a lady out of her jazz-crazed offspring—her mother enrolled her in the music program at Fisk University, in Nashville. Then, while Lil was away at school, she packed up and moved to Chicago. After completing two years at Fisk, Lil returned to Memphis for a year or so, then joined her mother in Chicago sometime between the summer of 1916 and 1918.

What happened to Lil upon her return to Memphis? What made her run to the domineering mother she had so desperately tried to escape since she was a young teen? Lil never said, but history shows that the summer of 1916 was a particularly violent one on Beale Street. Crump had consolidated his power with the help of Beale Street businessmen and black political ward chiefs. In an effort to tighten his grip on the city, Crump announced in 1914 he was running for sheriff and planned to hold both offices.

C. P. J. Mooney, editor of *The Commercial Appeal*, was outraged. He put the full force of the newspaper behind efforts to stop Crump, who eventually backed down and ran his own man for sheriff. Crump's man won, and Mooney grew more determined to break the Crump machine, which by that point had become not so much a political machine as a crime syndicate. The opportunity to put Crump away came in 1915, when the mayor refused to enforce newly enacted state prohibition laws. The liquor and cocaine trade was the basis of his political machine. Crump couldn't shut it down without shutting himself down. Mooney stepped up his attacks. The state attorney brought suit against Crump to oust him from office.

Because Crump publicly vowed not to shut down the liquor and drug trade, the state easily won its case; but Crump had found a loophole. The court's ruling applied to his current term only. He was subsequently elected to a second four-year term, to which the ruling did not apply. When Crump let it be known he would be returning as mayor, *The Commercial Appeal* made it clear it would oppose him every step of the way. Rather than fight the newspaper, he waited six weeks after the date he was supposed to take office, then arranged to be sworn in on a holiday when the courts were closed. He handpicked his successor, then promptly resigned, but not before collecting six weeks' back pay. Crump learned a valuable lesson that has been adhered to by organized crime interests in Memphis for almost a century: *The Commercial Appeal* is the only institution in the city powerful enough to challenge their interests.

The following year, in 1916, William Latura, who owned one of the city's well-known gambling establishments, began making threats against law enforcement officials. The threats were taken seriously. In 1908 Latura, who went by the nickname "Wild Bill," strolled into Hammett Ashford's Saloon at Beale and Fourth and gunned down seven black patrons. Joe Mack, who was in the club but escaped, told police what happened: "I was standing at the pool table furthest from the door when a white man whom I recognized as Latura entered the door. He came through the door slowly, looked around and began to shoot. I hid under a table or I think he would have shot me. I don't know how many times he fired. One of the boys whom he shot begged him, as he fell, not to shoot him again. Soon after Latura came in, another man walked in and stayed about five minutes and then went out. Then I called the police."

Latura was charged with the murders but never convicted. Over the next several years, he was arrested thirty-five times for liquor-law violations. Finally, he was brought in on gambling charges and sentenced to three years in prison. It was while his case was on appeal—and he was out on bond—that he made threats against the police chief. With Crump out of office, Latura, along with most of the city's five hundred or so club owners, felt desperate. Police Chief Oliver Perry's response to the threats was short and to the point: "Get Latura."

Two police officers, Sandy Lyons and Charlie Davis, who had been recently docked ten days' pay by the chief for looking the other way during Latura's criminal activities, confronted Latura outside his club. Latura cursed the police officers. "I said, 'Bill don't curse me that way,'" Office Lyons said in his report. "He had used some hard names to me. He said, 'Aw, I'll kill you, you . . .' I said, 'Bill, you are under arrest.' He said, 'Aw, you can't arrest me. I'll kill you sure enough.' Then he started to draw and I beat him to it."

Lyons and Davis pumped four shots into Latura. Then, fearing retaliation by Lutura's friends, they left him dying on the street and returned to headquarters. But they took their time—about forty-five minutes. When they arrived and made their report, the acting captain dispatched an emergency car to the scene. They found Latura lying in the street surrounded by curious onlookers. Latura's young daughter and his chauffeur were comforting the still-conscious man. Police officers loaded him into the car, but he died before they reached the hospital.

■   ●   ■

A wild nightlife was one thing, but the unrelenting violence common on Beale Street must have had an impact on Lil's tender sensibilities. Beale was not a huge district. Basically, the clubs, brothels, and gambling dives that supported the nightlife were located in a two-block area. Whether Lillian was influenced by the Wild Bill Latura incident or not, we may never know. We know that shortly after the shooting occurred, she left for Chicago. To her mother's horror, she took a three-dollar-a-week job as a demonstrator at a local music store. Sheet music, not records, was the hot-ticket item in those days. Stores hired musicians to entice customers into purchasing sheet music by performing the songs for them.

A slender, very attractive young woman, Lil quickly became a popular attraction at the store, a favorite hangout for jazz musicians. She was more comfortable playing Bach and Chopin than jamming with the jazzmen who came in the store, but when she was asked to audition for the New Orleans Creole Jazz Band, she jumped at the chance. She was hired and her income jumped to $27.50 a week. She was afraid to tell her mother she had joined a jazz band, so she told her she was working at a dance studio.

When her mother found out the truth, she blew her top. No daughter of hers was going to perform with a jazz band. Lil pleaded with her: at least meet the guys in the band before you decide. Finally, she agreed to a meeting. One can only guess at the level of fearsome skepticism with which she greeted the guys in the band, but they obviously were on their best behavior because she gave her consent for Lil to play in the band on condition someone walk her "little girl" home at night.

That gig lasted only a few months, but by that time Lil was hooked—not so much on the music, but on the money (in later years she recalled seeing someone tip Alberta Hunter three hundred dollars)—and she did what jazz musicians have always done when a gig comes to an end: she joined another group. Poor Mama Hardin! She must have been praying twenty-four hours a day at that point for the deliverance of her daughter from the clutches of the jazz demon.

By 1920 or so, Lil had joined King Oliver's Creole Jazz Band, one of the best-known groups of that era. They performed at Dreamland, Chicago's most elegant nightclub, and occasionally at an after-hours club frequented by mobsters. There are reports Mama Hardin herself sometimes showed up early in the morning to escort her daughter home. In search of a broader horizon, King Oliver took the band to California, but Lil was unhappy there and returned to Chicago, where she took a job as the house pianist at Dreamland.

After a while, King Oliver made his way back to Chicago and restructured his band. In 1922 he hired a hot young cornet player out of New Orleans named Louis Armstrong. That in itself is a mystery, since he hired Louis to play second cornet behind himself. Bands then did not contain two instruments of the same type, so his addition of Louis was viewed with suspicion by other musicians.

Pleased with his new acquisition, King Oliver took Louis by Dreamland to meet Lil. Louis was five-feet-four, weighed over two hundred pounds, and had an awkward appearance. Lil was not impressed. Everything he wore was too small for him, she later recalled. He was an atrocious sight. His necktie hung down over his potbelly, and his bangs draped over his forehead like a canopy.

Sparks flew, like King Oliver hoped, but they were the wrong sparks. Lil recently had married an aspiring singer, Jimmy Johnson, and she simply wasn't interested in Louis. It seems obvious King Oliver was trying to impress Louis. By that time, Lil had grown into a beautiful woman. Slender at a time when black women tended toward corpulence, she represented the epitome of elegance. More important, she was educated and could do what none of the other musicians could do, including King Oliver and Louis Armstrong: read music. Mama Hardin had done her job well. Lil was a class act.

Enter Louis Armstrong. For the past several years he had been working on the *Dixie Bell*, a riverboat that plowed the Mississippi River between New Orleans and St. Louis, with a twelve-piece band. The boat made regular stops at Memphis (by then Lil had already moved to Chicago). In 1918 Louis married Daisy Parker, a hot-tempered prostitute, who liked to work the dance halls frequented by black roustabouts. They fought like dogs and cats, frequently with knives, fists, or whatever they could find, and either or both were arrested on numerous occasions. Daisy was pretty, but she was illiterate, and Louis's associates felt it was beneath him to marry a prostitute, especially one who couldn't read. But Louis was in love and wouldn't listen to his friends.

Eventually, King Oliver persuaded Lil to return to the band. More out of sympathy than anything else, Lil befriended Louis and showed him around town and introduced him to her friends. King Oliver whispered into her ear that Louis was someone she should keep her eye on—and she did, even more so as her marriage deteriorated. When the group made its first recording in 1923, Lil noticed that King Oliver made Louis stand far away from the microphone, to reduce his presence on the record, and her heart went out to him. Before she knew it, she had fallen in love.

Louis was stunned to discover she was interested in him. By Louis's standards, Lil was an absolute goddess, not only in appearance but by breeding. He wasn't in her social class and he knew it. With the same determination she had shown in making a place for herself in a man's world, Lil set out to rehabilitate Louis. She taught him how to dress (he preferred secondhand clothing), she persuaded him to lose about fifty pounds (he had a voracious appetite), and she urged him to stand up for himself with King Oliver. Most important, she gave him confidence in himself as a musician. Then, having accomplished all that, she arranged for divorces for the two of them. Lil and Louis were married on February 5, 1924.

Lil's devotion to Louis's career did not go unnoticed by King Oliver, who tried to drive a wedge between them. He spoke badly of Lil behind her back. The disharmony spread to other band members. Baby Dodds, the drummer, once punched Louis off the stage. Tempers flared.

King Oliver started carrying a pistol. Lil knew she had to get Louis away from King Oliver if he was ever going to have confidence in himself.

Lil pushed Louis, then pushed him some more. Finally, he quit the band, though he didn't have the courage to tell King Oliver to his face. He sent a friend with the message. "Now what do I do?" he asked Lil. "Get a job," she said. Louis went to Sammy Stewart, the leader of a popular dance band. Stewart turned him down. All the band members had light skin, and Louis was dark. Louis then tried Ollie Powers, who was putting together a new group for Dreamland. To Lil's delight, Louis got a job as first trumpet. Lil stayed on with King Oliver for a while, then she and Louis went to New York to join Fletcher Henderson's big band.

Dissatisfied with New York, Lil contacted the manager at Dreamland and urged him to hire Louis as a headliner. The manager said no one knew who Louis was. Well, they know me, Lil told him. The manager agreed and allowed her to form her own group. She called it the Dreamland Syncopators; Louis played first trumpet.

Once they returned to Chicago, Lil was unrelenting in her efforts on Louis's behalf. Feeling the pressure, Louis sought out an agent, white Chicago nightclub owner "Papa" Joe Glaser. "I told him I was tired of being cheated and set upon by scamps and told how my head was jumping from all of that business mess," Louis confided to Larry L. King years later. "Lil, one of my wives, had sweet-talked me into going out on my own to front some bands and it was driving me crazy—and I told him, 'Pops, I need you. Come be my manager. Please! Take care of all my business and take care of me. Just lemme blow my gig!' And goddamn that sweet man did it!"

Over the next few years Lil devoted herself to Louis's career. Between 1925 and 1927 they recorded almost fifty songs, many of them written by Lil, including "Lonesome Blues," "Jazz Lips," and "The King of the Zulus." When Louis recorded with the Hot Five and the Hot Seven, Lil always played the piano and arranged the music. She didn't perform many solos on the recordings because piano riffs were not in vogue at the time. While she was performing, writing, and keeping Louis's career on track, she also attended school. In 1928 she got a teacher's diploma from the Chicago College of Music, and the following year received a postgraduate degree from the New York College of Music.

Unfortunately, Louis's eye began to wander. He saw other women. He and Lil fought over his affairs, and separated on several occasions, but Lil always took him back. Still, there was a limit to her patience. In 1931, in the wake of Louis's New Orleans homecoming appearance, she told him it was over. He was making a thousand dollars a week and no longer needed her help. There was no reason to continue the relationship; Louis agreed.

Lil returned to Chicago and focused on her own career. During the thirties she formed two all-girl bands (one named the Harlem Harlicans), led a male band, and became the house pianist at Decca Records. In later years she took a WPA sewing class and learned to design clothes. Some of her creations, such as a cocktail gown she named "Mad Money," became famous, and Louis himself is said to have turned to her for the design of his dress coats. In addition, she taught French, gave piano lessons, and wrote more than 150 songs, some of which— "Struttin' with Some Barbecue" and "Original Boogie"—became Louis's biggest hits. Lil wrote a song in the forties, "Just for a Thrill," that became a big hit for Ray Charles in the sixties.

Sadly, Lil never stopped loving Louis. She never remarried and continued to wear the rings he had given her. She kept the cornet he played in the early days and preserved old letters and photographs. In later years she retraced their steps, as if trying to relive the moments she shared with him, and often visited a Michigan resort where they had vacationed as a couple.

On August 27, 1971, six months after Louis's death, the city of Chicago held a tribute concert to honor his memory. Lil was invited to perform. Wearing a boldly patterned dress with long, elegant sleeves, she took the stage at the outdoor concert and, as if going full circle back to her Memphis roots, sat at the piano and played Handy's "St. Louis Blues." As she hit the final chord of the song—and as two thousand fans watched in stunned disbelief—she fell over dead, the victim of a heart attack.

Lil knew how to make an exit.

THE TWENTIES:
FURRY, MINNIE, SLEEPY,
AND ABE

n the 1920s Memphis music was dominated by four figures: Furry Lewis, Memphis Minnie, Sleepy John Estes, and "Fiddling Abe" Fortas. Judging by newspaper accounts, Fiddling Abe was the most popular. You might say he was the white W. C. Handy of his generation. When he left Memphis in 1933 to take a post in the U.S. farm bureau, the *Press-Scimitar*, the city's evening newspaper, ran the following four-column headline in bold type: FIDDLING ABE FORTAS, 22, LEAVES MEMPHIS DANCERS FOR HIGH LEGAL POST WITH UNCLE SAM'S FARM BUREAU.

The reference to "Memphis dancers" was not a joke. The man who was to become a U.S. Supreme Court justice—and one of the most influential men in President Lyndon Johnson's administration—was a product of the wild and woolly Beale Street music scene. The son of Orthodox Jewish immigrants who moved to Memphis from England at the turn of the century, Abe, born June 19, 1910, grew up on Pontotoc Street, a couple of blocks from Beale and about the same distance from the Lorraine Motel, where Martin Luther King was to be assassinated in 1968. Because his family was poor, they lived adjacent to a black neighborhood. Abe's father worked as a pawnbroker and jeweler, and was very much a player in the economics of Beale Street.

From the time Abe was a small child, it was apparent to his father he needed to find his son a career as a counterbalance to his slight, slender build. Because Abe's hands were noticeable for their delicate

Abe Fortas, c. 1930s.
Photo courtesy of the Mississippi Valley Collection,
University of Memphis, University Libraries

appearance, he encouraged his son to take violin lessons. By the age of thirteen, Abe was proficient enough on the violin to form a band, the Blue Melody Boys. The band earned eight dollars a night and became a popular attraction. Soon he was given the nickname "Fiddling Abe." Over the next four years, Fiddling Abe earned enough money performing to pay his way through a private college in Memphis, Southwestern University. For two years he led the school orchestra.

Abe never talked about Beale Street after he became successful. Like Lil Hardin and Alberta Hunter, he thought it prudent to avoid the subject. Actually, he had compelling reasons to do so. It was while he was experiencing the street's gritty nightlife that he probably first met the linchpins of Memphis's underworld community of drug dealers, criminals, bootleggers, and other nefarious types. Likewise, it would have been impossible for Abe not to have had at least a passing acquaintance with Memphis Minnie. They lived in the same neighborhood and competed for the same jobs. And for the leader of the Blue Melody Boys, the allure of an attractive black woman who had a reputation for being a genius on the guitar and a slave to passion must have been difficult to ignore, especially at Minnie's prices (reported to be two dollars a trick).

Throughout the 1920s Memphis maintained its distinction as the murder capital of the nation. Cocaine was sold by storekeepers in dime boxes, and drug addiction increased. Police officials estimated addiction rates in the black community at between 60 to 70 percent of the population. Cocaine had been introduced into the city in 1902 with the opening of the Coca-Cola Bottling Company of Memphis. The soft drink originally had been formulated by a pharmacist as a tonic, and cocaine was the key ingredient. The drug was dropped from the formula in 1905, but not before entrepreneurs forged a direct link with Colombian suppliers of the drug. But cocaine wasn't the only drug in demand on Beale. Morphine was also a popular drug, and published accounts indicate it had a street value of seventy-five dollars an ounce by the mid-1920s.

In that decade the city continued to be flooded with young women, many of whom became prostitutes and cocaine addicts. Typically, the brothels contained both black and white women. White male patrons were admitted until 3 A.M., at which time black male patrons were allowed in the back door to partake of the leftovers. It was the only socially sanctioned means by which black men could have intercourse with white women. To help combat the problems caused by the influx of young girls into Memphis, the city organized the Woman's Protective Bureau in 1921. Under the direction of Mrs. Anna Whitmore, the bureau was charged with investigating each police case that involved a young woman. In 1923 the bureau handled the cases of more than eleven hundred young women, an astonishing number when you consider the total female population of the city was only about seventy-five thousand. A police reporter for the *Memphis Press* asked Mrs. Whitmore why so many girls were coming to Memphis: "A girl who fails to find encouragement from her parents when she is ambitious, is liable to leave home to fight it out alone. . . . Other girls leave because they are unable to get the pretty clothes they desire. In the city, they think, they will be able to earn money to buy all the pretty clothes any girl could desire."

To deal with the growing cocaine problem, the city's narcotics division worked closely with the woman's bureau. In 1923 thirty young female addicts where held in jail until they "got off" the drug, and another fifteen were sent to a hospital for treatment. "The 'cure,' condemned in many cities, has been found to be successful there," reported the *Memphis Press*. "The 'cure' consists of placing the addicts in jail, and letting them stay there until they are off the drug. This has been condemned by doctors as a process of torture, which it really is. But police officials believe it is the only way to rehabilitate the addicts and place them back in society. A new world in another city is found for them so there will be no chance for their return to the land of the living dead."

Enterprising young men on Beale Street quickly learned the benefits of introducing impressionable young women to free cocaine and easy money. William Faulkner often wrote about the Memphis brothels of this era in his novels, but many people mistakenly supposed his accounts to be fictitious. Of course, Memphis was not unique in that respect. Brothels were found in almost all American cities at that time. What made Memphis unique was the way drug dealers—and in those days many legitimate Memphis store owners were selling cocaine on the side—learned to pair the demand for the drug with the demand for women as a means of building economic and political empires. As a result of that expertise, Memphians developed the blueprints for the modern-day drug syndicate.

E. H. Crump kept a low public profile in the early 1920s. Six months after his resignation as mayor, he was elected to the financially lucrative office of county trustee, a position he held for eight years. Not eager to tangle with *The Commercial Appeal*, he worked behind the scenes to strengthen his political machine, the likes of which the nation had never seen, not even in politically corrupt Chicago and New York. A profoundly cynical man, he paired the profits of vice with the political clout of black voters in such a way as to magnify the influence of each.

Crump considered running a candidate in the mayoral election of 1919 but decided against it and the day before the election endorsed an independent candidate, Rowlett Paine. When Paine won by a hefty margin, as Crump knew would happen, Crump took credit for the victory. When the Ku Klux Klan flexed its muscle against Paine and others across the mid-South who they feared were falling under the influence of black voters, Crump saw an opening: he supported Paine for reelection against a candidate supported by the Klan. A superb editorial writer, C. P. J. Mooney unleashed the editorial might of *The Commercial Appeal* against the Klan. Mooney felt some discomfort at finding himself on the same side with Crump, but did what he felt he had to do to stem the influence of the Klan. Although it wasn't apparent at the time, Paine's reelection elevated Crump to a Southern-boy godfather status in the eyes of the Memphis underworld. A wily fox, he beat *The Commercial Appeal* at its own game.

In 1926, while working in his office, C. P. J. Mooney, who despised nothing on earth as much as crooked politicians, dropped dead at his desk, opening the door for his nemesis, E. H. Crump, to reenter mayoral politics. The year after Mooney's death, Crump jumped back into mayoral politics by offering a handpicked candidate, Watkins Overton, to run against Paine. When the dust settled, Overton won by a margin of 19,806 to 7,080 votes.

With Mooney gone, Crump was free at last.

■　●　■

Throughout the twenties, Memphis music underwent significant changes. The sophisticated blues of the teens introduced by Handy were replaced on Beale Street by its long-neglected country cousin, the down-home blues. At eight dollars a gig, Fiddling Abe was one of the highest-paid musicians in the city. There were a few good-paying venues that wanted jazz bands, such as the ornate Peabody Hotel, which first opened its doors in the 1920s; but most of the musicians worked solo, and they performed wherever they could—in bars, at parties or barbecues, on the street corner—and their pay was measured in nickels and dimes, not dollars.

Walter "Furry" Lewis was one of the most talented bluesmen to prowl Beale Street in the 1920s. Born in Greenwood, Mississippi, sometime around the turn of the century (he was always a little fuzzy about the exact date), Furry moved to Memphis with his family as a teenager. He found work in the tent shows that came into Memphis on a regular basis, and occasionally he performed with Handy's band. As Furry told it in later years, Handy gave him his first quality guitar, a six-string Martin he used for decades, until he "wore it out." When Handy moved to New York, Furry went on the road with a medicine show, where he got more requests for jokes than music. When he came off the road, he took a job as a street cleaner for the city of Memphis at fifteen cents per hour. It was a job he held until 1966, when the city forced him to retire. It must have been difficult work for him. In 1916,

Furry Lewis, c. 1960s.
Photo courtesy of the Mississippi Valley Collection,
University of Memphis, University Libraries

while hopping a freight, he slipped and fell beneath the train; the wheels severed his leg. For the rest of his life he wore an artificial limb.

Furry is credited with inventing the bottleneck style of guitar playing. I am not sure how valid that claim is, though it is possible. Certainly he was one of the best at performing in that style. He made his own bottlenecks for playing by wrapping a cotton shoestring around the base of a bottle's long neck and setting the shoestring on fire. The heat enabled the bottleneck to be removed in a clean break. He would slip the bottleneck over his finger and use it to fret his guitar, sliding it up and down to create the sound he wanted. He also had a unique way of using his guitar as a percussive instrument, rapping it with his right hand as a rhythmic counterbalance to his left hand's fingering. In 1927 he took time off from his job as a street cleaner to go to Chicago to record five sides for the Vocalion label, which specialized in "race" music. Over the next couple of years he recorded another eighteen songs, some in Memphis at a makeshift studio, for Vocalion and a second label, Victor Records.

By 1958, when Furry met Don Nix, a major figure at Stax Records in the 1960s, the bluesman had faded into obscurity. "I worked downtown at a TG&Y store, and I remember seeing him sweeping the street," says Nix. "He had a guitar in the little buggy he pushed. I knew who he was, but it wasn't until a year later that I actually heard him. He'd sit in Handy Park and play."

By the mid-1960s Nix had adopted Furry. Often he let Furry stay at his house to recover from his frequent alcoholic binges. "One time I found him sleeping on these people's couch," Nix recalls. "He was real sick. He looked terrible, and I was afraid he was going to die. I took him to my house, and he stayed there the rest of the summer. One day he said, 'Don, I need some junk.' I said, 'Junk?' He said, 'Yeah, I need some souce and crackers.' So I went and bought him some rag souce [baloney]. I realized that if you left Furry alone, he would bounce back if he was going to."

Sometimes Nix would spend the night at Furry's house when the bluesman's girlfriend wasn't there to take care of him. She cleaned portable toilets for a carnival and was on the road during the summer months. When she was there she took good care of him. Furry lived in a black neighborhood south of Beale. For Nix, with his white, middle-class upbringing, staying at the two-room apartment was an exotic experience. "It was the blues place," Nix says. "I would stay the night, sleeping in his kitchen, and not think anything about it." Nix pauses, his eyes glazing over with the memory of it. "Now I wish I could go back and stay one more night."

■　●　■

Throughout the 1920s Sleepy John Estes drifted in and out of Memphis from his hometown of Brownsville, Tennessee, becoming a familiar figure on Beale Street. Born in 1904, one of sixteen children, John Adams Estes grew up in a rural area where music was homemade if it was made at all. As a child he constructed a guitar out of a cigar box and a broom handle and learned to make music on the single string he stretched along the handle. His father, a sharecropper, was impressed by what he heard and saved enough money picking cotton to buy his son a real guitar.

Sleepy John learned to play guitar by jamming with his neighbors. After mastering a few chords, he slung the guitar over his shoulder and hit the road. He performed wherever people would listen—at small gatherings, at harvest parties, at birthdays—but he never strayed far beyond the Memphis area. Usually, he received a free meal for his efforts. On occasion, someone would give him a dollar. It was during this time he met eleven-year-old Hammie Nixon, several years his junior; Hammie had a harmonica, so Sleepy John asked him to be his partner and go to Memphis with him. Hammie's mother wasn't too happy about that, but Sleepy John promised to bring him back the next day. They were gone six months.

For nearly thirty years Sleepy John and Hammie performed together. Using Beale Street as a base, they worked in and around Memphis until they got wanderlust, hopping a freight to hobo around the country until they got homesick, when they would return to Memphis. For many of the early bluesmen playing the blues was as much a lifestyle as it was a vehicle for artistic expression. Memphis may have

Sleepy John Estes, c. 1960s.
Photo by Don Nix

been home to Sleepy John and Hammie, but they never really liked the city.

Sleepy John was once asked which was the tougher town, Memphis or Chicago? Memphis, he answered, offering his opinion that Memphis was the leader of dirty work in the world. Hammie echoed his friend's sentiments in an interview with Margaret McKee and Fred Chisenhall. "Beale Street wasn't nothing but good timers and guys walking the street and telling fortunes and conning you and cheating you," he said. When traveling, he discovered it was better not to admit his Memphis connections. "You know, when I first went to Chicago, I couldn't hardly get a room," he said. "I thought maybe it would help me to say I was from Memphis, but come to find out, everywhere I go, they'd say, 'You from Memphis? Oh, I done already rent that room out.' And finally someone told me, said, 'What you say you from Memphis for? Don't tell nobody you from Memphis, man.'"

In 1929 Sleepy John made several recordings in Memphis for Victor Records, including "Diving Duck Blues" and "Broken Hearted, Ragged and Dirty Too." The following year he cut additional sides: "Poor John Blues," "My Black Gal Blues," and "Milk Cow Blues." Over the next decade he recorded over three dozen additional songs, building a national reputation as a country blues singer. But by 1949 the party had ended. Sleepy John and Hammie returned to Memphis, where Sleepy John married and started a family and Hammie found work as a chauffeur and cook. Two years later, Sleepy John lost his eyesight. With life in the city becoming more difficult, he moved his family to Brownsville, with Hammie in tow, and settled into the hard-times, rural lifestyle from which he had begun his life's journey.

After a decade of obscurity, Sleepy John and Hammie were "rediscovered" in the early 1960s by producer Bob Koester, who took them into the studio again and arranged for them to go to Europe with the American Folk Blues Festival. Sleepy John recorded new albums—*The Legend of Sleepy John Estes*, *Broke & Hungry*, and *Brownsville Blues*—and found a new, young, mostly white audience. But the years had taken their toll, and his failing health made performing a chore. On June 5, 1977, Sleepy John passed away. Hammie followed, as he was wont to do, in 1984, giving his traveling companion a good seven years' head start.

Memphis Minnie, born Lizzie Douglas, grew up in Walls, Mississippi, just outside Memphis. A headstrong child, her parents called her "Kid" because she couldn't stand her feminine moniker. She had a disdain for farm work and, as a teen, often ran away from home to explore the bright lights and dim alleys of Beale Street. As a teen she learned to play the guitar; she also learned to exploit her sexuality. An attractive woman with a petite build, she learned at an early age that Beale Street had what she wanted: money and recognition.

With W. C. Handy setting the musical standards, Memphis Minnie (she adopted the name early in her career) did not immediately find a home for her rough-edged, country style of blues. She did what restless youngsters of that era did when they felt stifled: she joined a circus. Touring the small towns that made up the circus circuit, she developed her own unique performing style. Circus life also taught her how to dress and capitalize on her good looks. By the time she returned to Memphis in the 1920s, Handy had moved on and the country style of blues she loved, as performed by Furry Lewis and Sleepy John Estes, was gaining popularity.

Memphis Minnie had a reputation as a fiery, sometimes violent, woman whose promiscuity-for-profit was the talk of the town. She craved sex, and she used sex, brandishing it as a weapon to get what she wanted. Once, after a recording session for Decca, Minnie offered to have sex with Hammie Nixon and the other players in exchange for their share of the money. Homesick James said he knew her before she got famous, when she was an outright streetwalker. Others said she liked to wear dresses when performing so that she could entice men into looking up her skirt. Not surprisingly, Minnie's music often reflected her experience as a prostitute. One song she wrote, "Hustlin' Woman Blues," tells of standing on the corner all night, not able to go home because she hadn't made enough money. Then there's "You Can't Give it Away," in which she taunts a prostitute for trying to sell something that "ain't good to eat" and "ain't good to smell." Minnie was a fearsome guitar picker, but she was no lady.

Whatever Minnie's contemporaries thought about her sexual activity, one thing was certain: no one ever criticized her, at least not to her face. Despite her small size, her elegant jewelry, and her gold-capped front teeth (a sign of status in the black community), she was feared, not so much for her physical strength as for her willingness to do whatever it took to win. Homesick James said she was tougher than any man he knew. When angered, she would reach for whatever was handy—her guitar, a pistol, a knife—and she was not timid about using violence to get her way. Johnny Shines said Minnie had a reputation for violence that outdid anything anyone had actually ever witnessed. "They tell me she shot one old man's arms off, down in Mississippi," Shines told Paul and Beth Garon. "Shot his arm off, or cut it off with a hatchet, something. Some say shot, some say cut. Minnie was a hellraiser, I know that! . . . She'd work Son Joe [her second husband, also a guitarist] over right on the bandstand, right in front of the whole audience. Bang, bop, boom, bop!"

Minnie dominated the Beale Street music scene throughout the 1920s. After she recorded her first record in 1929, she dominated the national blues scene throughout the 1940s and 1950s, along with her husband, Joe McCoy. She was the hottest woman blues artist of her day, recording an impressive string of over one hundred records. Many of her songs, such as "Bumble Bee," which she recorded in 1930, and "I'm Talking about You," became classics. As a guitarist, Minnie was without equal. Her influence extended long past her death. Bonnie Raitt once told me Memphis Minnie was one of the reasons she became a performer, figuring that if Memphis Minnie, a woman, could play the hell out of a guitar, so could she.

After working out of Memphis for several years, Minnie and Joe moved to Chicago in the early 1930s, where Minnie established herself among the city's other blues artists. After she and Joe parted company in 1935, she married guitar player Ernest "Son" Lawlar. Throughout the 1940s she often participated in guitar-playing contests, which would find her facing off challengers such as Muddy Waters. They would take turns playing, then the audience would pick the winner. Minnie usually took home the prize, a fifth or two of whiskey, and her male challengers usually conceded defeat with dignity, but not without pointing out that Minnie probably won because she was a woman and had a skirt to lift at just the right moment.

By 1958 recording sessions were a thing of the past for Minnie. She and Son moved back to Memphis, where she performed on a regular basis in black nightclubs, fish fries, and wherever she could find work. Minnie suffered a stroke, then Son died in 1961, prompting a second, more serious stroke. Minnie spent the remainder of her life in a wheelchair, unable to speak.

In 1968, after hearing about her desperate financial situation, a British blues band held a fund-raiser in London for the ailing blues legend. Proudly they sent the check to America. A party was held at the nursing home where Minnie lived, family members were called in, a newspaper reporter and photographer showed up to document the event, and Minnie was given the money with great ceremony: a total of $117.58. According to a reporter, she spoke only one word: "Thanks." The partygoers were lucky Minnie was paralyzed and unable to express her outrage at such a paltry offering. In better days she would have told them a thing or two.

Minnie died on August 6, 1973, and was buried in an unmarked grave. In the final years of her life, she spent her days in a wheelchair, weeping, a voiceless, pitiful creature, alone, without sex or music.

THE THIRTIES:
SLIP-SLIDING AWAY

s the 1930s began, the Great Depression was little more than a flickering firefly on the horizon. City leaders told Memphians not to worry, that King Cotton would insulate the city from the effects of the Depression. In good times or bad, Memphis maintained its distinction as the murder capital of the nation, a fact that attracted the attention of the national press. By mid-decade the situation had become so desperate that FBI director J. Edgar Hoover sent a special envoy to Memphis to examine the city's homicide records. Baffled by the slaughter, the FBI envoy told city officials that if they classified some homicides as self-defense, the city's murder rate would look better to the public. The police chief agreed to do that, but told reporters that the real solution to the city's murder rate was for the federal government to control the sale and distribution of firearms.

The plentiful supply of alcohol and cocaine in Memphis also was the subject of national speculation. In 1931 *Redbook* magazine noted that Memphis had a speakeasy for every three hundred inhabitants, making it worse than Chicago when it came to alcohol use among the "young society set." In 1935 *Colliers' Weekly* attacked the city for its tolerance of narcotics and prostitution.

As the 1930s began, Beale Street thrived, its dives and brothels filling the pockets of the crime families; but as the decade progressed and the dollars from the cotton plantations dried up, the entertainment district began a slow descent into economic oblivion. Country blues, as performed by Sam Chatmon, Bukka White, and Lillie May Glover, was still the main fare in the clubs, but the more refined musical interpretations of Jimmie Lunceford and Peter Chatman, better known as Memphis Slim, exerted subtle influences on the music scene that eventually had a major impact.

Jimmie Lunceford arrived in Memphis in 1926 by way of Fulton, Missouri, where he was born, and Fisk University, in Nashville, from which he received a bachelor of music degree. While teaching music at Manassas High School in Memphis, he put together a student dance band. They played in and around Memphis during the summer months, attracting a lot of attention. Encouraged, Lunceford added three professional musicians in 1929, all former students at Fisk, and put together a first-rate orchestra. By 1930 the group was really cooking, but Lunceford avoided any association with Beale Street, preferring more staid bookings as a dance band at white society functions. The degree to which white society accepted Lunceford is reflected in the fact that radio station WREC invited his orchestra to perform live on a regular basis.

There were no black radio stations in the city, and racial segregation was the order of the day, except on Beale Street, where the only color that mattered was green. All over the city, restrooms and water fountains were labeled for "whites" and "coloreds." Restaurants would not serve blacks, and hotels would not register them as guests. Theaters, if they admitted blacks at all, required them to sit in the balcony. The only way blacks could participate in white social events was as food servers or entertainers. I am sure black activists would today consider Lunceford an Uncle Tom—he led his orchestra with a long, white baton and dressed elegantly—but I don't think he was being accommodating to white society so much as living out a fantasy of how society should conduct itself.

Lunceford was a strict bandleader. He did not drink or use drugs. He preached to his orchestra about respectability, and he would not tolerate musicians who crossed the line. If you do not respect yourself, he told them, the public will not respect your music. Considering his disdain for any deviation from his strict Protestant upbringing (his father was a choirmaster), it is not surprising Lunceford left Memphis at the first opportunity. After touring in the Northeast Lunceford took the group—then named the Chickasaw Syncopators, after the Indian tribe that first settled the Memphis bluffs—into New York, where they took up residency at the legendary Cotton Club. Throughout the 1930s Lunceford's jazz orchestra was one of the most influential in the nation.

What Lunceford learned in Memphis was very much a music phenomenon unique to the city. His gift was as an arranger, not as a composer, but in much the same way Handy blended music styles, Lunceford blended instruments with spectacular results. He played a significant role in the development of swing, and by the 1940s Glenn Miller and Benny Goodman had built on his precise, melodic arrangements to take swing to a new level. Unfortunately, Lunceford did not make the transition to jazz during the 1940s and was content to maintain his status as a show bandleader. In that capacity, Lunceford appeared in a number of movies, including *Blues in the Night*.

"The music of Lunceford's mid-thirties' glory days was, for a moment in time, the very best that jazz had to offer," observes music historian Gunther Schuller. "The Lunceford band, second only to Ellington and for a few brief years even more consistent than his, reigned supreme for a while—until Basie and Goodman came along and, combined with Ellington's full maturing in the late thirties, pushed Lunceford to the sidelines artistically. But the Lunceford band at its best—and fortunately in recorded form it is still with us—was something wonderful to admire and cherish, a still timeless music, and a superior, significant part of our American musical heritage."

In the summer of 1947 Lunceford made a personal appearance at a music store in Seaside, Oregon. While signing autographs, he collapsed in the store and was taken to a hospital. On July 12, at the age of forty-five, he died. The cause of death was listed as food poisoning. There were rumors he had been murdered, but nothing was ever proved.

While Lunceford was basking in the bright lights of New York—and Fiddling Abe Fortas was joining the faculty of Yale law school—their country cousins on Beale Street were experiencing hard times. Between 1930 and 1932 unemployment in Memphis rose from four thousand to seventeen thousand as the city felt the effects of the Depression.

Fewer jobs meant fewer dollars for Beale Street, but the dollars that did get there were desperate for entertainment—and cocaine.

■　●　■

Among the best of the peripatetic country bluesmen who breezed in and out of Beale Street during this time was guitarist Sam Chatmon, a member of the Mississippi Sheiks and a relative of Memphis Slim, who spelled his name Chatman. From the turn of the century, the Chatmon family—there were at least nine full brothers and maybe as many half brothers, all the sons of a former slave—made up one of the best touring bands in the South. One brother (born Armenter Chatmon) billed himself as "Bo Carter" and had the most successful solo career, performing blues and so-called "hokum" or sexually suggestive songs. Another, Lonnie, was a fiddle player, who worked with both Bo and the Sheiks.

From their hometown of Bolton, Mississippi, they made their way through Tennessee and Illinois and occasionally into Georgia performing at white parties and picnics. They usually went by the name Mississippi Sheiks, but they sometimes called themselves the Blacksnakes or the Mud Steppers. They recorded their first records in the late 1920s, but it was during the 1930s that they made their biggest impact, recording nearly one hundred songs. Their most successful records were "Stop and Listen" and "Sitting on Top of the World," which became a national hit in the early 1930s and was covered in later years by Frank Sinatra, the Grateful Dead, and Bob Wills and the Texas Playboys, to name a few.

In the late 1920s Sam moved to Hollandale, Mississippi, a small Mississippi Delta farming town south of Memphis on U.S. 61, where he became a fixture on the local street corners. When he performed in Memphis, either with his brothers or solo, he always traveled by bus. The bus picked him up on the street corner on which he performed and deposited him in Memphis only a block or so from Beale Street. Sam performed at festivals and clubs all over the country for nearly five decades, but he didn't like to fly and always went by bus. He once turned down a booking in Europe because he didn't like the eight-

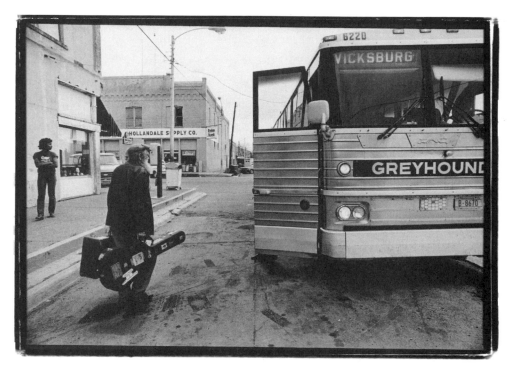

Sam Chatmon boarding the bus in Hollandale, Mississippi, for Memphis, c. 1980.
Photo © Steve Gardner

hundred-dollar paycheck and didn't want to fly.

"My boy told me once, say, 'Oh, Dad, go ahead over there with Memphis Slim. Boy, eight hundred dollars would be good for a week. You ain't going to die 'til your time come,'" Sam told Margaret McKee and Fred Chisenhall. "I told him, 'Yeah, but I'd look like a fool. I'd be way up over all that water and somebody else's time come and I had to follow him down for him to die. I'd look just like a fool following him down to die.'"

Sam never cared much for the Memphis nightlife. He preferred working in Jackson, Mississippi, or in New Orleans. Sometimes he worked as a sideman with Louis Armstrong in New Orleans. He had a high opinion of Louis's trumpet playing, but felt his singing was just "clowning." He also had a high opinion of Elvis Presley. He especially liked Presley's "Jailhouse Rock," which Sam once said knocked right at the door of the blues. Just a bit more, he said, and Presley would have walked right in.

By the end of the 1940s Sam's musical fling had ended. He worked at odd jobs in Hollandale throughout the 1950s and 1960s. He was "rediscovered" in the 1970s and toured extensively. He appeared on NBC television's *Today Show* and performed at every major music festival in North America, including the Mariposa Folk Festival in Toronto and the New Orleans Jazz and Heritage Festival. With his long white beard, he cut a striking figure on the blues revival scene. He died in Hollandale on February 2, 1983.

■　●　■

Within a month or so after I moved to Memphis in January 1982, I went to a downtown nightclub, Blues Alley, to sample the nightlife. It was there that I first heard Lillie May Glover, who liked to bill herself as "Ma Rainey Two," after the legendary 1920s blues recording star. Lillie May was a big woman and she had a big voice. Back in the 1930s she often was compared to Ma Rainey because of the power of her voice. She was in poor health and did all of her vocals seated in a chair on the bandstand. She shared billing with Little Laura Dukes, the daughter of Alex Dukes, W. C. Handy's drummer back in the old days. While Little Laura sang, Lillie May usually napped, her chin collapsed onto her chest. When it was Lillie May's turn to sing, the guitar player tapped her on the shoulder, bringing her back to life.

Lillie May began her career in the 1920s touring with the Rabbit Foot and Georgia minstrels. By the 1930s she had settled into a regular routine on Beale Street and at the Cotton Club across the river in West Memphis, Arkansas. She never found a national audience, but for nearly sixty years she was regarded as a local celebrity. In some ways, her personal life was more interesting than her musical career. Nicknamed "Big Mama" because of her imposing size, she developed a reputation as a street brawler and a practitioner of the ancient, black magic art of voodoo, or hoodoo, as it was more commonly called in those days.

Beale Street had a thing for hoodoo women. Almost from day one, they were there, casting their spells and doing their dirty work, usually for a handsome profit. The practice of hoodoo was illegal in

Lillie May Glover at a downtown concert, c. 1970s.
Photo courtesy of the Mississippi Valley Collection, University of Memphis,
University Libraries

Memphis, but Big Mama never let that stop her from casting a spell or
two. She had a small apartment just off Beale Street. Sometimes she
sent hustlers out onto the street to bring in customers, but usually
word-of-mouth referrals were enough to keep her busy.

She liked to tell the story of the woman who came to her in search
of a spell that would get rid of her abusive lover. Big Mama had the
woman bring her one of his socks. She sprinkled toilet water on the
sock and muttered magic over it. She told the woman that if she tossed
the hoodooed sock into a creek she would get rid of her lover and he
would never bother her again. Later, the woman's sister showed up on

Big Mama's doorstep, raising hell. Her sister had fallen into the creek and nearly drowned fooling with that damned hoodooed sock. Big Mama, doing some quick thinking, told the woman she should get down on her hands and knees to thank her. It was her hoodoo magic that saved her sister from drowning. Eventually the woman did get rid of her lover, and, of course, Big Mama took credit for it.

Hoodoo had two main purposes—or should I say *has* two purposes, because it still is practiced in Memphis: to give an enemy bad luck or to remove bad luck that has been inflicted by an enemy. Hoodoo was a powerful force on Beale Street. It appealed not just to the ignorant and the poor but to a wide spectrum of people.

The Hoodoo cartel was built on the same premise. Many Beale Street merchants sold cocaine from their stores. It didn't take them long to realize that the same people always came back for more. It also did not escape their attention that practitioners of black magic also catered to a repeat clientele. People who really wanted cocaine, whose bodies craved the drug, would do anything to get it. Similarly, people who desperately wanted a hoodooist to remove a curse would do whatever the hoodooist told them to do, even murder. Using the addictive powers of cocaine and hoodooism as controls, organized crime built a low-volume, under-the-counter cocaine and bootleg whisky business into a major economic force during the 1930s. It built up a network of black street vendors and used hoodoo to make them tow the line. Political contributions kept the heat off their vendors.

The money flowed in so quickly that the cartel invested in real estate. When large amounts of cash became difficult to explain, they diversified into dozens of small businesses. Who was to say that a small company that sold coathangers, for example, did not take in large sums of cash for coathanger orders? Small businesses were the perfect vehicle by which to conceal illegal profits. There was no need for the crime bosses to send cash out of the country to launder it. They could take care of that right there in Memphis.

Besides, the Memphis crime bosses never invested much trust in outsiders, as gangster Machine Gun Kelly found out in 1933. Sought by the FBI on a kidnapping charge, Kelly and his wife, Kathryn, hid out in Memphis and set up a bootlegging operation. For about two months he sold whisky in and around Memphis. Bluesman Thomas Pinkston told an interviewer that Kelly sold bootleg whisky to Sweet Mama's, located off Beale at 311 S. Fourth. It was Kelly's misfortune that the club was owned by a woman who was having an affair with a Memphis police detective. My guess is that Kelly's arrest was not the result of a sudden devotion to civic duty by the club owner or her cop lover. The Hoodoo cartel has never encouraged competition, but unlike the crime families in Chicago and New York, it seldom used violence against competitors unless it was indirect. Instead, it preferred to use its police "source" to put a hoodoo curse on its competitors.

There is no evidence Boss Crump was personally involved in drug trafficking and prostitution, but there is evidence his organization was financed by contributions from racketeers who were. In a biting article published in the January 26, 1935, edition of *Collier's Weekly*, writer Owen White linked Crump to the "commercialized vice" prevalent in the city: "Professional sinners, therefore—that is, men and women who run gambling houses, dance halls, blind pigs, policy rackets, houses of ill-fame and all that sort of thing—being cash assets for professional politicians, are not only encouraged to operate but are actually instructed to go ahead and provide everybody, both visitors and home folks, with as much wide-open wickedness as possible."

White told of parties he attended at which "coke and corn" were in abundance and where "unclad" dancing girls provided the entertainment. "Memphis (and I'm not talking about black Memphis now, but white Memphis) supports a population of about 7000 professional sinners whose sole business is to provide everybody with a good time," he continued. "They do it; they make a nice job of it, while furthermore they also do something else constructive, which is to take away from legitimate business the entire financial burden of supporting the political ring that actually runs Memphis and Shelby Country, and almost runs the entire state of Tennessee."

Actually, by 1935 Crump and his organization did run the entire state. With a firm grip on the mayor's office—in 1931 Crump's candidate won by a margin of 23,684 to 869 votes, and in 1935 ran unopposed—Crump looked for ways to expand the organization's influence beyond Memphis. He ran for Congress and was elected to two terms.

He voted for every New Deal initiative offered by the Roosevelt administration. His loyalty was not overlooked by Roosevelt, who quietly appointed Fiddling Abe Fortas to the Agricultural Adjustment Administration in 1933.

Not particularly infatuated with Washington, DC, but acutely aware of the economic plums there for the picking, Crump looked for someone to represent his interests. U.S. Senator Kenneth McKellar, a Shelby Country native, jumped at the chance to form an alliance with the "Boss." Together, they and their benefactors, of which the Hoodoo cartel was but one contributor, decided who would be elected in Memphis and who would win important state offices, who would get federal contracts and who would be prosecuted for crimes at the local, state, and federal level. That partnership lasted nearly two decades.

Noted historian V. O. Key, Jr., whose book *Southern Politics* was once a bible for the study of politics in the South, wrote about Crump in 1948 when the Boss still had political teeth: "Although Crump has no organized forces of Brown Shirts, some of his critics in the state have stayed away from Memphis in fear that a visit there would endanger their lives. An insult, a scuffle, a planted gun, a verdict of justifiable homicide in self-defense—all these expectation have been worked up in the minds of such persons by events in Memphis."

The thirties were critical to the development of Memphis's favorite fiddle player, Abe Fortas. After his graduation from Yale, he taught at the law school for a while, where he met his wife-to-be, Carolyn Agger, a cigar-smoking economist. She enrolled in law school and took classes under her husband, but the academic life was attractive to neither of them. Abe took a position with the Agricultural Adjustment Administration, better known as the farm bureau, then quickly moved on to the Securities and Exchange Commission. Carolyn landed a job with the National Labor Relations Board, then quickly moved over to the tax division of the Department of Justice.

During that time Abe was a tireless networker. While still teaching at Yale, he met a tall, aggressive Texan, Lyndon Johnson, who worked as secretary to a Texas congressman. They became friends and often visited each other's apartments, where they took turns cooking steaks. Throughout that time Abe maintained his contacts in Memphis. One can imagine the glee that greeted Abe's appointment to the SEC and Carolyn's appointment to the tax division of the Justice Department by that benevolent custodian of Memphis values, Congressman Boss Crump.

In a 1937 visit to Memphis Abe went by to see his mother, who still lived in the heart of Beale Street at 525 Pontotoc. Cornered by a newspaper reporter, who asked if he still played his fiddle, Abe said he did, but only for his own amusement. He said he often played with his wife's brother, a music instructor. "We get together and play and have a good time," Abe said. "I'm going in for serious music now and I play it rather badly."

■ ● ■

Not playing for their own amusement were Booker T. Washington White, known professionally as Bukka White, and Peter Chatman, better known as Memphis Slim. They played to put food on the table. They were both probably performing on Beale Street when Abe visited his mother in 1937.

Did the three men ever meet on the street? Did Abe take time to sample the music while he was in town, or did he spend all his time visiting his mother and meeting with his Memphis benefactors? We'll never know, but it's tempting to imagine Abe, stiffened somewhat by his straightlaced Yale education, walking the short distance from his mother's house to Beale Street, then ducking into the Green Mule or Sweet Mama's to mingle with the hot-blooded whores and coke dealers before heading back to Washington.

White had no hopes of attending Yale. An ex-con, he had moved to Memphis from Mississippi, where he had served two years in the state penitentiary. Details of the crime are sketchy. There was a crap game; a man ended up dead; White took the fall. As a guitarist, he was a master of the Delta blues—and several of his records, such as "Parchman Farm," describing life in the notorious Mississippi state prison, and "Aberdeen, Mississippi," are classics—but as a professional musician he was always just a step away from the poorhouse. He was a fixture on Beale Street throughout the 1930s, but he never made enough money to sustain a career. He eventually gave it up to open a secondhand furniture store.

In 1962 Bob Dylan focused new attention on White when he recorded one of his songs, "Fixin' to Die." As a result, White reemerged from his furniture store, took his nickel-plated steel guitar out of storage, and toured all over the United States and Europe, winning college audiences over with his brash voice and folksy style. He recorded a few more albums, including *Mississippi Blues* and *Big Daddy*, then retired from music again, this time for good, and returned to Memphis, where he lived in a rented room south of Beale Street. He died in 1977.

■　●　■

By the age of sixteen Memphis Slim was performing professionally in juke joints around the South. It was not an easy life. The only dependable way to get from one town to the next was by freight train, and that usually was frowned on by the railroad. He decided to return to Memphis after a wintertime trip to Chicago that left him shivering in the bitter cold. His clothing was too thin to allow him to hobo in the North.

When he returned to Memphis in the early 1930s—he was still a teenager, because he was born in 1915—he went straight to Beale Street. He hung around a club where bluesman Roosevelt Sykes, his hero, performed on a regular basis. Sykes left town one day to do some recording in Chicago, and Memphis Slim saw his chance.

"I went in there, and I had to be drunk, because I didn't have the nerve to go in there, and started playing the piano and singing like Roosevelt Sykes, and a guy came up and asked my name, and I said it was Peter Chatman," he says. "And he said: 'You Peter Chatman's son?' and I said: 'Yes.' They were all hustlers together. He asked if I wanted to work, and I got the job, not because I was Peter Chatman's son, but because I sang like Roosevelt Sykes. And then I really had them coming in listening to me."

Memphis Slim's father was well known for having owned a string of juke joints in Memphis and across the river, in Arkansas. He was an amateur musician but never tried to make a living at it. Despite his father's background—or perhaps because of it—Memphis Slim encountered opposition as a child whenever he showed an interest in the blues. "I was called a 'good-for-nothing mannish boy' when I was eight and singing," he recalled years later. "Now when you start at eight, they call you 'genius.'"

As a blues musician, he was in the minority on Beale Street because he played piano at a time when most blues performers played guitar, but he played with great style—he had a tendency to perform a lot of bass-note flourishes when he was in a boogie-woogie mode—and he was a local star by the time he got out of his teens. His pay was usually $1.25 a night, plus two bottles of cheap whisky. Compare that to the $8 a night Fiddling Abe earned a decade earlier. A good blues musician in those days, he once recalled, could judge his worth by the number of fights that broke out during his performance. "When you were singing and touched somebody, they started fighting, and that meant you had success," he says.

By 1939 Memphis Slim had enough of the tough Beale Street nightlife and the pitifully low wages he earned as a performer. He moved to Chicago and recorded for Okeh Records using the name Peter Chatman. The next year he recorded for Bluebird. This time he used the nickname he had picked up on Beale Street: Memphis Slim. He joined popular bluesman Big Bill Broonzy's band, and over the next few years made a name for himself in Chicago as one of the best boogie-woogie piano players on the circuit. By 1944 he was popular enough to form his own band, Memphis Slim & His House Rockers.

Throughout the 1940s and early 1950s he continued to build audiences with songs such as "Having Fun," "Wish Me Well," and "Everyday I Have the Blues," but it wasn't until the late 1950s that he was caught up in the blues revival sweeping white college campuses and found a large audience. By that time he had added several outstanding musicians to his band, including guitarist Matt Murphy, who later performed with the Blues Brothers.

During the late 1950s and early 1960s he performed with Pete Seeger and Joan Baez at clubs in Greenwich Village and at the Newport Folk Festival. It was during that time that Memphis Slim began making his first tours of Europe. He was especially popular in France, where he often was booked at the Parisian cabaret Les Trois Maillets. By 1961 his marriage was falling apart. He returned that year from a tour of Europe, took a hard look at his marriage and at his opportunities in the United States, and promptly turned around and returned to Paris, where he married the daughter of a Paris cabaret owner and began a new life.

In 1978 Memphis Slim returned to Memphis for a homecoming performance with the Memphis Symphony at the Orpheum, an ornate theater at the western end of Beale Street. He confided to reporters that he was apprehensive about returning to Memphis: "I've been to Newport. I've been to Carnegie Hall. I've been to Monterey, but coming home? I'm nervous about it." His performance at the Orpheum marked the first time he had ever been allowed downstairs in the theater. Growing up in Memphis, he had been required to sit in the fourth balcony, the area designated for African Americans. Times had changed, even in Memphis.

"I can remember when I was on Beale Street, the white people were only allowed there on Thursday nights," he told a *Press-Scimitar* reporter. "That was for the 'Midnight Rambles' at the Palace Theater, and all the police in town would be down there to protect them. Any other time that any white people went down there, they were told: 'You're on your own,' and if something happened to them, they were told: 'We told you not to go down there.' It was rough. The white police—that's all they had—didn't come down much on other nights, because it was so tough."

Memphis Slim was pleased to be honored by his hometown, but the event brought out deep-seated conflicts within himself. In Paris he was a star, a real somebody. He had recorded over five hundred songs, half of them his own compositions. He was a headliner at folk and blues festivals all over the world. Even the U.S. Senate had acknowledged him by proclaiming him "America's Ambassador at Large for Good Will," an honor previously held by Bob Hope and Louis Armstrong. But in Memphis, indeed throughout most of the South, he was just another blues musician. Every town in the South had one or two on the street corner.

Memphis Slim was gracious, but during the visit he struggled to

Memphis Slim at the Mississippi Delta Blues Festival, 1976.
Photo © Steve Gardner

come to terms with Memphis—and, by necessity, his own life. "It's a pitiful thing, that when I was a young man, blues were very strong in Memphis, but later on when people realized how strong blues was going to be, they started making the black people feel ashamed of the blues, and that's why the blues is not as strong here now. Today, when I talk to people, even in Memphis, they are still ashamed of the blues. They call the blues all kinds of other names, because the black man who owned the blues is still ashamed of the blues."

Memphis Slim returned to Paris and lived another ten years. He died there in 1988 of kidney failure at age seventy-two. He died a long way from the home of the blues, but in the end, home was not so much where his heart was as where he was best able to define himself. "I didn't know I was a poet until I went to Europe," he said. "But I am a poet. Really a poet."

On September 3, 1938, an event occurred in Memphis that had a disastrous effect on Beale Street and radically changed the way organized crime pursued its interests. On that evening, eight of the city's most prominent citizens gathered at an establishment called the Saddle and Spur Club. A private club, it was located in a white neighborhood in a secluded grove near the Fairgrounds. At the club that night were Memphis's heavy hitters, who would become known as the Memphis Eight after tragedy struck that night.

Abe Plough was the founder of the company that is now known as Schering-Plough. Plough's first product was an antiseptic "healing oil" he manufactured himself and sold from a horse and buggy on Beale Street. By 1938 Plough's company was a major player in the national patent medicine and cosmetics industry. A. R. Orgill was a member of a prominent family whose wholesale hardware company was the oldest still-operational business in Memphis. It had begun in 1847 and specialized in fine cutlery and guns imported from England. The list continues with Dr. Eugene Rosamond, a prominent pediatrician, Julian Wilson, a judge, and Julius Marlowe, president of a coal company that would have had an interest in Boss Crump's decision early in his career to let the city take over operation of its privately owned power plant.

The Memphis Eight were playing a friendly game of poker at a private club in the heart of suburban Memphis. They sat at a poker table, awaiting a midnight snack that was being prepared by the club waiter, when three black men armed with pistols burst into the room. The bandits entered from three different doors. "This is a stick-up and hold up your hands," said the man who entered from the south entrance. Before anyone could respond, he leaped forward and shot Dr. Rosamond in the neck from a distance of about three feet, point-blank range. When he took the bullet, Rosamond, who was sitting next to Plough, fell over into his friend's arms. Plough cradled the critically wounded pediatrician as Dwyer and the waiter ran for the door. The gunmen squeezed off several rounds but missed. As Dwyer and the waiter exited the club, they were fired at by another man waiting outside. Those shots also missed, and the two men took cover in the grove.

The gunmen calmly went from person to person, collecting their money. The gunman went through Plough's pockets, taking about a hundred dollars in cash. Then as quickly as they had entered, the gunmen left the room, dropping most of the money as they fled.

Police officials told reporters the bandits were professionals. Three days later, after an intensive city and county search, detectives cornered two men they identified as the bandits. While they were being handcuffed, the men knocked down one of the detectives and ran away. Oddly, the detectives did not fire at the suspects and allowed them to escape. When asked about the incident later, police officials said the detectives had not fired at the suspects because it was police policy for officers to fire only if fired upon.

The Saddle and Spur Club robbery was staged as a warning to one or more of the club's members. Clearly Dr. Rosamond was not the target of the message. Was the Hoodoo cartel the sender of the message? We may never know. We know the police were not very interested in apprehending the bandits. We know that retaliation by misdirection is the trademark of the cartel. And we know the robbery resulted in major changes in the way organized crime—and Beale Street—went about its business.

For almost a year after the Saddle and Spur Club incident, Boss Crump struggled to maintain control of the city. The murder rate still soared. The national media still slammed the city, but now, instead of blaming uneducated blacks for the high crime rate, writers blamed prominent white Memphians for their involvement in the booming vice trade. Crump, caught in the middle of a power struggle between competing crime families, was indecisive for months as the rivalries festered. Abruptly, the Memphis turf wars were resolved in 1939, when Tennessee repealed Prohibition. In one swift move the state put the city's bootleggers out of business.

The wisdom of the day had it that Crump was caught off guard by the state's actions. I doubt that. The legislature's action didn't overly concern Crump because his supporters had already moved away from bootlegging drugs and alcohol into the more lucrative area of government contracts. By 1940 organized crime had moved its base of operations from the street into plush offices. Clearly, Crump's concern was not so much over his economic base as over his power base. He had to take action to shore up that base. But what?

In 1939 Crump announced that he was running for mayor. That shocked everyone. He already controlled every office in the city and most state offices. Why would he "step down" to run for mayor? As usual, he had his reasons. When the votes were counted in the mayoral election, Crump won by a margin of 31,825 to nothing (he had no opponent). That is not to say people weren't speaking out against him. A coalition composed of newspaper editor Meeman at the *Press-Scimitar*, lawyer Lucius Burch, and Edmund Orgill, brother to the Saddle and Spur Club Orgill, pleaded with voters, but no one wanted to listen. In 1940 Crump was sworn in as mayor. Treating it as a joke, he promptly resigned and went to a football game. He didn't really want to be mayor. He just wanted to prove to the Saddle and Spur Club, and anyone else who doubted it, that he was still the Boss.

But he wasn't finished. Without warning or debate, he ordered Beale Street shut down. The gin joints, the whorehouses, the casinos, the street vendors who sold cocaine, the juke joints that sold bootleg alcohol—all were shut down. Memphis musicians were tossed out on the street. Boss Crump may have been old and crazy, but he was no fool. Some of his supporters were still involved in vice, but so were some of his enemies. His main supporters had moved on to white-collar crime: that was where the real money was.

■ ● ■

The decade ended with a visit on December 1, 1939, by W. C. Handy, who returned to Memphis for a heralded championship football game between two of the city's black high schools. It was billed as the Blues Bowl. The city honored Handy with a parade that began on Beale Street and ended at the stadium. Handy said a few words to the audience and then played his trumpet. For the first time in over two decades, he played the "Memphis Blues" in the city that inspired it.

"Handy was resplendent for the occasion in a black topcoat, gleaming white muffler, gray spats and walking cane," reported the *Press-Scimitar*. "The 'Daddy of the blues' certainly found that his child was being nourished and cherished in its birthplace—Beale Street."

There is no record Crump attended the football game or tried to contact Handy during his visit. Whatever Handy felt upon his return to Memphis, the next morning's headline in *The Commercial Appeal* certainly must have put it in perspective: HANDY TOOTS A GOLDEN HORN: DARKIEDOM SQUEALS IN GLEE.

5

THE FORTIES:
THE DOOR SLAMS SHUT

eale Street was devastated by Crump's 1940 crackdown on vice. Black leaders had provided unquestioned support of Crump's candidates because the vice trade, unsavory as it was, was the only area of the Memphis economy open to black entrepreneurs. By turning his back on the black underworld in favor of white-collar machinations, Crump burned bridges between the races that would not be rebuilt for nearly three decades.

The vice crackdown of 1940 did not result in the closing of all the nightclubs on Beale Street, but since it eliminated the source of much of the ready cash spent in the clubs, it crippled the ability of musicians to make a decent living. Many blues musicians stayed on the street, but most moved on to greener pastures. West Memphis, Arkansas, took up the slack by accommodating some of the prostitutes and drug dealers, and nightclubs with gaming tables popped up along the Arkansas side of the river in the shadow of the Memphis skyline. Memphis musicians looked for opportunities wherever they could find them.

Out of Crump's crackdown, or perhaps because of it, Memphis music, a life force embedded deep in the belly of the city, looked toward new technology for ways to survive. It would find nourishment and then rebirth first in radio, then in the recording industry. As the decade began, Lillie May Glover was still performing on Beale Street, as were Sam Chatmon and Sleepy John Estes on a sporadic basis. However, one

Sonny Boy Williamson.
Photo by Chris Strachwitz, courtesy of Arhoolie Records

of the most enterprising bluesman of the early 1940s was Rice Miller, known professionally as Sonny Boy Williamson 2. Born in Mississippi around 1910 (the actual date is disputed), Sonny Boy spent much of the thirties as an itinerant musician, performing with hard-core bluesmen such as Robert Johnson. Much of his early life is a historical blur, because in later years he told different stories to different people. He appropriated his professional name from John Lee "Sonny Boy" Williamson, a Chicago blues musician who was murdered outside a Chicago nightclub in 1948. Miller was using the name long before the other "Sonny Boy" died, and despite a number of outstanding records by the Chicago "Sonny Boy" in the mid-to-late 1940s, there can be no doubt Miller was the more important musician of the two. He was a wizard on the harmonica and his vocals were earthy and passionate. He was one of the first bluesmen ever to use the harp as a lead instrument.

In 1941 Helena, Arkansas, a Delta river town about sixty miles south of Memphis, got its first radio station. It was christened KFFA, call letters that showed deference to an organization that was popular in that area, the Future Farmers of America. Because the economy was almost exclusively agricultural, the radio station designed its programming to appeal to a rural audience. That usually meant country music and crop reports. The nearest large city was Memphis. Technically, Helena residents, being loyal Arkansans, acknowledged Little Rock as their capital, but because, as in most Delta towns in Arkansas and Mississippi, black residents composed a significant percentage of the population, Memphis was considered their spiritual capital.

To travel to Memphis it was necessary to either ride the train (usually too expensive) or take the ferry across the river to Delta Landing. The ferry, incidentally, was operated by Harold Jenkins, country singer Conway Twitty's father. From Delta Landing, you could drive about fifteen miles to U.S. 61 and then have a straight shot into Memphis.

Sonny Boy often worked the juke joints around Helena. KFFA went on the air at a time when the area's clubs (where he worked) were still reeling from Crump's crackdown. When Sonny Boy heard about the radio station, he asked the white station owner if he would air a blues show. The owner liked the idea, but told him he needed a sponsor. He sent him over to talk to Max Moore, owner of the Interstate Grocery. When he heard Sonny Boy's idea, Max was very interested. He had his own line of flour and corn meal and saw a blues show as a way to market his products in the black community. He agreed to sponsor the show. Because King Biscuit was the name of his four, he decided to call the show *King Biscuit Time*. To promote the corn meal, he renamed it "Sonny Boy Corn Meal." The package boasted a picture of Sonny Boy sitting barefoot on a tow sack.

King Biscuit Time aired daily at noon. Sonny Boy became a household name, not just among blacks, but among whites as well. The format of the show was simple: fifteen minutes of live blues, interspersed with commercials for King Biscuit Flour and Sonny Boy Corn Meal. The show was broadcast from the KFFA studio on the fifth floor of the Helena National Bank building. From 1941 to 1981 it did for the blues what the Grand Ole Opry had done for country music. For many years, the show replaced Beale Street as a venue for Memphis blues musicians.

During that time the show had two white announcers, Hugh Smith and Sunshine Sonny Payne. I never met Smith, but I met Sunshine in 1988 when I produced a weekly syndicated radio program based on the old "King Biscuit" format. Sunshine, then in his sixties, was one of my announcers. He was reserved to the point of timidity, but when the tape started rolling, the big booming voice that had been a trademark for *King Biscuit Time* for four decades filled the room with the resonant good humor that made him a household name in the Delta. Small in stature but stocky in build, he was always immaculately dressed, a walking advertisement for the well-mannered Southern gentleman.

Sunshine told me about his first meeting with Sonny Boy. Two things stuck out in his memory. Sonny Boy showed up at the radio station wearing a derby hat—and Sunshine had never seen a derby hat. The other was Sonny Boy's appearance. "I don't mean to be insulting, but he had a nose just like a buzzard's beak, " Sunshine says. "A lot of the blues performers called him the Buzzard Beak."

Sonny Boy put together an outstanding house band. Alternating on guitar were Robert "Junior" Lockwood, Houston Stackhouse, and Joe "Willie" Wilkens. On drums was James "Peck" Curtis. Joe "Pine Top" Perkins came down from Memphis to play piano. The routine was always the same. They showed up at the studio a few minutes before the show aired. The musicians sat down to play their instruments, but Sonny Boy stood and faced the microphone at eye level. Every day Sunshine asked him what he was going to sing so that he could announce it, and every day Sonny Boy said he didn't know yet. But when the show began, he sang and the band played on cue, usually something they made up on the spot.

"When he came in, he always had a big smile on his face," says Sunshine. "He would greet all the musicians and naturally the guy who would be hosting the show, in most cases myself. After that, everything was strictly business. He got serious. He didn't want anybody to foul up. He wanted you right then and there on the spot to do your thing and do it right. That was the easiest way to make him mad. He got real serious about his music." Pine Top Perkins, on the show on a regular basis from 1943 to 1948, agreed with Sunshine on that point. "Me and Sonny Boy could get along all right," he says. "He was kinda' crabby, but he never did bother me too much."

Sonny Boy was paid fifteen dollars a week. Compared to normal wages of that era—fifty cents to one dollar a day—that was good pay, especially for a fifteen-minute workday. As a result of the program, Sonny Boy's fame spread. In the late 1940s he sold a radio station in West Memphis on his idea for a blues format. For a while he did both shows, living in Memphis and commuting to Helena and West Memphis. Then in 1951 he teamed up with Elmore James and recorded his first record, "Dust My Broom." By 1955 he was ready for the big time. He went to Chicago and signed with Chess Records. "Bring It on Home," "Don't Start Me to Talkin" (a Top 10 hit on R&B charts in 1955), and "Help Me" established Sonny Boy as one of the leading bluesmen of the postwar period. An excellent songwriter, his songs were marked by biting wit and a fatalistic view of society. He went to Europe and played a significant role in the development of the British blues-rock invasion that hit America in the 1960s. While in Europe he performed with the Yardbirds and the Animals, who later offered American audiences their own version of Sonny Boy's "Bring It on Home."

Sonny Boy was in and out of Helena during the late 1950s and early 1960s. When in town he always stopped by KFFA to perform on *King Biscuit Time*. In 1964 he returned for one of his regular visits, but this time there was something different about him. Sonny Boy told Sunshine he had come home to die.

Shocked, Sunshine told him, "No one ever knows when they are going to die. That's God's thing."

Sonny Boy shook his head. "I know," he said.

He rented a room upstairs over the Dreamland Café. A few months later Sunshine was at the radio station when he got word that Sonny Boy had died in his sleep.

"I didn't believe it," he told me. "I felt somebody was kidding me. They used to try to wake him up and they couldn't get him awake. That was the first thought that entered my mind, that somebody was snow-jobbing me. When I actually saw his body, I knew he was gone and it hurt." Years later, Sunshine still couldn't talk about it without the grief slipping into his voice. The two races may not have eaten or slept together during those segregationist years, but they cared about each other and often forged lifelong friendships. Sunshine was devastated by Sonny Boy's death. "I felt kind of dead myself," he says. "I cried."

■ ● ■

Sonny Boy Williamson ignited a spark in Memphis with his radio program. It was a slow-burning fuse that didn't detonate until 1948, but throughout the early-to-mid-1940s it inched forward with a slow, steady burn. One of Sonny Boy's regular listeners in Indianola, Mississippi, was a youngster named Riley Ben King. When *King Biscuit Time* went on the air in 1941 King was sixteen years old. He attended school in cold weather and worked in the cotton fields in warm weather. For King and thousands of other working black youngsters like him, *King Biscuit Time* was the main source of entertainment. "We would be in the fields and we would go home for lunch," King says. "We hurried so we would be there when 12:15 came so we could catch the King Biscuit program. I heard them so long, it seemed like I really knew them."

Riley Ben King went on to become the legendary B. B. King, but that was later, much later, and in the interim *King Biscuit Time* not only entertained him, it gave him a vision of a better life. He could hear black men participating, not just in the mainstream of Southern life, but in the forefront of new technology. Just as important, he could hear black men and white men bantering together on the airwaves, communicating man to man. It instilled a sense of pride in him.

In 1946 King went to Memphis to visit his cousin, bluesman Bukka White. He stayed several months, making the rounds of the clubs with Bukka, watching him perform. Back home in Indianola, King sang in a quartet, but Memphis was the big time and he didn't have the nerve to ask Bukka, or anyone else, if he could perform. Instead, he found work as a laborer and spent his earnings partying on Beale Street like everyone else. "Where I came from, they only had one nightclub,"

King says. "They had several on Beale. People seemed more into what was happening. Where I came from, you wore your work clothes to work and you came home in them. On Beale you couldn't tell people were working. Everybody would be dressed up and looking neat in the evenings. They had places to go for socializing that we didn't have at home."

Beale Street also offered a more liberal view of race relations than he was used to in Mississippi. "It was different, somewhat. Most of the white people I saw were people who had stores on Beale Street. They seemed to be accommodating. Everyone knew each other. You didn't see the race thing until the police came around. I remember this squad car we called Number One. They weren't too friendly when they came around. But most of the people, the people who worked in the stores, they treated you kindly."

As visits with relatives are prone to do, this one ran out of steam after several months, and King returned to Indianola to work on the plantation. In 1947 he visited Bukka again; then, the following year, he moved to Memphis to stay. He took the guitar Bukka had given him as a child and he started performing under the name Riley King. His first job was at the 16th Street Grill across the river in West Memphis. He was paid twelve dollars. Today, King laughs when he thinks about it. "I had been working on the plantation for twenty-two fifty a week— and I got paid twelve dollars for one night! I had never heard of that much money in the world."

By 1948 West Memphis was wide open. Whorehouses, gambling halls, and dope dens, all the exotic pleasures that had fled Memphis, found a home in West Memphis. Performing in one of the whorehouses on a regular basis was a thirty-eight-year-old Arkansas farmer, Chester Burnett. During the day he was a typical field worker. He looked the part, too. A large, muscular black man with an enormous face and a rock-solid jaw, he didn't always take time to change from his farmer's overalls when he went into town to perform. Apparently, no one cared. With a booming, rough-edged voice that bellowed like a demon in the throes of a godly presence, he captivated his audiences and vocally wrestled them into submission.

It didn't take long for West Memphis radio station KWEM to hear

B. B. King, c. 1980s.
Photo © Steve Gardner

about Burnett. By then he was using a stage name, Howlin' Wolf. The station offered him a job as a deejay and as a featured performer. For fifteen minutes a day Howlin' Wolf talked, sang, then—after the farm reports and advertisements for fertilizer and assorted farm products were run—sang and talked some more. Sonny Boy Williamson had proved in Helena that radio and the blues were a solid mix. So when he approached KWEM about doing the same thing there, the station jumped at the idea. For a time Sonny Boy and Howlin' Wolf were filling the airwaves with their down-home humor and captivating performances. B. B. King told me it was Sonny Boy who gave him his first radio exposure. King, a fan of Sonny Boy's show, showed up at the radio station one day and asked Sonny Boy if he would put him on the air. "He made me audition for him," King recalls. "But he must have liked what he heard because he put me on the show that very day."

As an art form, the blues had been airborne in Arkansas and some parts of Mississippi for seven years, but Memphis had been slow to make use of black programming. All that changed in a big way in 1947 when the owners of radio station WDIA—two white men named Bert

Ferguson and John Pepper—decided to convert to an all-black format. The station was losing money and they figured they had nothing to lose by giving it a try. In 1948 there were no black radio stations in America, so they had to make it up as they went along. Not only did Ferguson and Pepper want the station to air black music, they wanted to staff it with black personnel. No American radio station had ever done that. It was a revolutionary concept that would radically change American broadcasting.

For their first deejay they hired Nat D. Williams, a popular columnist for the black-owned newspaper the *Tri-State Defender*. When Williams went on the air with a program called *Tan Town Jamboree*, the station was flooded with letters of protest from white listeners who demanded Williams be taken off the air. But the station owners wouldn't budge. They not only kept him on the air, they expanded black programming as well.

Listening with great interest was Riley King.

Early in 1949 King summoned all the courage he could muster and walked into the WDIA studios at 2074 Union Avenue. For what seemed like an eternity, he stood at the picture window of the control booth, watching Nat D. Williams. During a break Williams poked his head out the door, and asked, "What you want, son?" King said he wanted to make records. He wanted to be a big shot and get on the radio. Williams liked what he saw. He called over the stations owners, Ferguson and Pepper, and when King left the station that day he was the host of his own daily program. The ten-minute show was scheduled to air each day at 3:30 P.M.

"Mr. Ferguson started this product called Peptikon, and it was my job to advertise it," King says. "It was a competitor to another tonic called Hadicol." King wrote the jingle himself. Fifty-four years after the fact the jingle was still fresh in his mind when he sang it for me in 1995:

Peptikon sure is good. Peptikon sure is good.
You can get it anywhere in your neighborhood.

Within a month, King, using the name Beale Street Blues Boy, was one of the most popular deejays at the station. His program was expanded to fifteen minutes. He abbreviated his name to Blues Boy, then shortened it even more to "B. B." The program attracted so much attention that Lucky Strike cigarettes decided to cosponsor it, becoming the station's first national advertiser. To play piano on the Lucky Strike jingles, and to vocalize when necessary, Pine Top Perkins was recruited by King for the show. Pine Top would later move on to become Muddy Waters's pianist and a recording artist in his own right, but in those days he divided his time equally between Memphis and Helena, just trying to survive.

The impact WDIA had on the development of American music—and American culture—was far-reaching, both economically and spiritually. To put it in perspective, consider that blacks in 1948 were still restricted by law as to where they could eat, sleep, or socialize. Racism was not an unreasonable attitude, it was the law of the land. The hit records in 1948 were Dinah Shore's "Buttons and Bows," Spike Jones's "All I Want for Christmas Is My Two Front Teeth," and Kay Kyser's "Woody Woodpecker." The top-grossing movies of 1948 were *The Road to Rio,* with Bob Hope and Bing Crosby, and *Red River*, with John Wayne and Montgomery Clift. With few exceptions, black culture was all but invisible to white America.

B. B. King treaded ground no one had ever walked before. It was like being the first man to set foot on the moon. King still marvels at the experience. "Bert Ferguson had rules that were different from any other place I had ever gone," he says. "At the station, you gave honor to whom honor was due. You didn't have to say, 'yes sir' or 'yes ma'am,' simply because a person was white. Most of us learned at an early age that you respected people. But if a person was named Tom, then you called him Tom. Of course, you never addressed a lady by Laura or Lucille unless they were at a level with you. If it was a married lady, it was Mrs., but you didn't have to do it because she was white. Mr. Ferguson will be Mr. Ferguson to me for the rest of my life because I respected him. The atmosphere was like it would be today if you went to the American Embassy in Russia. You feel like you are at home. That's the way I felt at WDIA. It wasn't intimidating. It was like a college of learning for me."

For King, WDIA was a safe refuge in a land seething with danger.

Crump may have closed the door on black musical aspirations with his Beale Street crackdown, but WDIA, located just two blocks off Beale Street, had inexplicably risen out of the ashes of that despair to give hope to a new generation typified by B. B. King.

Bolstered by his success on radio, King recorded four or five songs in WDIA's Studio A for Bullet Records, a company based in Nashville. Unfortunately, the company went out of business shortly after the songs were recorded. But King pushed on. In 1949 he recorded a song on mobile equipment set up at the YMCA. The song, "Three O'clock Blues," was released in 1950.

Memphis had become a hotbed of recording activity for black musicians. But because there were no studios, sessions were held wherever they could find an empty room. Most of the sessions were for record companies based in Chicago. By the late 1940s Chess Records had recruited a talent scout from Mississippi: Ike Turner would later find international fame as leader of the Ike and Tina Turner Revue, but in those days his first big "find" was Howlin' Wolf, whom he recorded on portable equipment for Chess in 1948.

Across town from WDIA, a white employee of radio station WREC watched with great interest. Sam Phillips had moved to Memphis in 1945 to work at the station, and after four years the ambitious Alabamian was on the lookout for new opportunities. What he heard on black radio in 1948 and 1949 excited him. White radio had overproduced pop music and folksy announcers. Black radio had Howlin' Wolf, Sonny Boy, and B. B. King. The airwaves exploded with the sexual bravado of liberated black manhood—and the people of Memphis were noticing. Something was in the air.

THE FIFTIES:
SOWING THE SEEDS
OF REVOLUTION

Sam Chatmon didn't look like anyone else I knew. He had a bushy white beard at a time when most men were clean-shaven. He wore funky hats. Not the straw work hats or cloth caps worn by most of the field hands, but arty, bebop hats that made you do double takes. But it wasn't the clothes, or even the beard, that most set Sam apart. It was his eyes. Unlike most of the black men you'd meet on the streets of Hollandale, Mississippi, Sam looked you straight in the eye. It wasn't a stare. There wasn't anything creepy about it. It was like crossing a railroad track and looking up to see the light of a freight train bearing down on you. You paid attention.

After my father died in 1952, my mother, my sister, and I moved to Hollandale, to live with my maternal grandparents. My grandfather had a department store on Main Street, and I worked there on Saturdays from the time I was eight. Sam Chatmon would come into the store and sometimes I would wait on him. I remember selling him white socks packaged three pair for a dollar. I would also see him on the street corner near Booth's Drug Store, where he would lean back against the building out of the sun and play the blues late in the afternoons and into the evenings. I must have walked past him a thousand times. He was a gentle man and I never heard him raise his voice above a murmur. Sometimes I stopped to listen. He was the first person I ever saw play a guitar. That was the only time Sam would not look you straight in the eye, when he was playing his guitar.

Sam Chatmon at home in Hollandale, 1980.
Photo © Steve Gardner

Sam Chatmon was a part of my growing up in the 1950s. When he wasn't sitting on the street corner or working as a night watchman, he was waiting for the bus to take him to Memphis to lay the groundwork for a cultural revolution. There were dozens more like him, white and black, all drawn to Memphis from across the South, as if by a beacon. There were two sides to Memphis in those days. On the outside, it was a Norman Rockwell painting. In 1950 it was chosen the "Nation's Cleanest City." The murder rate plummeted. So did drug addiction. Prostitution, gambling, and cocaine were holed up across the river in Arkansas. Boss Crump outlawed the sounding of car horns, and the city was given a national award for being the nation's quietest city. To make sure his cleanup was being enforced, Crump perpetually drove about the city in his chauffeur-driven limousine. If he saw a piece of paper, he got out and picked it up. If he saw a pothole, he sent a stinging reprimand to the city engineer. By the end of the decade the national press was in love with Memphis. *Look* magazine gave the city an award for urban renewal.

Beneath the surface, Memphis was primed for revolution. Dozens of Sam Chatmons infiltrated the city, performing in the few clubs left on Beale Street or on the street corners, but mostly looking for opportunities to make records or be heard on the radio. The contrast between white and black Memphis had never been greater. The economic boom brought about by World War II had lulled white Memphis into a cultural complacency. In 1950 the hit records were Patti Page's "The Tennessee Waltz" and Red Foley's "Chattanooga Shoe Shine Boy." Two of the biggest grossing movies were *Cinderella* and *Cheaper by the Dozen*. There was no talk in white Memphis of making records or getting on the radio. It was as if half the city had an erection and the other half was asleep on the porch.

Black Memphis throbbed with jive talk. Hey, man, let's *do* it, went the refrain. Everybody had a scam to get on the radio or make records. Beale Street had once been the place for action. Now talk was king. That and high fashion. Clothing stores such as Lansky's sold bright, gaudy apparel—pimp duds—that symbolized the simmering passions on the street. By 1950 B. B. King was a major celebrity in the black community, but he was by no means the only celebrity. Howlin' Wolf had his fans. So did Ike Turner (and not far away in Nutbush, Tennessee, so did his future wife, Annie Mae Bullock). Before long they were joined by Little Milton, Junior Parker, James Cotton, and Bobby "Blue" Bland. Using modern technology—radio and the recording industry—black Memphis, not thinking it, mind you, but feeling it, quietly redefined Beale Street, priming the revolution with generations of sweat piped in from the plantations.

U.S. 61 was the pipeline that supplied the revolution with foot soldiers. Because U.S. 61 runs through Hollandale, my hometown was a beneficiary—and sometimes a training ground—for the Memphis experiment. In the summers I often waited until dark, then walked two blocks downtown and climbed the chinaberry tree next to the icehouse. I peered across the railroad tracks into Blue Front, the black entertainment strip that during the day appeared deserted and run down, but came alive at night with teeming crowds that packed the nightclubs, all-night cafés, and brothels. I listened to the forbidden music that made the night air come alive with exotic rhythms and sweet harmonies. I watched pickup trucks and cars filled to capacity dodge pedestrians in the dimly lit street, and I saw brightly dressed prostitutes dance in and out of the headlights as the music of Jimmy Reed, Little Milton, and dozens of other faceless musicians wafted overhead to melodic heights and then fell stonelike across the tracks on the white side of town. There were no juke joints for whites in Hollandale in those days. That privilege was reserved solely for the town's black residents, who made up about 80 percent of the population.

■　●　■

Radio was the key to the magic taking place in Memphis. It instilled pride; it energized emotions. "All of the radio stations prior to WDIA were informative, but they didn't seem to touch us where we lived," says B. B. King. "When I left home in Indianola, every time I heard something about a black person it was when they did something wrong. It was never praising them. Rarely would you hear of anything positive being done by a black person. WDIA was like a light."

With two notable exceptions, white Memphis just didn't see it.

In 1950 a fifteen-year-old immigrant from Mississippi, Elvis Aron Presley, lived with his parents in a two-bedroom apartment in a housing project not far from Beale Street. His first summer in Memphis, he worked as an usher at a movie theater, but the next summer he got a more lucrative job, earning twenty-seven dollars a week at Precision Tool Company. Elvis wasn't like the other boys. He sang at high school programs and at church gatherings. Beale Street intrigued him, and he started hanging out on the street, listening and watching, soaking up the atmosphere, but still keeping his distance. Before he knew what had happened, he was making the talk, doing the walk.

In 1950 Sam Phillips took the plunge. After two years of listening to black radio and feeling the excitement—it was so raw, it was sexual in its overtones—he leased space in a building at 706 Union Avenue and opened Memphis's first recording studio. He called it Memphis Recording Service. At that time Union was the main east-west thoroughfare that connected midtown with downtown. Traffic on Union was usually heavy. Directly across the street from Memphis Recording

Service, with a small triangular median in between, was the east end of Beale Street. Several blocks to the west was the entertainment district. Phillips wasn't on Beale, but from his front door he could see it, and that counted for something. Phillips rounded up all the black talent he could find and started recording. The idea was to record songs that could be sold to Chess in Chicago or Modern/RPM, on the West Coast, the two main labels that signed black artists.

At the start of the decade B. B. King became the undisputed leader of the pack when his song "Three O'Clock Blues" made the national R&B charts. It was the first time a Memphis radio personality had placed a hit record on the national charts, but it would not be the last; it would happen again in the 1960s with Rufus Thomas and once again in the 1970s with Rick Dees. Despite the notoriety the record brought him King kept his day job at WDIA, but continued performing at local clubs and recording at every opportunity for the Los Angeles-based Bihari brothers. "We went to homes, the YMCA, wherever the Bihari brothers could find me," says King. "They would set up portable equipment and put blankets against the wall to make it sound better. Then I learned about Sam Phillips's studio and the company I worked for made a deal with Phillips's studio that anything I wanted to record, and they had the time to do, they would let me in."

Joining King, first as his chauffeur, then as a musician, was Bobby "Blue" Bland. Born in Rosemark, Tennessee, his family moved to Memphis when he was a child, and he grew up singing in churches around the city. Even though B. B. King was just five years his senior, Bland idolized him and jumped at the chance to become his driver as he toured around the mid-South. Eventually King, spotting his talent, invited him to join his band. Years later, Bland looked back on those days with affection. The only bad part was the pay. "We worked for Sunbeam Mitchell at Beale and Hernando and we got about five dollars a night, with food," says Bland with a laugh. "But it was a good time."

Bland did some sessions in 1951 with Ike Turner, and one of the songs, "Cried All Night," was released on Modern. His career came to a screeching halt in 1952 when he was drafted. After his discharge in 1954 he was signed by a Texas-based label, Duke Records. From 1954 to 1972 he recorded a number of Top 40 hits for Duke, including "Cry Cry Cry," "Stormy Monday Blues," and "Turn on Your Love Light," an upbeat tune that was enormously successful with white college audiences in the 1960s. Like many of his sessions, "Turn On Your Love Light" was recorded in Nashville. It was raining that day, he recalls. "We didn't really think it would do anything," he says. "But it turned out to be one of the biggest things we ever did."

Bland still lives in Memphis and, with the exception of a seven-year stint in Texas, has always made the city his home. Sadly, Memphis has never claimed him, perhaps because he recorded in Nashville for a Texas label. I once asked him about Memphis's neglect of its blues heritage. "Memphis is sorta' swishy-swatchy," he sniffed. "But they will never get rid of the label, 'Home of the Blues.' W. C. Handy saw to that."

■ ● ■

B. B. King did some recording at Memphis Recording Service, but not much. Phillips was trying to sell his own discoveries to Modern/RPM, and the Bihari brothers apparently thought it wise not to get too cozy with Phillips, the wild man from Memphis. In the beginning Phillips would record anything that moved. Weddings, speeches, and birthday greetings; nothing was beneath the dignity of Memphis Recording Service. If it made a sound, Phillips could give you a good reason for preserving it on tape—and for a fair price. But Phillips was a dreamer. He wanted to make records like the ones played on the radio. Pop music was out of the question. There were no musicians in Memphis sophisticated enough to do pop. Country was the hottest thing going, but Nashville had that tied down, and besides, there didn't seem to be any good country musicians in Memphis. That left R&B. With R&B talent scouts from Los Angeles and Chicago visiting Memphis on a regular basis, Phillips knew the odds for success were better if he concentrated on black music. In those days the market for R&B among whites was almost nonexistent. Few whites purchased R&B records. They might listen on the radio, but they wouldn't be caught dead buying the records.

In February 1951 Ike Turner brought his band, the Kings of Rhythm,

Sam Phillips, 1985.
Photo by Dave Darnell

into Phillips's studio. Phillips booked the session on the recommendation of B. B. King, who had heard the group in Mississippi. With Turner's band was Jackie Brenston, a new saxophonist who had written a song called "Rocket 88." When they recorded the song Brenston, not the regular vocalist, did the vocals. Chess bought the master. To the surprise of everyone, the record went to No. 1 on the national R&B charts. Not only was "Rocket 88" the first No. 1 record Chess ever had, it was the only No. 1 record Ike Turner ever had, with or without Tina.

Many people consider "Rocket 88" the first rock 'n' roll song ever recorded. That is debatable, because there were a number of similar songs recorded around that time that could quality for that honor. What is not debatable is *where* the first rock 'n' roll record was recorded: Phillips's Memphis Recording Service wins that honor, hands down.

Lightning had struck for Phillips. His studio, still in the toddler stage, had produced a No. 1 hit record. Encouraged, he stepped up his efforts to recruit black talent. It was a courageous thing to do. Segregation was still the law of the land. Socializing between the races was not just frowned upon, it was against the law. If he had taken Ike Turner and

Jackie Brenston into the café next door to celebrate the success of the record, they all would have been arrested. Years later, when asked why he had focused on recording black music, Phillips attributed it to the fact that while growing up on a farm in Florence, Alabama, one of the black laborers, Uncle Silas Payne, often sat him on his knee and sang to him. When the R&B records he recorded with black artists became hits with white teens, Phillips was not surprised. "These records appealed to white youngsters, just as Uncle Silas's songs and stories used to appeal to me," says Phillips. "To city-born white children who had never had an Uncle Silas, it was something new, and it became their nonsense—like fairy tales."

To hell with the law, Phillips was on a mission. His memories of Uncle Silas—and his obsession with success—propelled him with a reckless abandon for the social consequences. A stream of talented black musicians poured into his studio: Walter Horton, Doctor Ross, Joe Hill Louis, Willie Johnson—and, of course, Howlin' Wolf.

Phillips had heard Howlin' Wolf on the radio, so he had this visual image of him in his imagination, but when he first came into his studio in the summer of 1951, Phillips could scarcely believe his eyes. The Wolf stood at six-foot-six and had the largest feet Phillips had ever seen. Howlin' Wolf was his stage name; his friends called him "Big Foot Chester." If Phillips, who is in the five-foot-six range, felt intimidated, it gave way to awe when the Wolf cranked up his band. Phillips later said that watching the Wolf sit in his studio, his enormous feet spread apart, the veins on his neck bulging, and his eyes burning with fire as he sang and played his harmonica, was one of the greatest shows on earth. When he performed, the Wolf was as raw as the Arkansas earth he tilled as a farmer. His voice had a primeval quality to it. It was not a big, deep voice as you might expect from his size; it was long and dark, like a tunnel, filled with the anguish (or angst, as it would be called in the 1980s) of a thousand painful lifetimes. Despite his size, the Wolf had a vulnerability, expressed in his voice, that was appealing, and that was a major contributor to his success.

The Wolf recorded two songs during that first session, "Moanin' at Midnight" and "How Many More Years." More sessions followed.

Phillips placed some of the songs with Modern/RPM, then, after a dispute with that label, sold the Wolf's next masters to Chess. Modern/RPM responded with a lawsuit against Phillips and Chess. Then, while Phillips was recording the Wolf for Chess, Modern/RPM hired Ike Turner as a talent scout and asked him to record the Wolf for them.

Turner set up a portable studio and re-recorded the first two songs the Wolf had done with Phillips. By September the Wolf had records from both Chess and Modern/RPM on the national R&B charts. Years later the Wolf admitted he had "messed up" by doing dual sessions, betraying the man who first took a chance on him, but he attributed the competition to a dispute between Turner and Phillips. The Wolf's last session with Phillips was in July 1952. Leonard Chess ended the rivalry by taking the Wolf away from both Phillips and Modern/RPM. He offered the Wolf four thousand dollars in cash and a new car if he would move to Chicago. Phillips couldn't compete with that, and Modern/RPM didn't know about it, so the Wolf turned his farm over to his brother-in-law and loaded up his new car and struck out for Chicago, where he lived until his death in 1976. He signed an exclusive contract with Chess and had a number of R&B hits over the years, including "No Place to Go," "The Red Rooster," and "Smokestack Lightin'."

By the late 1950s the Wolf's primitive style of music had fallen into disfavor with black audiences, and he was looked down on by black jazz musicians, who considered his rough edges an embarrassment. The Rolling Stones rediscovered the Wolf in 1964 and introduced him to the British public. From that point on, the Wolf performed almost exclusively for white audiences. In 1970 he teamed with Eric Clapton, Steve Winwood, Bill Wyman, and Charlie Watts in a London studio to record an outstanding album, *The London Howlin' Wolf Sessions*, released by Chess in 1971. It was an important session for the blues rockers—Ringo Starr even sat in on one song—but if they thought the Wolf, by then in poor health, was in awe of them, they were mistaken. Outtakes from the session reveal a somewhat paternal Wolf, reminiscent of Phillips's Uncle Silas, willing to explain chord changes, but resistant to Clapton's invitations to join in when he didn't want to participate.

Frustrated by his dealings with the record labels in Chicago and Los Angeles, dealings that he considered marred by questionable business tactics on their part, Sam Phillips decided to start his own record label in 1952. He called it Sun Record Company. The label's first release was "Drivin' Slow," by saxophonist Johnny London. People told Phillips he was crazy to start his own label. They told him he couldn't compete with the majors. But he didn't believe them, not even when "Drivin' Slow" proved a bust. For a year after that failure, he put Sun Records on the back burner, while he struggled to keep the studio going. Meanwhile, he still had his day job at the radio station. He also had a night job at the Peabody Hotel, where he monitored the equipment for big band broadcasts from the rooftop.

By 1953 he was ready to gear up Sun Records again. WDIA had just added a new deejay, Rufus Thomas. A high-energy announcer with a glib delivery, the thirty-six-year-old Thomas had toured with the Rabbit Foot minstrel shows since leaving high school in 1936. Going from town to town (they called it the chitlin circuit), he learned the basics of being an entertainer. "It was truly an experience," says Thomas. "They had high-stepping dancers, comics, singers; they had it all. That was during the days of separation, where the whites were on one side and the blacks were on the other. Man, we had some of the greatest shows ever."

Thomas looked like a winner to Phillips. He was a high-profile announcer on WDIA and had nearly twenty years' experience as a minstrel entertainer. To hedge his bets even further, Phillips decided to have Thomas cover a recent R&B hit, Big Mama Thornton's "Hound Dog." They took the "Hound Dog" melody and set new words to it, calling the result "Bear Cat." Phillips released the record and held his breath. It was a hit. Encouraged, Phillips released two more songs: "Just Walking in the Rain" by the Prisonaires and "Feelin' Good" by Little Junior Parker. Both were hits.

Unfortunately, Phillip's celebration over "Bear Cat" was short-lived when he was hit with a lawsuit over copyright protection of Thornton's "Hound Dog." The expense of the suit—and Phillip's continuing problems with black acts like Howlin' Wolf and Ike Turner who freely sold their music to different labels (lacking loyalty to tiny Sun Studios, a cardinal sin in Phillips's eyes)—may have led to his decision to lose interest in Thomas and the other black artists on his roster. I asked Thomas about that in 1989 and was surprised to hear an undercurrent of bitterness in his voice when he talked about it, even after all those years. "Sam dropped all of the black artists," says Thomas. "That is the only thing I dislike about the whole picture—Sam not carrying along the good black artists with the good white artists."

■　●　■

As it happened, 1952 was a big year for Memphis. Not only did it mark the birth of Sun Records, it was the year Memphis businessman Kemmons Wilson opened America's first Holiday Inn. But it was two years earlier, in 1950, that the fireworks really began. That was the year Tennessee's new senator, Estes Kefauver, an arch-enemy of Boss Crump, took over as head of the Senate Crime Investigating Committee. Over a two-year period, Kefauver used the committee hearings, many of which were televised, to expose a vast network of organized crime in every major American crime city but one: Memphis. Looking back, it is obvious Kefauver used the hearings to taunt his enemies in Memphis. He had no intention of exposing them (not all of his supporters in Memphis had clean hands), but he obviously wanted his enemies to know he *could* expose them.

Whatever his motivation—it could have been merely defensive, to protect himself and his Memphis supporters, or it could have been a genuine desire to combat organized crime—the results mesmerized the entire nation. The Accardo-Guzik-Fischetti syndicate in Chicago and the Costello-Adonis-Lansky syndicate in New York were exposed by Kefauver, as were syndicates in St. Louis, Kansas City, New Orleans, Tampa, Las Vegas, Cleveland, and Detroit. The media were so enthralled by the process that no one noticed Kefauver had omitted Memphis from his inquiry. For some mysterious reason, the "murder capital" of America's escape from the committee's scrutiny was overlooked by the press.

When the committee issued its findings many seemed tailor-made for Memphis. It said lawyers had helped racketeers defraud the government. The committee advocated that firms doing business with the government be required to publish the fees paid to their lawyers. It said organized criminals had infiltrated legitimate businesses, ranging from liquor to sports to news services. It identified gambling as the principal support of racketeering, a finding that must have galled Memphis's organized crime families, who had vowed to someday reinstate gambling in Memphis. The results of Kefauver's excursion into the underworld were predictable. All of the gangsters identified by name said they were innocent and had never heard of organized crime. After receiving death threats, Kefauver stepped down from the committee in 1952, citing a desire to work for "international peace." Later that year he ran for president against fellow Democrat Harry Truman. He lost, but entered the race again in 1956 and ended up with the vice presidential nomination.

Kefauver's work on the committee may not have done much to stifle organized crime and official corruption in America, but it had a profound effect on Memphis. Boss Crump may have been down, but he was not out. In the 1952 elections Crump's candidate for governor, Frank Clement, defeated the incumbent, Gordon Browning. Clement's solid block of votes in Memphis proved Crump still had clout, as did his continued control of the mayor's office despite continued pressure from the Meeman-Burch-Orgill coalition. But Crump's clout was fading. In the Senate race that year, Crump's main political ally, Senator McKellar, was defeated for reelection. Crump was devastated. At age eighty, his health began to fail.

For almost the entire decade Abe Fortas kept a low profile. With his old political base eroded, he cultivated a new one with Lyndon Johnson, but mainly he devoted his efforts to making money through his Washington law firm. Using information he gained while working for the government, he became a legal gunslinger to help clients in opposition to the government. Fortas also returned to his Memphis musical roots. He and his wife, Carolyn, were earning enough money to buy a fancy Georgetown home and a summer house in Westport, Connecticut, expensive Chinese art, 150 pairs of shoes for Carolyn, and a classic Rolls-Royce. He often was spotted roaming Washington in his chauffeur-driven Rolls-Royce, playing his fiddle in the back seat. At parties, and there were many, he introduced himself as a musician. He formed a quartet, a Georgetown version of the Blue Melody Boys.

■　●　■

In early 1953 Scotty Moore, a guitar picker fresh out of the navy, went by Memphis Recording Service to talk to Sam Phillips about the Starlight Wranglers, a country group he was fronting. At that time Sam was using the studio for two types of recordings: vanity recordings for weddings and birthdays, and speculative recordings for sale, he hoped, to record companies. Because Sam was still concentrating almost exclusively on black artists, the Starlight Wranglers did not fit into either category. Sam wasn't eager to put out a record by a country band, but he had an open-door policy and he didn't discourage Scotty from hanging out at the studio. At every opportunity, Scotty mentioned the exploits of the Starlight Wranglers. Finally, Sam relented and let the group into the studio. The session produced a record, "My Kind of Carrying On," that, according to Scotty, sold "twelve copies, maybe."

Undeterred, Scotty continued to hang out at the studio. It was during that time that Elvis Presley stopped by the studio to do a vanity recording, a birthday greeting for his mother. Since his family had moved to the projects his musical interests had grown, but for the most part he preferred gospel music to pop. He often attended gospel concerts at a downtown theater, Ellis Auditorium. Somehow he summoned the courage to go backstage to meet the performers. For years Memphis had been a hotbed of activity for gospel music. Just as the major labels sent recording teams to the city to record blues musicians, the labels that specialized in gospel music sent teams to record Christian music. Thus, the city that invented the "devil's music," the blues, also was a major center for Christian music. The Memphis-based Blackwood Brothers, one of the most successful gospel recording groups in history, often performed at Ellis Auditorium. That was where Presley met J. D. Sumner, the bass singer for the Blackwood Brothers. They remained close friends for the remainder of Presley's life.

Scotty Moore today.
Photo by James Dickerson

By the time Presley walked in off the street to make that recording for his mother, the Memphis airwaves were dominated by blues and gospel music. The excitement in the air was palpable, so strong you almost could reach out and touch it. Presley felt it every time he turned on his radio, every time he stepped out onto Beale Street. What he felt when he recorded that birthday greeting at the age of eighteen one can only imagine. Marion Keisker, Phillips's secretary, was there when Presley made the recording. She was impressed enough by Elvis that, when she took the four dollars for the recording, she asked for his name and address in case her boss ever needed a singer.

About a year later, during one of Scotty's daily pilgrimages to the studio, Scotty, Sam, and Marion went next door for a cup of coffee. Scotty figured that if he knew what Sam was looking for, he would give it to him. He tried the direct approach.

"What exactly are you looking for?" Scotty asked.

Sam wasn't sure. He wanted it to be something different. It couldn't be the same old same old, like everybody else was doing. It was at that point, recalls Scotty, that Marion joined in the conversation: "She said, 'Mr. Sam, you remember that boy who came in to record that song for his mother?'

"He said, 'Yeah, I remember him. He was a dark-haired boy.'

"She said, 'Well, you said you thought he had a pretty good voice. Why don't you get him to come in and try it?'

"Sam said, 'Yeah, I'll probably do that.'

"That was all I needed to hear," recalls Scotty. "I worried him to death." From that day on, Scotty's daily visits to the studio always began with the same question: "Have you called that boy yet?" Finally, Sam relented and told Marion to dig out Presley's name and phone number.

"When I saw his name, I said, 'What kind of a name is this?'

"Sam said, 'I don't know. It's his name. Give him a call. Ask him over to your house and see what you think about him'" Scotty gave Elvis a call. They made arrangements to meet at Scotty's house the next day, on a Sunday, July 4, 1954. Scotty also invited his bass player, Bill Black.

Scotty's wife, Bobbie, was looking out the window when Elvis arrived. He was wearing white buck shoes, a white lacy shirt, and pink pants with a black stripe down the legs. She gave Scotty one of her "if he's coming inside, I'm going out the back door" looks and she left the house. When Elvis came in, Scotty was impressed at how clean and neat he was. "He sang everything from Eddy Arnold to Billy Eckstine," says Scotty. "It was uncanny to me how he knew so many songs. Bill came over and listened for a little while and got up and left. I told Elvis I would talk to Sam and we probably would be in touch."

After Elvis left, Bill, who lived just down the street, returned to compare notes with Scotty. "I asked him what he thought," says Scotty. "He said he thought he had a pretty good voice. I said I thought he had good timing."

Scotty called Sam that afternoon and Sam set up a session for the following night. Scotty, at age twenty-two, played guitar. Black was on bass. Elvis, at age nineteen, did the vocals and also played guitar. Sam was in the control room. They did several songs, none of them very impressive, but they knew they were just experimenting. It was not meant to be a real session. They would record a song, then Sam would back the tape up, and they would record the next song over the previous one. During a break Elvis jumped up and started playing his guitar. "I mean he was beating the fire out of that guitar," says Scotty. "Then he started singing, 'That's All Right, Mama.'"

Sam stuck his head out the control room door.

"He said, 'What are you doing?' I said, 'We're just goofing around.' He said, 'Well, it didn't sound too bad through the doors. Try it again.' We did it three or four times for Sam and he put it on tape. He played it back for us and said, 'Yeah, that's good. It's different. What is it?' I said, 'Well, you said you were looking for something different.'"

"That's All Right, Mama" had been written and recorded in 1940 by blues singer Arthur "Big Boy" Crudup. Elvis almost certainly heard the song on WDIA. But when Elvis sang it, it didn't sound like a blues song. It was . . . well, different. Sam knew he had a record. He told them he needed a song for the B side. For a couple of days they tried out songs. Nothing seemed to work. Then, in a return to the spontaneity that gave birth to "That's All Right, Mama," Bill jumped up and started slapping his bass, singing "Blue Moon of Kentucky" in a high falsetto voice. Elvis joined in. Sam stuck his head out the door and hollered above the music: "That's the one."

Finally, Sam had the "something different" he had been looking for. Within two weeks they had the record pressed and ready for the radio. Marion took Elvis by the *Press-Scimitar* to meet the entertainment writer, Edwin Howard. An item appeared the next day in the newspaper. Years later Howard wrote that Elvis had been very shy during the interview and let Marion do most of the talking. When Elvis spoke, he recalled, it usually was to say "yes, sir" or "no, sir." His hair was brushed back in a ducktail and his face was covered with pimples. He wore a "funny looking" bow tie. He wasn't what you'd call a lady-killer.

Sam took "That's All Right, Mama" to Dewey Phillips (no relation), a deejay at WHBQ who was doing for white radio what WDIA had done for black radio. Sam and Dewey were good enough friends that Sam could take tapes by for Dewey to play on the air during his *Red Hot and Blue* show. If listeners called in Sam knew he had a hit; he would rush back to the studio and cut an acetate on equipment he had in the studio. When Dewey played "That's All Right, Mama" the station's white listeners went wild. Elvis was the talk of the town. Sleepy Eyed John, a deejay for a country station, picked up on the flip side, "Blue Moon of Kentucky." At night Sleepy Eyed John moonlighted as an announcer at a nightclub called the Eagle's Nest. Jack Clement, a guitarist and singer in a band that was playing the Eagle's Nest at that time, awoke one morning to hear Sleepy Eyed John introducing "Blue Moon" on his radio show. "Sleepy Eyed was saying, 'Here's the record everyone is screaming about,'" recalls Clement. "I said, 'Oh, man, that's it. I want to hear that again.' It was an instant hit from day one."

A week and a half after the record was released, Elvis performed at the Overton Park Shell, an outdoor amphitheater. The afternoon show, headlined by country crooner Slim Whitman, was a dud. When Elvis returned for the evening performance, he was nervous. He sang an up-tempo song. The audience went wild. The women screamed and shouted. "That's when he got into all that shaking," recalls Scotty, who played guitar that night. "When Elvis played the guitar standing up, he would go up on the balls of his feet and keep time to the music. He was doing it, I'm sure, when we cut the record. When we did the show, all those people started screaming and hollering and we didn't know what was going on. When we went offstage, someone made the comment that it was because Elvis was shaking his leg. From then on, he just starting adding a little more to it and made it into a fine art. But it was a natural thing for him."

Sam knew he had a hit with Elvis. What he didn't know was how to package him. The songs they recorded were bluesy, but they weren't blues and even if they had been, he couldn't package him as a blues singer because white men didn't sing the blues. Earlier that year, in May, Louis Armstrong had come to Memphis for a performance on Beale Street. A newspaper story described Armstrong as "the great negro trumpet player" and announced that he would be giving "a show for whites at 8 p.m. and a dance for negroes at 10:30." No, it wouldn't do to bill Elvis as a rhythm and blues performer, not at a time when race mixing could land you in jail (or worse). The songs had a country feel to them, but Elvis wasn't like any other country singer making records. Sam compromised. Since "rock 'n' roll" had not been coined, Sam, or his secretary, made up a phrase he thought represented a mix of the two styles. Elvis was billed as the "Hillbilly Cat." By the end of the summer he succeeded in booking the Hillbilly Cat on the Louisiana Hayride, a top-rated country radio show broadcast from Shreveport, Louisiana.

On October 16, 1954, as Elvis walked onto the stage of the Louisiana Hayride, Boss Crump, at age eighty, lay dying in his bed at 1962 Peabody Avenue in Memphis. He had fallen ill earlier in the summer. As Elvis performed that night, initiating a new era in American music, life flowed from Crump's ravaged body. He died that night without appointing a successor to his empire. What he thought of the music emanating from his radio all summer is not known.

Buoyed by the success of Elvis's record in Memphis and his reception at the Louisiana Hayride, Sam Phillips booked Elvis anyplace and every place he could. John Evans, who would later play keyboards on the first No. 1 pop record recorded in Memphis, "The Letter," recalls seeing Elvis perform at the grand opening of a laundry down the street from his house. "My brother held me up to where I could see," says Evans. "People came from all over the neighborhood and swarmed down on the place."

Sam loaded up his car with records and promoted them at radio stations across the South. Then he sent Elvis, Scotty, and Bill out on the road. Soon "That's All Right, Mama" and "Blue Moon of Kentucky" were solid hits across the South. For the first time, Sun Records looked like a viable business. Sam stopped scheduling sessions with black musicians and focused all his efforts on Elvis. When they returned to Memphis, the trio performed at local venues and worked in the studio with

Sam. Through the summer of 1954 and into the fall of 1955 a string of regional hits flowed out of the studio, including "Mystery Train," "Baby, Let's Play House," and "Good Rockin' Tonight."

It was during this time that Jack Clement met Elvis. With the success Ray Price was having on the country charts, Sleepy Eyed John organized an eight-piece western band at the Eagle's Nest. Jack was the lead singer and the MC. Elvis, Scotty, and Bill were booked as the floor show, which meant Jack introduced them each night. "The first time, Elvis said, 'Give me a big buildup, Jack,'" he recalls. "I said, 'OK, I will.' When they came on, just the three of them, with Elvis on acoustic, Scotty on electric guitar, and Bill slapping the bass, it was magic. My girlfriend, Doris, was there. I later married her. Elvis was always flirting with her, but he didn't get her. I got the girl that time."

Although Sam, Elvis, Scotty, and Bill didn't coin the term "rock 'n' roll"—that honor went to Cleveland deejay Allan Freed—they invented and then defined the music that took the name. It didn't take long for the major labels to feel the tremors radiating from Memphis. Sam received many offers for Elvis over the next year but turned them down. Then, in the summer and early fall of 1955, something happened to make Sam change his mind.

Abruptly, in November 1955, he sold Elvis's contract to RCA Records for forty thousand dollars (thirty-five thousand to Sam and a five-thousand-dollar advance to Elvis). People were stunned. It was a bad deal. Why would Sam sell an artist he knew was worth millions? It became one of the great mysteries of rock 'n' roll. In a 1959 interview Sam said he never regretted the decision: "Selling that contract gave us the capital we desperately needed at the time for expansion. To understand why I have never regretted the decision, you have to remember something. At that time, most of the experts thought Elvis was a flash-in-the-pan. Even RCA wasn't sure they had made a good deal." That's Sam's story, but it has always raised more questions than it has answered. Jack Clement once asked him point-blank. "I said, 'Tell me the truth,'" says Clement. "'Did you want to sell Elvis or did Elvis want to leave?' He said, 'No, Elvis wanted to stay.'"

The month before Sam sold Elvis's contract, he made history by starting up the nation's first all-female radio station. His partner was fellow visionary Kemmons Wilson. The station was given the call letters WHER and housed in a Holiday Inn on Third Street south of Crump Boulevard. Not only had Memphis, within a period of seven years, given birth to rock 'n' roll, the first all-black radio station, and the first national motel chain, it now was the home of the first all-female radio station. A sign was hung over the control room designating it as the "Doll Den." Two attractive and effervescent sales executives were given the keys to a Rolls-Royce and told to sell, sell, sell.

In his book *Last Train to Memphis* Peter Guralnick makes the case that Sam was in desperate financial straits and felt he had no choice but to sell Elvis's contract. I have my own theory. Sam was—and still is—a brilliant businessman. The exact nature of his involvement with Kemmons Wilson's Holiday Inn project has always perplexed me. Kemmons has said he loaned Sam twenty-five thousand dollars for the radio station on condition they would be partners if the station was successful. Apparently, if the station was not successful, Sam was not expected to pay the money back. Why would a man who was trying to get a hotel chain off the ground loan someone who was facing bankruptcy that much money on such speculative terms? Guralnick found evidence that Sam told people, particularly family members, that he was on the verge of bankruptcy; I don't dispute that, but telling people you're broke and actually being broke are not the same. Do people who are considering bankruptcy start up radio stations?

Once you understand the history of the Hoodoo cartel—and its decades-long dominance of Memphis's political and economic development—it is difficult to believe the cartel was not interested in Elvis's career. Elvis was painfully shy and naïve to the ways of the world. He was the type of youth an older man of Sam's sensibilities would feel a need to protect. I don't think there was anything out of line with Sam's partnership with Kemmons. They are both scrupulously honest men. However, I have often wondered if Sam sold Elvis's contract to RCA in an effort to keep him out of the cartel's grip, using the Holiday Inn project—and threats of bankruptcy—as an excuse. If the Memphis mob could have Crump at its beck and call for four decades, then it could turn Sun Records inside out with a mere flick of the wrist. I don't think Sam sold Elvis down the river; I think he tried to save his career. In my eyes, Sam Phillips is a hero.

Memphis sizzled with excitement. It's not surprising that dreamers flocked to the city in droves. It was the only place in America where a shy country boy could become a king, where black men and white women could not only get on the radio, but have a hand in management. For those who had been shut out of the system, Memphis offered new hope. The revolution was underway.

One of the first to respond was Carl Perkins, who drove in from Jackson, Tennessee, to introduce himself to Sam Phillips. Within twelve months he would be followed by Johnny Cash from Arkansas, Jerry Lee Lewis from Louisiana, and Roy Orbison from Texas. Carl wasn't sure what to expect when he walked into the studio. After an audition, Sam signed him to a recording contract. "I'd sent tapes to every record company I could," says Carl. "I'd get them back and they'd say, 'We don't know what it is and we don't know what to do with it.' Most of the tapes were never even opened." If the majors didn't know what to do with Carl, Sam certainly did. Among the first songs they recorded was one Carl wrote while living in the projects in Jackson. He titled it "Blue Suede Shoes." It was released early in 1956 and immediately became a hit on all three charts: pop, country, and R&B.

Meanwhile, RCA had taken Elvis to Nashville for a session. In January 1956 they released the first single, "Heartbreak Hotel." As "Blue Suede Shoes" and "Heartbreak Hotel" battled it out on the charts, Carl appeared the clear winner. Arrangements were made for him to receive a gold record for the song on Perry Como's television show in New York. In late March 1956 Carl and his band left a concert in Norfolk, Virginia, to drive to New York. Outside Wilmington, Delaware, they were involved in an accident that almost killed Carl. A little over three weeks after the accident, "Heartbreak Hotel" went to No. 1 on the *Billboard* charts. "Blue Suede Shoes" stalled at No. 4. Fate, as if to rub Carl's nose in his misfortune, gave the No. 2 slot to Perry Como for "Hot Diggity/Jukebox Baby." Elvis sent a wire to Carl suggesting that Carl might have been No. 1 if he had not had the accident.

Carl recovered from his injuries quickly enough to receive a new car from Sam Phillips on April 10. Carl told a reporter he was going to drive the dark blue Cadillac "mighty careful." Carl's photo with the car appeared the next day in the *Press-Scimitar*. Back in the studio with Sam, Carl followed "Blue Suede Shoes" with "Your True Love" and "Pink Pedal Pushers," but subsequent records bombed and his career fizzled until the 1960s, when the Beatles recorded three of his songs: "Matchbox," "Honey Don't," and "Everybody's Trying to Be My Baby."

Sam took Carl's plunge in stride and moved on to the next in line, Johnny Cash. Sam had signed Cash to a contract early in 1955, and his first release, "Hey Porter," backed with "Cry, Cry, Cry," was a hit, as was the follow-up, "Folsom Prison Blues." But Sam apparently thought Johnny was too country to fit the new rock 'n' roll mold, and with the success of Elvis (and then Carl), Sam gently nudged Johnny to the back burner. Despite his day job as an appliance salesman, Cash stayed busy writing new songs. When Sam called him back in the studio after Carl's automobile accident, he was ready. In 1956 he scored with three self-penned Top 10 hits: "I Walk the Line," "There You Go," and "So Doggone Lonesome."

Elvis now recorded solely in Nashville, but he still lived in Memphis and he stopped by Memphis Recording Studio on a regular basis. Like everyone else, he quickly became a Johnny Cash fan. By then Colonel Tom Parker had become Elvis's manager. Because Parker also managed Johnny Cash's future wife, June Carter, a member of the popular Carter Family, he often booked Elvis and June together at fairs. "I used to do a little comedy act in the beginning and do my little set and then Elvis and Scotty and Bill went on," says June. "I was introduced to Johnny Cash by Elvis. He used to go into every little café and play Johnny Cash records. He used to tune his guitar by listening to 'Cry, Cry, Cry.' . . . I met Johnny Cash because Elvis was such a fan of his." June Carter Cash's comments about touring with Elvis Presley were made to me in 1985 in Nashville. More about her recollections of that period can be found in my book *Coming Home: Conversations About Memphis Music*.

Johnny Cash became Sun Record's biggest-selling artist, with sales surpassing those of Elvis while he was with Sun. It was during this period that Roy Orbison entered the picture. Johnny heard him perform in Texas and suggested he send a demo to Sam. Roy sent in a tape of

"Ooby Dooby," an up-tempo song written by some of his schoolmates. Sam liked the song and called him, but when Roy told him Johnny Cash had recommended him, Sam snapped that Cash didn't run his studio and hung up. When he cooled off, he offered Roy a contract and re-recorded "Ooby Dooby." The song, with a solid rockabilly riff and nonsense lyrics, did well, but wasn't a major hit.

By the summer of 1956 Sam decided he needed some help in the studio. Jack Clement had a job in a hardware store, but he performed at night and on weekends. That summer he set up a studio in a garage on Fernwood Street with a truck driver, Sam Wallace. As they were learning to use the equipment, Jack did a recording session with Billy Lee Riley in a radio station. He took the tape in to Memphis Recording to be mastered and when he told Sam he was setting up a garage studio, Sam offered him a job. If you ask Jack if he was hired as an engineer, he will laugh. He prefers the word "operator," since he considers engineers technical experts and not music experts. "Actually, I was one of a new breed," says Jack. "Prior to that, everyone who had run a board had been an engineer. I was a musician. So suddenly a musician is playing with those knobs instead of an engineer. I did a lot of things wrong. But some of them worked. That was the neat thing about doing things wrong—sometimes it works."

On June 15, 1956, Jack Clement reported for his first day of work at Memphis Recording. He remembers the date because he had enlisted in the Marine Corps on June 15, 1948. If he had picked up a copy of *The Commercial Appeal* that morning, he would have read a front-page story about a political meeting that had taken place the evening before at the fairgrounds, near where the Saddle and Spur Club used to meet. The newspaper reported that "45 Negroes" had attended a meeting to elect the Shelby County chairman of the Democratic Party. Ordinarily that story would have appeared on the inside of the newspaper. The fact that "45 Negroes" were there made it front-page news, even though they sat in a special section and did not mingle with the whites.

The first artist Sam assigned to Jack Clement was Roy Orbison. Sun already had released "Ooby Dooby" and was in need of a strong follow-up. "Musically, Roy was ahead of his time," says Jack. "He wanted to

Jack Clement, 1950s.
Photo courtesy Jack Clement

do things in the studio that were a little bit over our heads produc-
tion-wise. Memphis wasn't quite ready for that. We didn't have organized vocal groups and strings. He was thinking orchestrally. He was
wanting to cut what he ultimately did cut. I told him, and he never
let me forget it, that he would never make it as a ballad singer."

Jack and Roy became good friends, and Roy moved into his house
while they were working together in the studio. Roy was shy, says
Jack, but not as withdrawn as he appeared later in life. "We went out
at night and hung out," says Jack. "Roy was a lot of fun. He was very
comfortable with the people around us. Now, if you brought in other
people, he might be a little shy, but he was very comfortable with our
little group. He was a genuinely nice person. Always was."

Jack's official job title was engineer, but with Sam staying less and less at the studio, Jack organized the sessions, booked the players, and operated the equipment. He recorded a number of songs with Roy—the better cuts were "Rock House," "Sweet and Easy to Love," and "Mean Woman Blues"—but they never got another song that did as well as "Ooby Dooby." Sam wanted Jack to push Roy more toward rock 'n' roll, but Roy wanted to be a ballad singer. Frustrated, Roy left Sun Records in 1957 and moved to Nashville, where he wrote and recorded the hits for which he is best known: "Oh, Pretty Woman," "Cryin'," and "Blue Bayou."

One day in autumn of 1956 Jack was in the studio when the receptionist came into the control room and told him there was a man in the outer office who said he played piano like Chet Atkins played guitar. Jack invited him into the studio. "I'm JerryLeeLewis," the man said, running the words together so that they sounded like one word. "Sure enough, he played 'Wildwood Flower' on the piano and it sounded like Chet Atkins licks," says Jack. "I said, 'Can you sing?' He said, 'Yeah,' and started singing these wonderful George Jones songs. I taped four or five songs. I asked him if he knew any rock 'n' roll. He said no. I liked the tapes so much I played them for anybody who came in the door. For some reason, I didn't get around to playing the tapes for Sam for several weeks. I was busy, he was busy, whatever."

When Sam heard the tapes, he told Jack to schedule a session with Jerry Lee, but before he could call him, Jerry Lee showed up at the studio sporting a newly grown goatee. Jack thought he looked pretty scruffy and gave him hell. Jack told him that if he would stick around town a few days, they would cut some songs. That suited Jerry Lee just fine.

Sam was in Nashville attending a disk jockeys' convention when they did the session. They recorded a song Jerry Lee had written, "End of the Row," then they tried four or five other songs. Nothing really clicked. Jack asked if he knew "Crazy Arms." Jerry Lee said he knew a little of it. Jack turned the tape on. The bass player was in the bathroom. The guitar player had put down his instrument. It was just Jerry Lee on piano and the drummer. Jack let the tape run because he figured they would redo it when the bass player returned. "There wasn't anything but drums and piano on the record, except at the very end when

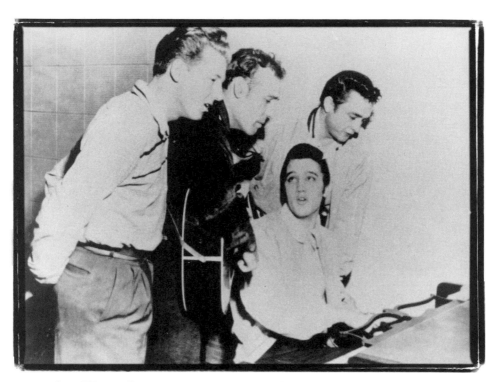

The Million Dollar Quartet. L to r: Jerry Lee Lewis,
Carl Perkins, Elvis Presley, Johnny Cash.
Photo courtesy of the Center for Southern Folklore Archive © 1995

the guy who was playing bass walked in and picked up the electric guitar and made a bad chord because he thought we weren't recording. That's all there was to 'Crazy Arms.' It was on tape, so we went on to something else."

After Jerry Lee left Jack listened to the tape again. He fell in love with "Crazy Arms." He played it for everyone who came into the studio over the weekend. "The next Monday, when Sam came in, we went back into the control room," says Jack. "I put the tape of 'Crazy Arms' on. It started and before it ever got to Jerry Lee's voice, Sam reached over and stopped the tape. He said, 'I can sell that. Just from the piano intro.' Then he wound it back and played it through. That night he made an acetate and took it to Dewey Phillips, and Dewey started playing it, and everyone wanted to buy it. Now, that was when the music business was fun. We make a tape on Thursday, and it's on the radio the next Monday, and on sale in the stores the next Thursday."

Based on public reaction to "Crazy Arms" and "End of the Road," Sam offered Jerry Lee a contract and promised to use him as a session player whenever possible. Meanwhile, Jerry Lee went out on the road, shocking audiences by kicking his piano bench across the stage and jumping up on top of the piano. That fall Johnny Cash, probably at the suggestion of Jack Clement, took Jerry Lee out on the road with him. ""He gave me my first tour," says Jerry Lee. "We left town in a '56 Buick and I was getting a hundred dollars a day and I thought I was getting rich. We went all over Canada on gravel roads and wore the car completely out. When I got home, I had sixty dollars in my pocket."

In December 1956 Sam scheduled a session with Carl Perkins. He told Jack to bring Jerry Lee in off the road and book him on piano for the session. While Carl and Jerry Lee were rehearsing, Johnny Cash showed up. Carl had invited him to the session and was expecting him. Then, to everyone's surprise, Elvis strolled into the studio. He often stopped by when he was in town.

"Elvis played the piano for about an hour and then Jerry—he was brand new—he asked if he could play the piano," says Johnny. "Well, when Jerry sat down at the piano, Elvis didn't play it anymore." Johnny laughs. "Nobody followed the 'Killer.'"

As the four of them gathered around the piano, Sam called a newspaper reporter to photograph the group that would later be dubbed the "Million Dollar Quartet"—and Jack turned on the tape machine. "I set up a couple of microphones here and there in the room and started taping," says Jack. "I wasn't trying to make a record. I kept that going for an hour and a half or so. Some people say Johnny Cash is not on the tape. He says he is. I'm not sure."

Unfortunately, nothing substantial resulted from the session. The songs recorded by the Million Dollar Quartet weren't released until 1981, and the only good thing to come out of Carl's individual session was "Matchbox," which was not a hit for Carl, but was a hit for the Beatles.

The year 1956 ended with Elvis firmly entrenched as the king of rock 'n' roll. It had been a good year for Memphis music. Elvis had four No. 1 hits: "Don't Be Cruel/Hound Dog," "Heartbreak Hotel," "Love Me

Tender," and "I Want You, I Need You, I Love You." Carl scored with "Blue Suede Shoes," and Johnny had a string of country and regional hits. Elvis became a movie star with the release of *Love Me Tender* in November 1956. By the end of the movie's run in 1957, it had grossed $4.5 million, making it the tenth most-profitable movie of the year. At the top of the list was *The Ten Commandments*, with Charlton Heston, which grossed $18.5 million.

By 1957 Memphis was soaring. In a year that saw Pat Boone, Frank Sinatra, and Perry Como all score with No. 1 hits, Memphis countered with Jerry Lee Lewis's "Whole Lot of Shakin' Going On," which peaked at No. 2, and another string of No. 1 hits from Elvis: "All Shook Up," "Jailhouse Rock," "(Let Me Be Your) Teddy Bear," "Too Much," and "Love Me." Elvis starred in his third movie that year, *Jailhouse Rock*, but it was the beginning of the end for Elvis the artist. Between 1956 and 1972 he starred in thirty-three movies. His music took a back seat to his film career; Elvis, by then earning $1 million a picture, was too busy savoring his success to notice what was happening to his music—or to his friends. To impress his mother, he bought a two-story, limestone mansion in Memphis for one hundred thousand dollars. He kept the name that came with the house: Graceland.

Unnoticed in the commotion over the motion picture deals was the way Elvis's band was being pushed to the sidelines. By then Scotty and Bill had been joined by D. J. Fontana on drums. When Elvis filmed *Love Me Tender*, the music director, Ken Darby, refused to use Scotty, Bill, and D. J. in the movie. He wanted to use his own trio. Elvis's manager, Colonel Tom Parker, agreed to exclude them from the soundtrack. To make it up to the Memphis boys, Elvis flew them to Hollywood to record "Too Much" and his second RCA album, *Elvis*. It was a nice gesture, but it was too little, too late. When they first went out on the road, they had a 50-25-25 split agreement. Elvis got half and the other half was split by Scotty and Bill. When D.J. joined the group, he was given a salary of $100–$125 a week. When Elvis's manager got involved, the group's financial structure changed.

"We discussed it and decided that Bill and I would go on salary, too, " says Scotty. "They decided to make a corporation out of Elvis. We got a hundred dollars a week when we weren't working and a hundred and fifty a week when we were. Later it went up to two hundred dollars." That arrangement worked for a while, but when Elvis started making $1 million per movie, it created waves. "We had to buy our own meals and clothes," says Scotty. "When it got to where he was really raking in the bucks, and we were at the same level, well . . . our union wasn't strong enough, so the only thing to do was to quit."

Scotty and Bill walked out in 1957. Elvis did a show without them in Tupelo, Mississippi, then Parker asked them to do a tour of the Northwest that took them to Seattle, Spokane, and Los Angles. Scotty and Bill agreed to do it for $250 a show, but when the tour ended they went their separate ways. Then Elvis went into the army. Scotty didn't perform with Elvis again until the NBC-TV "comeback" special in 1968.

After the departure of Scotty and Bill, Elvis's music sank into a soundtrack mind-set, but with the enormous success of the movies no one, least of all Elvis, noticed that his music had lost the raw, reckless, Memphis-homeboy synergy that had made him a recording star. Elvis would have many hit records over the years, but not until he returned to his Memphis roots in 1969 would he again make a good record.

If 1957 was an ominous year for Memphis music, 1958 would prove to be disastrous. Jerry Lee would have a No. 2 hit with "Great Balls of Fire," but would then self-destruct by marrying his thirteen-year-old cousin. Elvis would have two No. 1 hits with "Don't" and "Hard Headed Woman" and a No. 2 hit with "Wear My Ring Around Your Neck," but he would be devastated by a double whammy: in March he was drafted into the army and in August his mother died of a heart attack. Elvis was devastated by his mother's death. Some say he never recovered from the loss.

Jerry Lee was stunned by public reaction to his marriage. Before the marriage took place, he told Elvis what he was going to do. Elvis thought he was joking. When he convinced him he was serious, Elvis reportedly said: "God bless you, Jerry Lee. You just saved my career." Sam advised him not to do it, but Jerry Lee was hardheaded. Why would people get mad about that, he reasoned, when they approved of all the other outrageous behavior he engaged in? Jerry Lee was fond of telling about the time he and Elvis went to a party at Jack Clement's house and got buck naked and rode motorcycles around Memphis at 2:30 A.M. Jack doesn't remember the incident now but admits it may have happened without his knowledge.

Not happy with the way his career was progressing at Sun Records, Johnny Cash signed with Columbia Records and left Memphis in 1958. Jack Clement was working with Johnny at that time and still considers the breakup a mistake for both Johnny and Sam. "I think Johnny left because he got his feelings hurt," says Jack. "One day Johnny dropped by and wanted to talk to Sam or have lunch or something and Sam was too busy. He was doing something with Jerry Lee. I think John felt slighted. I think that's what started it."

Johnny says Jack played the role of "Henry Kissinger" between himself and Sam. After Johnny signed with Columbia, Sam sent Johnny a curt letter instructing him to come into the studio to complete the recordings agreed to in their contract. When he showed up at the studio, Sam wasn't there. Sam left instructions with Jack to get everything he could out of Johnny. "I did every song that Jack asked me to do," says Johnny. "I really don't think I would have done it for anyone else in the world. I could have played off sick or pulled this or that excuse. Jack said after we got to working, 'I don't like this any better than you do.' I said, 'Well, I'm really kind of enjoying it.' I recorded everything he asked me to do." The session produced enough material for Sun Records to release Johnny Cash singles long after he was gone.

■　●　■

By 1959 Johnny Cash and Roy Orbison were gone, Elvis was in the army, Jerry Lee was being ridiculed by the press and his concerts were canceled by nervous promoters, and Carl Perkins had returned to the juke joints from which he had sprung. Despite the hard times, Sun Records scored a No. 4 hit with Bill Justis's instrumental "Raunchy," and Fernwood Records, co-owned by Scotty Moore, had a No. 8 million-selling hit with Thomas Wayne's "Tragedy." Scotty produced the record, using himself and

Elvis Presley as he leaves the induction center in 1957 after passing his physical for the U.S. armed forces. With him is Dorothy Harmon, a Las Vegas showgirl.
Photo courtesy of *The Commercial Appeal*

Bill Black as the only musicians. For the vocal he recruited his paperboy, Thomas Wayne Perkins. When a reporter asked Sam Phillips in 1959 if rock 'n' roll was dead, he answered an emphatic no; the music was simply "modifying the beat." But as the decade ended, Sam prepared to move into a new building on Madison Avenue. The old Memphis Recording Service building would be left vacant.

That fall, three black students integrated the all-white Memphis State University. That sent shock waves through the community, but it would be several years before the public schools would be desegregated. As the decade ended, it was still against the law for black Memphis residents to eat in white restaurants, go to white movie theaters, or check into white hotels.

But there was hope. Back during the 1955 mayoral campaign,

Crump's man, incumbent Mayor Frank Tobey, suffered a heart attack and died. His only opponent was former mayor Watkins Overton, also a Crump man. Under pressure from reformers, Edmund Orgill entered the race and—to everyone's surprise—won with the help of black votes and organized labor. In 1958, during the last year of his term, he entered the governor's race at the urging of Estes Kefauver. Orgill lost the election by a small margin. The following year he ran for reelection as mayor, but was forced to withdraw because of a blocked artery. Henry Loeb, a young reformed-minded county commissioner, entered the race and was elected by a landslide.

As editor of the *Press-Scimitar*, Edward J. Meeman maintained that newspaper's dominance, but there was a new star in the ascendancy at *The Commercial Appeal*. In 1957 Michael Grehl began work at *The Commercial Appeal* as an obit writer. By the end of the decade he was well on his way to becoming its managing editor. Under his direction, the morning newspaper would assume the leadership role previously held by the *Press-Scimitar*. Grehl may have missed the birth of Sun Records, but he would be there to direct news coverage of the second flowering of Memphis music in the 1960s and he would be instrumental in its attempted rebirth in the 1980s.

THE SIXTIES: FROM SWEET SOUL TO SOUTHERN ROCK

t the age of forty Estelle Axton had settled in for the duration of middle age. After teaching grades one through eight in a one-room school in Middleton, Tennessee, she moved to Memphis, where she got a job as a bookkeeper at Union Planters Bank. With a husband, two children, and a home in suburbia, she had everything, statistically speaking, an American woman of the 1950s could want. The social, economic, and musical revolution taking place in Memphis did not interest her in the least. She was more concerned with raising a family and earning a living.

Estelle's younger brother, Jim Stewart, was more introspective. By age twenty-eight he had served a two-year stint in the army, earned a degree in business from Memphis State, accepted a job in the bonds department of First National Bank in Memphis, and married Evelyn White, who worked for the bank. But beneath the banker's exterior—he wore schoolteacher glasses and conservative business suits—simmered a passion for music. Jim Stewart led a double life.

While attending classes at Memphis State, he played fiddle in a series of swing bands and occasionally performed on WDIA, which in its early years sandwiched brief country segments between its staple R&B formats. On weekends he sometimes played at the Eagle's Nest, where he once met Elvis: "I remember [Elvis] . . . telling me he was going to have to quit because they couldn't afford gas to go on the road." Jim would never have told his co-workers at the bank about playing at the

Estelle Axton in 1995.
Photo by James Dickerson

Eagle's Nest or hanging out at a black radio station, nor would he have told them when he bought a tape recorder and dreamed of making records. Jim wrote a country song, "Blue Roses," and asked Fred Bylar, a radio announcer, to sing it. He thought Bylar, with his radio connections, would be able to get them a record deal. He couldn't, and Jim watched with disgust as his first recording disappeared into the black hole of American music. Jim blamed the failure on their equipment, or lack of it, and the fact they had to use a garage for a studio.

"So Jim came to me," says Estelle. "He played the song for me, even though I was more into popular music than country music. He said, 'Would you like to get in the music business?' I had never thought about it. I said, 'Well, I don't have any money.'

"He said, 'I know you don't have any money, but you have a house and you have several years paid into it.' He said, 'Maybe you could mortgage it. All we need is twenty-five hundred dollars.'

"I talked to my husband. He said, 'No way.' He wasn't into music and just wasn't interested in it. I had to talk to him for a long time and convince him that if we invested in something, it might come out, even though none of us knew anything about the recording business."

Estelle's husband was understandably hesitant. They had bought the house in 1940 for $3,800. Their monthly payments were low—$23.63 a month—so a $2,500 mortgage would take a big bite out of the equity they had in the house. "Back then, that was a lot of money," recalls Estelle. Then she chuckles, "We sold [that house] later on and got $50,000."

In the end, Estelle was victorious. With the $2,500 she received from the mortgage of her home, she and Jim bought a one-track Ampex recorder and set it up in a vacant grocery store in Brunswick, a small community just outside Memphis. They named their new company Satellite Productions (Russia's Sputnik had made *satellite* a household word). For about a year they experimented with the equipment, recording the store owner's sixteen-year-old daughter. When it became obvious Brunswick didn't have a deep talent pool, they looked to Memphis. "We knew we would have to get into Memphis to be close to the talent," she says.

Enter Lincoln Wayne "Chips" Moman, a twenty-two-year-old guitar

Petula Clark with Chips Moman in the studio, c. late 1960s.
Photo courtesy of the Mississippi Valley Collection, University of Memphis, University Libraries

picker, who had hitchhiked to Memphis at the age of fourteen from his home in Georgia. As a child he had lain awake at night listening to black gospel music with the radio hidden beneath the covers, the sound turned low so his father, Abraham Lincoln Moman, would not hear and suspect he had secret musical dreams. His father was a former professional baseball player, a Southern jock, and although he later was proud of his son's success—"Music was born in him, I reckon," he once told me. "I don't see how he does it myself. It's amazing to me"—he did not feel music was something his son could make a living at.

By contrast, Chips's mother, who played piano, encouraged his interest in music, first by buying him a ukulele when he was three in exchange for a visit to the dentist, then later by getting him his first guitar, a Gene Autry model, from Sears, Roebuck. For several years

Chips was in and out of Memphis, traveling around the country as an itinerant laborer. He chopped onions in Texas. He painted houses and service stations. "For a kid my age, I was really successful," says Chips. "I was making four to five hundred dollars a week. I painted fridges, post offices, flag poles, anything. When I got a chance to play in bands, I just did it. Some people just got to play it, can't help it."

By the late 1950s he had made a name for himself as a session player in California. "People would hire me as a guitar player, but they were really hiring me to put the sessions together," says Chips. But he was unhappy living away from home and returned to Memphis, where he painted by day and played music by night. In 1960 fate would throw Chips together with Jim and Estelle for the beginning of Memphis's second musical revolution. Chips had met Jim shortly after he bought the tape recorder, and he had worked on several projects with him, including his abortive "Blue Roses" record. When he heard Jim and Estelle were looking for a place to put a studio in Memphis, he found them a bargain, an empty movie theater at 924 East McLemore Avenue.

"The guy who owned it rented it to us for a hundred dollars a month," says Estelle. "Can you imagine a whole theater for one hundred dollars? We ripped out all of the seats and put a partition down the middle to compact the sound." They put the tape recorder up on the stage where the screen used to be and opened a record store in an abandoned barbershop next door. "When I was working at Union Planters, I took orders from the people I worked with," says Estelle. "They would tell me what they wanted, and I would go to Poplar Tunes (a record store) and buy records for sixty-five cents and sell them to them for one dollar. I took that profit and bought enough records to set up a record shop."

Chips, Jim, and Estelle were an unlikely threesome. With his arms marked with self-inflicted tattoos and a cocky attitude shaped by years of survival on the road as a teenage vagabond, Chips was a social rebel with a penchant for playing cards and hustling pool (he wasn't given the name Chips for nothing). Jim was the quintessential Walter Mitty, a mild-mannered banker who kept whatever rebellious thoughts he had to himself. Estelle was a slender, outspoken, forty-year-old redhead with two kids, a nervous husband, and a twenty-five-hundred-dollar mortgage. I never saw the three of them together, but knowing all three of them, I can imagine what it was like. Estelle would have spoken her mind, Chips would have disagreed on principle, citing his experience in a man's world, and Jim would have disagreed with both of them yet said nothing. There were rough days ahead.

As Jim and Estelle ripped out theater seats, Memphis music underwent major changes. In 1960 Sam Phillips closed the doors at Memphis Recording Service and moved into his new studio at 639 Madison Avenue, changing the name of his company to Sam Phillips Recording Service. In the spring of 1959 Phillips and Jack Clement had a falling out. In retrospect it was a signal flare from a sinking ship. "We'd been recording all day," recalls Jack, who by then had become Sam's right-hand man. "There was this guy named Cliff who was one of Elvis's entourage. He hit another member of Elvis's entourage over the head with a tennis racket, and Elvis threw him out of the house. For some reason, Cliff was staying with me. At that time, I lived over in Frasier, which was across the river. It got into the evening and Bill Justis had been having a few cocktails, and Sam came in and he had a few cocktails. Cliff also had a few cocktails. I wanted to go home because it was snowing and I wanted to get across the bridge before it froze up. So somehow I worked in the control room, and Sam was there telling jokes, and they were having a big party. I said, 'Cliff, we need to go.' Sam interpreted that as meaning 'You don't want to stay here and talk to this idiot.' In the meantime, him and Justis had been arguing. I just wanted to go home."

Jack and Cliff left. When he returned to the studio the next day there was an envelope addressed to him. "Sam had fired me," says Jack. "I saw another envelope there for Justis. He fired him, too. The next day I think he was sorry about it and we probably could have reconciled, but I was ready to go. Sam still don't know to this day why he fired me. We still argue about it."

Jack moved to Beaumont, Texas, where he set up a studio for a while, then he moved to Nashville, where he produced a number of hit albums for Johnny Cash. Sam had a minor hit in 1960 with Charlie Rich's "Lonely Weekends," but not since Jerry Lee Lewis recorded

Stax Records studios. The Satellite Record Store is partially visible to the right, beyond the old movie theater marquee.
Photo courtesy of the Mississippi Valley Collection,
University of Memphis, University Libraries

"Breathless" and "Great Balls of Fire" in 1958 had he had a major hit. In 1963, after his contract with Sun Records expired, Rich signed a contract with RCA-Victor. Sam sent a telegram to RCA notifying them that he still had a verbal agreement with Rich. RCA suspended the contract, and Rich sued Sam for breach of contract. The lawsuit was settled, Rich moved to RCA, and his first release, "Big Boss Man," was a hit. But it was the beginning of the end for Sun Records.

Jumping ship before the decade ended were three of Sam's session players: Ray Harris, Bill Cantrell, and Quinton Claunch. They teamed with a group of Memphis investors, including Joe Cuoghi, the owner of Poplar Tunes, one of the largest wholesale and retail record distributors in the South, to start up a new label, Hi Records. They built a studio in a movie theater in a black neighborhood on South Lauderdale and named it Royal Recording Studio. Impressed with the success of Bill Justis's hit instrumental "Raunchy," Cuoghi decided to build the label's reputation on instrumentals with a repetitive R&B groove. Hi's first hit came in 1960 with the Bill Black Combo's "Smokie Parts 1 & 2." Cofounder of the Bill Black Combo was Reggie Young, a native of Oscelo, Arkansas, who went on to become one of the best session guitarists in the country. Over the next ten years the combo racked up eighteen more hits. Playing on some of those sessions was saxophonist Ace Cannon, who scored with a hit solo effort in 1961, "Tuff."

In those days, the best band in town belonged to Willie Mitchell, a light-skinned black trumpet player whose pencil-thin mustache and dapper good looks made him a big hit with the ladies, then and now. In 1995 I was driving into Memphis from Nashville when I tuned my radio to a rock station. The deejay, commenting on a ceremony the night before at which Willie Mitchell had won an award, took a call from a young girl, who, judging by her voice, was in her early twenties. "Wasn't Willie Mitchell the best-looking thing you've ever seen?" gushed the caller. The deejay paused. "But he's in his sixties or something, isn't he?" "He might be," said the caller. "But he was still the best-looking man there."

Hi Records recruited Willie, first as a trumpet player, then as an arranger and producer. To turn out the instrumentals Hi wanted, he

Willie Mitchell on the steps of his studio, c. 1980s.
Photo by Greg Campbell

put together a first-rate house band that included Al Jackson on drums and Lewis Steinberg on bass. It was still illegal for blacks to go to white theaters or use white restrooms, but at Royal the two races worked together as equals.

In March 1960 Elvis was discharged from the army. He returned to Memphis, but he wasn't given much time to relax at Graceland. Within two weeks he was recording new material at a Nashville studio. Without even knowing the name of the first release, record stores had placed advance orders for 1.2 million singles. No one was surprised when the first release from that session, "Stuck on You," went to No. 1. After recording six songs in two days, Elvis reported to Hollywood to star in his next movie, *GI Blues*. It grossed $4 million that year, but it was a terrible movie; even Elvis was embarrassed. He asked the Colonel to find him better roles.

Elvis returned to Nashville in April for another two-day recording session. The Colonel was pushing him hard. "Stuck on You" had dropped from the charts by July, and Roy Orbison had scored with a hit, "Only the Lonely." One of the songs from Elvis's April session, "It's Now or Never," went to No. 1 in August and stayed there for five weeks. It was his biggest-selling single of all time, with sales exceeding twenty million. By fall he was filming another movie, *Flaming Star*, which offered him his first dramatic, nonsinging role. Under the guidance of the Colonel, Elvis became the biggest "star" in America in 1960, but he paid a stiff price for that stardom. His music entered a period of decline that would not be reversed until the end of the decade. Instead of building movies around his music, his handlers adapted his music to the movies.

Despite the financial success of his comeback year, Elvis was miserable. That Christmas he sent for Priscilla Beaulieu, a fourteen-year-old ninth grader he had met in Germany. The following year, Elvis asked her father if she could live in Graceland under the supervision of his father. In 1962 she moved into Graceland and enrolled at Immaculate Conception High School. When Jerry Lee Lewis found out, he must have been livid. He had done the "right thing" and married his teenage cousin, yet it cost him his career. Elvis was living in sin with a teenager and no one said a word. Where was the justice? By 1964 Jerry Lee's sales on Sun had dwindled to a trickle, so when his contract came up for renewal he left Sun and signed with Smash. His first album on Smash did well on country charts but didn't make a dent in the pop charts. Under the circumstances, he had no choice but to become a country artist. As a rock 'n' roller, he was history.

■　●　■

As Jim and Chips worked to get the new studio at Satellite Productions organized, Estelle stocked the record shop. It was a good idea. Without the profits generated by the record shop that first year, it is doubtful the studio would have survived. Both Estelle and Jim kept their day jobs. When they got off work at four, Jim would go to the studio and Estelle would go to the record shop, which she kept open until nine.

The first few sessions Jim undertook were unproductive. Then one day Rufus Thomas stopped by to pitch an idea to Jim. They had met at WDIA when Jim played his fiddle on the country segment. Rufus had written a song, "Cause I Love You," that he thought would make a good duet. He suggested he sing it with his sixteen-year-old daughter, Carla, who was then performing with a popular high school group, the Teen Town Singers. Jim liked the idea.

"In May of 1960 we brought out 'Cause I Love You' on Satellite," says Jim. "I didn't know what rhythm and blues was then, but I was in what you'd call a soulful environment. It sold about fifteen thousand locally, and to us that was like having a million-seller."

When Jerry Wexler, head of Atlantic Records in New York, was tipped off by a pressing plant operator as to how many units of "Cause I Love You" were being sold, he called Jim and Estelle and offered to distribute the record. It wasn't a hit, but it did sell thirty-five thousand units nationwide, giving Jim and Estelle their first national exposure as record executives. They were offered one thousand dollars for the master, plus a small royalty on sales. Estelle breathed easier about her mortgage. They signed what they thought was a leasing and distribution deal with Atlantic. Years later they discovered it was something else, but for the moment, at least, they were on top of the world.

Rufus and Carla recorded more songs, but they didn't sound like hits. One day they were sitting around the studio, tossing around ideas. "Carla said, 'I've got a song,'" recalls Estelle. "She said it was called 'Gee Whiz.' As soon as Jim and I heard that song we knew it was a hit. It's funny. When you hear a song, you know if it's got something in it that will sell."

Jim and Estelle used part of the thousand dollars they received from Atlantic to record "Gee Whiz." They hired strings and asked Chips to produce the session. When Wexler heard the recording, he signed Carla to a five-year contract and released "Gee Whiz" on Atlantic. In March 1961 it went to No. 13 on the pop charts, establishing Carla as a star and Satellite Productions as a player in the music business. "It took me a while to see the significance of what I was getting into," says Carla. "What I thought was fun was a business. Being young, black,

Rufus and Carla Thomas, 1979.
Photo courtesy of the Mississippi Valley Collection,
University of Memphis, University Libraries

and in the sixties, it was a thrill to just record." To understand her feelings, consider that six months after "Gee Whiz" became a hit, Memphis desegregated its public school system, but it would be another year before blacks, including Carla, would be allowed into movie theaters or permitted to use the public library. To the rest of the world, Carla was a teen queen; but to most of Memphis she was still a "nigger" who would have been arrested if she had gone to a movie theater.

■　●　■

At Satellite Productions, racial integration was in full bloom, as it was at Hi Records. As usual, music led the way in Memphis. Once Jim and Estelle got the studio cranked up, Chips was given free rein. He had used black players occasionally in his bands, so he thought nothing about using them in the studio. Booker T. Jones was one of the first young black musicians Chips worked with in the studio. Booker, though still a teenager, was playing bass then with Bowlegs Miller and Willie Mitchell at the Flamingo Club. He switched to organ after hearing Jack McDuff's combo one night at the club. McDuff used an organ and played the bass line himself on the pedals. Booker was so impressed that he took piano lessons. "No one was playing organ much then," says Booker. "I was able to get attention and get a job by playing the organ. It fascinated me because I had heard Ray Charles and I liked the way he played it." Chips saw Booker playing with Willie and Bowlegs and used him on bass a couple of times in his own club band. Inviting Booker to the studio was a natural thing to do.

Most of Memphis was totally unaware of what was happening musically in the city. There had always been two coexisting cultures in Memphis, one white, the other black. Now there were three. White male teens, witnessing the success Elvis, Jerry Lee, and the others had with members of the opposite sex, saw music as a way to score with girls. In the beginning, rock 'n' roll was more about sex than art. For that reason, teenage boys all over the city schemed to get into the studio with Chips. Among them was Packy Axton, Estelle's son. Some of his high school friends, Steve Cropper and Donald "Duck" Dunn, had put together a guitar band they called the Royal Spades. "My son was determined to be a musician," says Estelle. "He wanted to get in the band that Steve was in." Because the Royal Spades didn't need another guitar player, Packy learned to play sax. "He drove us crazy learning to play that thing," says Estelle. "He knew a little about music, but not much. He learned it himself. He never took lessons." When Packy asked Steve if he could join the band, Steve told him they didn't need a saxophone. Then Packy told him his mother owned Satellite Productions: "You know, the studio where Chips Moman works." Instantly, Packy became a Royal Spade in good standing.

Jim wasn't that crazy about having his nephew hanging round the studio (it would have offended his long-suffering sense of professionalism), but Estelle pushed it and Chips was desperate for musicians. Chips worked up a three-chord instrumental riff with keyboard

The Mar-Keys at home in Memphis. Top, clockwise: Don Nix, Terry Johnson, Duck Dunn, Wayne Jackson, Packy Axton, and Steve Cropper.
Photo courtesy of Don Nix

man Smoochie Smith during an intermission one night at a nightclub. He used the Royal Spades to flesh out the song in the studio. He cut take after take, using whoever was in the studio, adding a trumpet, additional saxophones, but as far as he was concerned the song never jelled. Jim never liked it, either. Chips took the tape to Nashville during the Carla Thomas sessions and got no reaction from the people he played it for there. When the tape came back, it had an erasure.

"I thought it was a hit," says Estelle. "I keep bugging Jim. Then I started in on Chips. I said, 'Look, this is a hit record.' They said, 'Forget it.' Finally, I got them to agree to it. They said for Packy to get the tape mastered and take it down to the pressing plant. That's when we discovered sixteen or eighteen bars had been wiped out." Estelle called Jim at the bank. "He said, 'Well, we did that song fifty times. Get Packy to find another front end, same tempo, and let him splice it on the front, and that's what Packy did. Whenever I hear that song, I can still hear the splice. There's about a half-a-note difference."

Satellite released the song, "Last Night," in July 1961. By then the Royal Spades had become the Mar-Keys. They had renamed themselves the Marquees, after the movie marquee outside the studio, but when no one could pronounce it, they changed it to Mar-Keys. To Jim's and Chips's enormous surprise, "Last Night" went to No. 2 on the pop charts in August, becoming the hottest-selling record in Memphis music history. Estelle felt vindicated. Maybe there was a place for women in the rock 'n' roll business after all.

Jim and Chips organized a touring band to promote the record. The Mar-Keys became Steve Cropper on guitar, Duck Dunn on bass, Packy on tenor sax, Smoochie Smith on keyboards, Terry Johnson on drums, Wayne Jackson on trumpet, and Don Nix on baritone sax. That group of musicians would become the core of the Memphis music's second revolution. One unexpected result of "Last Night's" notoriety was the threat of a lawsuit from another record company named Satellite. To avoid a legal hassle, Jim and Estelle changed the name of their company to Stax Records, a name formed by combing the first two letters of their last names. Some copies of "Last Night" were sold on Satellite and others on Stax.

The Mar-Keys could hardly believe their good fortune. "It was a high school band that lucked into a hit record—just seven people trying to have a good time," recalls Don Nix. "It was the big time to us. At that time, guys our age doing that was really crazy." To no one's surprise, Memphis ignored their success. It was an attitude musicians would come to expect from Memphians for the remainder of the century. "You get to where you don't expect them to [be supportive]," says Nix. "I remember at the time not caring. I didn't want to be famous in Memphis. I wanted to be famous in New York City. That was where all the girls were."

■　●　■

With two hits under their belts, Jim, Estelle and Chips slapped Stax Records into overdrive. Estelle used the record store as a workshop. Whenever Packy and his friends came by the studio, Estelle pulled them into the store and told them about the records that were selling and why she thought they were hits. She did the same thing with young black musicians. In effect, she became both a housemother and an educator. "I was a mama to all of them," says Estelle. "If they were having some personal problems, they would come to me. I was there when they needed somebody to talk to because Jim wasn't that type of person. They couldn't talk to him. Having the record shop was the most important thing for those writers and musicians in the studio. They could come to the record shop and see what customers were buying and why."

Chips was a magnet for the teenage boys who flocked to the studio. Unlike Jim and Estelle, neither of whom spent much time associating with musicians away from the studio, Chips performed in the local clubs and was idolized by younger musicians. He became the unofficial talent scout for the label. One of the first singers he brought into the studio was twenty-two-year-old William Bell, who had made a reputation for himself in local black clubs. He played a song for Chips and Jim that he had written himself. They recorded the song as a demo, but they liked it so much they released it as a single. The song, "You Don't Miss Your Water," was a smash hit in the South and made the national pop charts. Bell was drafted into the army shortly after the record was released and was out of the Stax loop for a couple of years, but the mold for future Stax hits had been set. Jim, Estelle, and Chips had found a soulful "sound" that would not only define the record label, but change the direction of American music as well.

In the summer of 1962 only one Memphian had a hit record, and that was Elvis, with his imminently forgettable single "She's Not You." Despite the success of "Gee Whiz," "Last Night," and "You Don't Miss Your Water," Jim wanted something for the country charts. He set up a session with a country singer and booked Steve Cropper on guitar, Booker T. Jones on keyboards, Al Jackson on drums, and Lewis Steinberg on bass. While waiting for the country singer, who never showed, they jammed to kill time.

Jim had heard Booker and Steve play a slow blues song, "Behave Yourself," in the clubs. They decided to record it. "Jim didn't want to release it without a B side, so he said, 'Why don't you guys record something for the B side and we'll have a record,'" says Booker. "Steve and I knew each other, and we had been fooling around together with some chords and stuff. We had this idea for 'Green Onions.' We had been fooling around with it on the piano a couple of weeks before . . . . Something just caused me to play it on the organ this time. It sounded a lot better on the organ than it did on the piano. That was a thrill for us to see that come together by accident."

"Green Onions" peaked at No. 7 on the pop charts. Whereas "Gee Whiz" had been a joint effort among Jim, Estelle, and Chips, Jim had not been involved with "Last Night," and neither Estelle nor Chips had been involved with "Green Onions." Tempers flared; egos were bruised. "Jim and Chips had a disagreement," says Estelle. "Chips was trying to take over the place. That's when the breakup came between Jim and Chips. I think their agreement was that if Chips would come back in a couple of weeks and agree to go along with Jim, then he would accept him back." Memories are fuzzy after thirty years, but it appears the breakup occurred after it dawned on Chips that he was helping build a company in which he had no equity. "Chips wanted half the company," recalls Estelle. "I was left out, and I was the one who put all the money up for it."

Whether Chips asked for 50 percent or 25 percent is immaterial because, considering the dynamics involved, it was a conflict that had no solution. Estelle had mortgaged her home to put up the money. There was no way she was going to take less than 50 percent. Jim wasn't about to become subordinate to his sister, not when the whole thing was his idea, his dream. Chips had the rough appearance of a

Booker T. and the MGs, with *Billboard* trophy for Top Entertainment Group, 1967. L to r: Al Jackson, Booker T., Steve Cropper, and Duck Dunn.
Photo courtesy of the Deanie Parker Collection, the Center for Southern Folklore Archive © 1992.

Southern roustabout, but beneath that exterior was the sensitive underskin of an artist. How could he give his heart and soul to a company that considered him nothing more than an employee? Jim and Chips exchanged harsh, bitter words, according to witnesses, and Chips stormed out of the studio and filed a lawsuit against Stax Records.

Amid that chaos, Booker T. and the MGs were born. Steinberg was replaced on bass by Duck Dunn, giving the group a racial mix of two whites and two blacks. "Steve and I had a little bit more rock 'n' roll in us and Booker and Al were the R&B—and the mixture worked," says Duck. "We were just playing with the people we loved to play with. We never thought about it as a racial thing."

"For us, music had no color," says Cropper. "What went on politically, we were not involved with . . . there were a couple of instances on the road later when we ended up leaving in the middle of something, but that only happened a couple of times . . . . If we went to a place and played in a town where things were segregated, we just stayed on the outskirts of town. We didn't worry about it."

In the studio, Cropper filled the leadership void created by Chips's departure. Using Cropper as a bandleader and a producer, Jim merged Booker T. and the MGs and the Mar-Keys to form the nucleus of his studio band. I once asked Jim how he got the idea to use that unique instrumentation for which Stax was famous. Jim laughed. He said the Stax horn sound developed because he couldn't find any Memphis singers who could get along well enough in the studio to sing background. The horns were a substitute for human voices. I asked Estelle the same question. She, too, laughed. "I think that when 'Last Night' came out so well, that's when they started paying attention to horns," says Estelle.

Into this cauldron of creativity tiptoed Otis Redding.

There are differences of opinion on whether he showed up at Stax Records by accident or design. Some accounts have him driving Johnny Perkins and the Pinetoppers to Memphis from Macon, Georgia, for a scheduled session at Stax. Others say his appearance was calculated to advance his own career. However it happened, Jim had some time left after he completed the session with Perkins, and he suggested Otis give it a try. Booker T. Jones had to leave, so Steve Cropper moved over to organ. Perkins played guitar, Lewis Steinberg was on bass, and Al Jackson was on drums. They recorded a couple of songs, one a Little Richard soundalike and the other an original tune written by Redding called "These Arms of Mine." Everyone was impressed with Otis's voice, but no one was particularly impressed with the results of the session.

When he returned to the studio the next day, Booker listened to the playback. "I had never heard of him, but you could tell there was something special about him," says Booker. "'These Arms of Mine' seemed new and different, and it was obvious that this man had quite a future."

Jim released the record locally on his new subsidiary label, Volt, but there was little reaction. To help things along, he gave a Nashville deejay a percentage of the publishing on that one song. The record died in Memphis, but the Nashville deejay played it so often that it became a minor regional hit. Jim didn't invite Otis back into the studio until June 1963, nine months after the first session. They recorded

Otis Redding, c. mid-1960s.
Photo courtesy of the Mississippi Valley Collection,
University of Memphis, University Libraries

two songs, "That's What My Heart Needs" and "Mary's Little Lamb," both disasters. Otis was slow to develop, but everyone knew there was something there. "That voice was different," says Estelle. "The way he expressed his songs—he didn't do them like anybody else." Otis returned in September and recorded one of his own compositions, "Pain in My Heart." The song scored on the R&B charts. Finally, Otis was on his way.

By then Booker T. and the MGs was one of the hottest groups in America. Encouraged by that success, Willie Mitchell stepped up his efforts to put together an instrumental group. Not to be outdone, Rufus Thomas brought Jim a new song he had written titled "Walking the Dog." "It was a nursery rhyme," says Rufus. "We used to do it in the neighborhood—'Mary Mack dressed in black'—this may sound strange, but I played all the games in the neighborhood, the girls' games as well as the boys'. So it was a nursery rhyme from when I was a child."

"Walking the Dog" was an enormous success, particularly with college students, who associated it with the newest dance craze, the dog. Some people consider "Walking the Dog" one of the first rap songs ever recorded. The song was so successful that an upstart British rock group, the Rolling Stones, recorded their own version on their debut American album the following year.

■　●　■

Stax had its fourth biggest hit. "Walking the Dog" peaked at No. 12 on the pop charts in December 1963, but in November, as it had been climbing the charts, President John F. Kennedy was assassinated in Dallas, Texas. As Vice President Lyndon Johnson ascended to the presidency, one of the first people he called was Memphis's own "Fiddling" Abe Fortas. Two months earlier, Senator Estes Kefauver had dropped dead of a heart attack.

With Crump's political machine gone, Memphis politics throughout the decade was defined solely by racial issues. Two men, Henry Loeb and William Ingram, alternated as mayor, with the primary issues centered around the two "-ations": integration and unionization. With the city spellbound by those two issues—and with Kefauver gone and Fiddling Abe fueling a pipeline to the White House—citizens and reporters alike lost sight of what organized crime was doing in the city.

After the Kennedy assassination, Fiddling Abe became the second most powerful man in Washington. President Johnson sought his advice on every major domestic issue. Fortas and Johnson were opposed to setting up a commission to investigate the assassination, but public pressure was such that Johnson had no choice. He put Fortas in charge of establishing the Warren Commission. In addition, he became the president's chief advisor on civil rights and his unofficial minister of culture. It was Fortas who helped draft legislation for the Kennedy Center for the Performing Arts. Fortas projected a complex, dual image. On the one hand, he was a high-profile lover of music and culture. He stepped up his musical performances and entertained often at his Georgetown home. On the other hand, he was a cynical, behind-the-scenes power broker, whose services were offered to the highest bidder.

In June 1964 Martin Luther King was jailed in St. Augustine, Florida, for trying to enter a "whites only" restaurant. Anticipating the same type of trouble in Memphis, King hired lawyer Lucius Burch, of the old anti-Crump coalition.

In July President Johnson signed the historic Civil Rights Act of 1964. "The purpose of this law is simple," said Johnson. "It does not restrict the freedom of any American so long as he respects the rights of others . . . . It does say that those who are equal before God shall now also be equal in the polling booths, in the classrooms, in the factories, and in hotels and restaurants and movie theaters and other places that provide service to the public."

By 1965 Fortas had become invaluable to the president, who decided to put him where he would be of the most help: on the U.S. Supreme Court. Shortly after the appointment, he autographed a photograph for his friend: "For Abe," Johnson wrote on the photograph, "the Isaac Stern of the Supreme Court. My first string man."

THE SIXTIES: STAX, AMERICAN, AND HI SPIN HITS GALORE

n the summer of 1964 two carloads of students from the University of Mississippi, better known as Ole Miss, struck out for Memphis for a late-night rendezvous on Beale Street. The students left behind a campus that only two years earlier had been racially integrated at gunpoint by federal marshals. The campus was still seething with racial tension, as, indeed, was the entire region. When President John F. Kennedy was assassinated in Dallas the previous November, the Ole Miss campus had erupted into rebel flag-waving celebration at the news.

In the two Memphis-bound cars were six male members of a band, the Strokers, and one female student, who had hitched a ride at the last minute. I was the keyboard player. I rode in the car with Bunker Ex Hill, the bassist, and a blonde coed who carried a box of fried chicken in her lap. The other four band members rode in the second car. Because it was a weeknight and a violation of school policy for coeds to be out of their dorms after 11 P.M., the coed left with the knowledge she would be risking expulsion. Perhaps for that reason she refused to tell us her name. The less we knew, the safer she felt. The less we knew, the safer *we* felt. She was dressed in a pink skirt and sweater and her makeup had a pinkish tint to it. We called her Pink Lady. That suited her just fine.

In 1964 Ole Miss had a well-deserved reputation as a party school. It was one of the largest venues in the country for popular music. On any given weekend there were probably as many nationally known recording acts performing at one of the dozen or so fraternity houses as there were in New York or Los Angeles. Music was everywhere: rock, rhythm and blues, pop, even jazz. I remember a weekend in which I listened to Julie London, backed by the Bobby Troup band, sing her scorcher "Cry Me A River," Rufus Thomas sing his hit "Walking the Dog," and Hot Nuts belt out ribald lyrics designed to solicit sure-fire squeals from the coeds. Most of the bands were black. The racial politics of the era were strident, but students were always willing to park their prejudices at the door for the sake of a decent party. As a result, Ole Miss was one of the most popular venues in the country for black R&B performers.

There were only two or three local bands that performed on the campus on a regular basis. The Strokers played once or twice a week at sorority "swaps" and on weekend nights at the fraternities. Ole Miss students were accustomed to the best bands in the country. To be accepted by them was a compliment of the highest order. I don't know how good the Strokers were. I do know the band's name was a source of controversy. Once I was riding in a car with some people I had just met. A young girl, a freshman, asked me if I had heard of the Strokers. I said I had. She had never heard the band, she said, but the sorry bastards had nearly kept her out of college. It seems her mother had heard of the band and told her daughter she could not enroll in Ole Miss as long as the Strokers were prowling the campus. After weeks of tearful pleading, she was allowed to enroll on condition she not get within a hundred yards of the band. She made a solemn vow to keep her distance—or else. I could have ruined her day, but didn't.

For whatever reason, the Strokers were booked at the Flamingo Club. It was on Hernando Street, just off Beale Street, in gritty downtown Memphis. On the way to Memphis we listened to WDIA, our favorite radio station. The Pink Lady sat between Bunker and me. She said very little. All her efforts were focused on that box of fried chicken.

"Yum, yum," she said, licking the bones clean as a whistle. "I could do this all day long." Her long, pink tongue flicked with serpentine accuracy, leaving a trail of chicken bones all the way to Memphis.

The Strokers at the Flamingo Room with Tommy Tucker (in suit).
Photo courtesy of James Dickerson

It was almost dark when we pulled up outside the Flamingo Club. By 1964 Beale Street had become a seedy, dilapidated caricature of its former self. The Flamingo Club was an all-black club. We knew that, but despite the racial tensions of the day, thought nothing about performing there. Black musicians had performed at Ole Miss for years. What we didn't know then—what I didn't discover until more than two decades later—was that all-white bands simply did not perform in black clubs in Memphis. The Strokers earned a footnote in history by becoming one of the first—if not *the* first all-white band—to perform in a black nightclub in Memphis.

At dusk the tall urban shadows bobbed and flickered in the fading light, transforming the most innocent of pedestrians into potential muggers. Some of the band members were packing heat. I protested that much firepower. The pistols were collected and put into a canvas bag for safekeeping on the organ bench. I think the idea was that I could squeeze off rounds with one hand, then, with my free hand, toss the extra pistols to the other band members. Maybe we were watching too much television.

That night the Flamingo Club was packed. We opened with some new music we had worked up. That spring a new British band, the Beatles, had released their first American album. We thought they showed promise. To the bafflement of everyone in the club, we opened with several Beatles songs. The audience was stunned.

"What kind of music is that?" a man in the audience shouted. "That music don't do nothing for me." Suddenly, a young black girl leaped onto the stage. She ran up to the microphone. "How 'bout a little honky tonk?" she said. The crowd went wild.

As the band belted out a raunchy Bo Diddley number in the key of E, the young girl, who was actually a professional stripper, or a shake dancer, as they were called in those days, did some dances we had never seen at Ole Miss. Pink Lady, who sat perched on the organ bench next to me like a pet parakeet, squirmed the entire time. When the song ended, the shake dancer gathered up her things. She looked at the band and cooed: "That was r-e-a-l good."

"I'm hungry," Pink Lady said. "I wish I had some more chicken."

We kicked off with another R&B song and stayed in that groove for the rest of the night. A second British band had released its first American album that year. They called themselves the Rolling Stones. Their first album sounded like a tribute to Memphis music. Because we had worked up songs from that album, including Rufus Thomas's hit "Walking the Dog," we added them to our playlist that night. After our first set, there was a commotion in the audience. A line of perhaps a dozen women snake-danced among the tables. Or were they women? Lord, no. They were men: a transvestite review. For one dollar, the patrons could have their photographs taken with the transvestite of their choice. Each time they snaked past the bandstand, the transvestites shouted out, "Kiss, kiss, kiss."

As we began the second set, the club manager took the stage. Without a word to us, he announced that Tommy Tucker, whose song "Hi-Heel Sneakers" was a tremendous hit on college campuses, was going to perform with the band. We were stunned.

As the audience went wild, Tommy Tucker, wearing a dapper suit, jumped up onto the stage. He turned to the band: "You know my song?" Luckily, we did. Tucker sang with us for the rest of the evening. The audience loved him and forgave us for playing Beatle music. Things were going so well I didn't pay much attention to Pink Lady's request for ten dollars for another box of fried chicken. I told her to get it from our manager. She left the bandstand and I forgot about her.

At the end of the night Tommy Tucker asked if we would back him at an upcoming engagement at Club Paradise, the biggest blues supper club in the city. We jumped at the chance. We loaded up the cars and went to Club Paradise, where Tucker met us. When the deal was proposed to the club manager, he looked at Tucker with amusement. The manager shook his head. "Not with no white band, you ain't," he said.

Tucker apologized and we parted company. It was then I realized Pink Lady was missing. The band gave me hell. "You gave her *money?*" they said in unison. Bunker and I left to look for the girl, while the others headed back to Memphis. In the wee hours of the morning, we made the rounds of the all-night downtown cafés. Finally, we found a night clerk at a cheap motel who recognized her description. "I know where she is," he said. "Room three-twelve."

"Who's she with?" I asked.

"Big guy," said the desk clerk. "Big as the two of you put together."

As we walked out the door, I turned back to the desk clerk. "How much are rooms here?"

"Ten dollars," he said.

For what seemed like hours, Bunker and I sat outside the motel in the car. Finally, the door to 312 opened. Out stumbled King Kong, adjusting his fly as he staggered along the walkway. We waited until he left the parking lot, then went up to the room. Pink Lady let us in and returned to the vanity to primp. "Nothing happened," she said, without being asked. I was just a kid, but I knew enough to understand that if a woman ever protests her innocence without being asked, you are better off not inquiring further.

On the long drive back to Ole Miss, I started nodding off. It was around 5 A.M. "Why don't you put your head on my shoulder and get some sleep," Pink Lady said. Her shoulder was hot and sweaty, and she smelled of sex. I slept like a baby.

I had an eight o'clock class across the street from the cafeteria, so

Bunker dropped me off there. Pink Lady said she was hungry. We made a strange-looking pair in the cafeteria. I was still dressed in my band uniform: a pink shirt, a burgundy blazer, and white pants. Pink Lady looked like a poster girl for Hookers Anonymous. As we approached the checkout counter, Pink Lady touched my arm.

"Let me treat you," she said.

She pulled out a thick wad of bills and paid the cashier.

■　●　■

In 1965 Beale Street resembled a ghost town. The nightlife was gone and only a few stores remained. Windows were boarded up. Trash littered the sidewalks. Bill Browder, who later changed his name to T. G. Sheppard and found success as a country music artist, worked as a sales clerk at Lanksy's, a clothing store on the west end of Beale. For years the store specialized in gaudy, pimpish clothing, but with the sudden burst of recording activity in Memphis it became a favorite shopping place for musicians. Elvis shopped there frequently. So did the Stax and Hi artists. "It was basically a black area, but a lot of white entertainers came down to Beale to buy clothes," says Sheppard. "Elvis would come down to buy from Lanksy's because they carried all those loud clothes entertainers like to buy."

After Chips Moman left Stax, the label struggled throughout 1964, without success, to get on the charts again. The only Memphis artists who made the charts that year were Elvis, with the embarrassing "Kissin' Cousins," and Roy Orbison with "Oh Pretty Woman." By no coincidence, it was the year the Beatles invaded America and totally dominated the charts. By April the Beatles held the top five slots on the pop charts with "Can't Buy Me Love, "Twist and Shout," "She Loves You," "I Want to Hold Your Hand," and "Please Please Me."

If 1964 was one of the worst years in Memphis music history, 1965 was one of the best. Between 1965 and 1970 Stax would do its best work, Hi Records would come into its own, Sam Phillips's studio would have one last hit, and Chips Moman would accomplish recording feats that seem incredible in retrospect. By then Chips had settled his lawsuit with Jim and Estelle and used the money to set up his own studio

The Gentrys at the Overton Park Shell where Elvis got his start.
Photo courtesy of Mike Gardner

on the north end of town. He chose a rundown black neighborhood for his studio, which he named American Recording Studios. He assembled a first-rate studio band, made up of Reggie Young on guitar, Bobby Wood on piano, Gene Chrisman on drums, Mike Leech on bass, and Bobby Emmons on organ.

Despite the flurry of activity at Stax, American, and Hi in 1965, the biggest hit of the year was a song recorded at Sam Phillips's studio. Domingo Samudio, a native of Texas, had been performing with his band, the Pharaohs, throughout Texas and Louisiana since the early 1960s. While working the club circuit, he made his way to Memphis and into Phillips's studio, where old rockabilly hand Stan Kesler recorded a session with him for MGM Records. Twelve weeks after "Wooly Bully" by Sam the Sham & the Pharaohs was released, it was the No. 2 record in the country.

American's first hit was an uptempo rock song, "Keep on Dancing," recorded by a group of white Memphis teenagers who called themselves the Gentrys. The song peaked at No. 4 on the pop charts. Chips never liked the song—he once told me he hated the song so much he mixed it with the sound turned off, setting the mix by the meter alone—but it opened the door for other, even bigger hits. For the first time since the early days of Sun, Memphis was again a hit factory.

American's next big hit came from Sandy Posey, the studio receptionist who scored with a No. 14 hit, "Born a Woman." But it takes more than two hits to sustain a studio, producers, and musicians, and Chips worked night and day to make ends meet. He engineered sessions for whatever he could get, he continued playing in bands, and he fought a deep depression that threatened to immobilize him at times. "I wouldn't turn anything down," says Chips. "There was a ten-year period in which I might have averaged three hours of sleep a night. I recorded one time for nine days without going home. I would fall unconscious behind the board and people would pick me up and shake me and say, 'Can you do one more mix?'—when they should have taken me straight to a hospital."

Chips clawed and scratched for everything he got. Thirty years later, I asked Estelle Axton how long it took for the hard feelings between them to fade away. "I don't think they ever did," she says. "I think Chips was going to prove that he could do it—and he did. There's no doubt he was talented."

Frustrated with a record label's refusal to send a check, Chips went to New York to collect the money himself. He was warmly greeted by the record executive, who stroked his ego, but when Chips asked for his money, all he got were excuses. Chips grabbed the record executive by the lapels and dragged him to a window of the skyscraper.

"You've finally pushed me to the point where I'm ready to die for this," Chips says. He pressed the record executive against the window. "Is this something you're ready to die for?"

Chips left with his check.

Extreme as Chips's behavior was, it was behavior Jim Stewart should have emulated in his dealings with Atlantic. Though he didn't know it at the time, he was being drawn into a financial morass from which he would never be able to extricate himself. No longer content merely to distribute the records produced at Stax, Jerry Wexler assumed a more activist role by signing artists to Atlantic and then persuading

Jim to work with them at Stax. Among the first were Sam Moore and Dave Prater, who recorded under the name Sam and Dave, and Wilson Pickett, whose first session at Stax produced his signature song, "In the Midnight Hour."

By 1965 the Stax family had grown. Jim brought Al Bell aboard as national sales director. Although Booker T. Jones and Al Jackson played prominent creative roles at the label, there had been no blacks involved at the executive level. Bell was a tall, aggressive African American who had been a successful deejay at a Memphis radio station. He was Jim's opposite, offering a much-needed balance. Cropper still was working both as producer and guitarist, using players from the MGs and the Mar-Keys, but new black faces started popping up in the studios: Homer Banks, who worked as a clerk in Estelle's record shop, and Isaac Hayes and David Porter, who made their way into the studio by way of Estelle's "workshops."

"I was really close to the writers," says Estelle. "Maybe my earlier experience as a schoolteacher may have had something to do with that. I'll never forget how David Porter became a writer. He was working at a grocery store across the street from the studio. The minute he got off, he'd come over to the record shop and talk to me. He was so young they wouldn't let him in the studio. He wrote a song and wanted my opinion. That song had eight sheets of words. I said, 'No way, David.' I said, 'You have to concentrate it, shorten it.' I would play him records that were hits. Today, he gives me credit for teaching him how to write songs. It makes me feel so happy I helped someone. He and Isaac Hayes are the best writers around."

By the time David Porter got into the studio, he found one of his school chums, Isaac Hayes, already there playing piano. They teamed up to write songs, with David doing the words and Isaac the music. After the first few sessions with Sam and Dave didn't yield any hits, David and Isaac submitted some of their ideas. One of their first songs, "Hold On, I'm Comin'," gave Sam and Dave their first hit and established Stax as the leader of Southern-based soul. David and Isaac followed that up with "Soul Man."

Meanwhile, Otis Redding was slowly building a fan base while recording a string of records that, while not hits, always seemed on the verge of being hits. Everyone knew Otis was going to be big, they just didn't know *when* he was going to be big. "Otis was not our biggest-selling Stax artist," says Jim. "But he was one of the most talked about and recognized. He started developing a market and was always good for a certain amount of sales. And each one he did would surpass the others. He was a superstar in Europe when he was best known over here among blacks and college kids. But it was obvious he was going to eventually be a pop star."

Otis's trembling, unisex voice was perfect for the times. He was sexual, but in a nonthreatening way, without orientation. White college students, particularly those at Ole Miss, wanted their soul music sweet as iced tea. It supported their view that blacks, at their core, were a benign race who possessed a glorious view of the world. Sweet soul music was never a reflection of the black experience so much as it was a creation of white college students who idealized the black experience. Most of the sweet soul music created in the early years was done to satisfy a white college audience. Black music, when written by and for a black audience, had a hard edge to it that flirted with violence. Otis wanted no part of that audience. His kinship was to the white Southern boys who wanted their soul sweet. It is the reason he worked so well with Steve Cropper.

David Porter saw two sides of Otis. "You know Otis didn't talk the way he sang," says Porter. "He might sing like a kid with a speech problem sometime but offstage he was soft-spoken and quite articulate. Another thing. When Otis strutted the stage he walked pigeon-toed, but offstage, he didn't walk that way. When he was on-stage that personality just came out of him and it would just knock you out. Otis worked on his style and even after he was rich and a polished performer, he could maintain the raw edge, the emotionalism of his music. That's because he was a pro."

Collaboration was the key to success at Stax. Jim worked on the principle that if you have the best musicians, the best songwriters, and the best singers in the country, something good just had to happen if you tossed them into a room together. Interestingly, while the same core group of musicians played on all of the recordings made in the studio, seldom did Jim ever pair his artists with each other. The major exception was Otis Redding and Carla Thomas. "We were in Memphis at the same time," says Carla. "Most of the time, when we got together it was for a social gathering and never in the studio. When we got together this time Jim Stewart said, 'Hey, everyone is doing duets. Why don't you and Otis?' First, it was kinda something that was thrown out for fun. I said, 'Hey, I'm used to singing soft ballads like 'Gee Whiz.' I don't know if I can keep up with Otis Redding.'"

The song Jim had in mind was "Tramp," a pre-rap extension of the trademark Stax groove. The song featured dialogue in which Carla berated Otis for his country ways, but Carla wasn't sure she could talk to Otis that way. Otis was a star. "They said, 'Oh, talk to somebody like you're mad and be yourself,'" she says. "It worked." The song reminded Carla of Rufus's hit "Walking the Dog." "My father's stuff really started that rap stuff," says Carla. "I remember he did a record called 'Jump Back, Baby, Jump.' He sang that to us when we were little kids when he was down on Beale Street."

What impressed Carla about Stax in those days was the way everyone pitched in to offer ideas or constructive criticism. "We were young and we did a lot of playing around in the studio," says Carla. "We weren't all that sophisticated. We didn't have sixteen tracks like they did in New York. We sat there and threw out ideas. The horns might say, 'Hey, how about a little something there,' and Duck [Dunn] might say the same thing. It was all put together by us. All those merging of ideas."

That sense of camaraderie extended beyond Stax's immediate family. While a student at Ole Miss, I often spent time in the rehearsal rooms in the building where music classes were taught. I had formed a band called the Dynamics that featured a trumpet and sax (I played sax), but I wanted to play keyboards and went by the rehearsal rooms every day after class to practice on the pianos and organs. Late one night I was trying to get "Green Onions" down when there came a knock on the door. A guy a few years older than myself stuck his head in and asked what the hell I was doing. He said he was from Memphis, where he played in a band. I asked what band. The Mar-Keys, he said. For years it was a point of pride that Smoochie Smith taught me to play "Green Onions."

Not to be outdone by what was happening at Stax and American, Willie Mitchell, now in charge of production at Hi, developed a competing instrumental style, exemplified by the 1964 hit "20–75." He set out to discover artists who reflected his own sophisticated view of Memphis soul.

Don Bryant had sung with Willie's club band for years, so it was natural that Willie would want to record with him first. "Don't Turn Your Back on Me," their first release, was a big hit in the South in 1965 but didn't make the national charts. Willie kept at it. For several years, Hi and Stax shared the same rhythm section, with Al Jackson on drums and Lewis Steinberg on bass, but Willie's concept of instrumentation was different from the Stax sound. At Stax, the horns offered rough edges and melodic repetition. At Hi, the horn sound was smoother, more sophisticated.

Willie needed singers who could complement that sound. One night Willie was at the Rosewood Club listening to Bowlegs Miller when Bowlegs brought a nineteen-year-old woman up from the audience to sit in with the band. At five-foot-three and ninety-nine pounds, Ann Peebles didn't take up much space on the stage, but when she sang, her voice filled the room. Willie knew he had found what he was looking for. After the set, Bowlegs introduced them.

"Where do you live?" asked Willie.

"St. Louis," she said.

"Not any more," answered Willie.

Ann Peebles didn't move to Memphis right away, but she commuted from St. Louis to work with Willie in the studio. In 1969 they released their first single, "Walk Away." It did well on the R&B charts, but didn't make the pop charts. Willie paired her with Don Bryant and other writers who were working with him in hopes of getting a breakout song. The pairing was more complete than Willie expected: Don Bryant and Ann Peebles got married.

As Willie waited patiently for Ann to develop, he kept working with new artists. Another female singer he worked with in 1965 was Annie Mae Bullock, who had been brought in by Ike Turner. By then she and

Rufus Thomas, Ann Peebles, and Al Green in 1976.
Photo courtesy of the Mississippi Valley Collection,
University of Memphis, University Libraries

Ike had married and she had changed her name to Tina Turner. Willie
worked with Tina from 1965 until 1977, recording seventeen albums
with her, and although she enjoyed a lot of success on the club circuit, she didn't become a superstar until the mid-1980s. In 1988 I
asked Willie if he was surprised by Tina's strong comeback. "I don't

think Tina ever needed to make a comeback," said Willie. "She was always there. She always had the talent, the looks, everything." Willie had good reason to be excited about Tina's good fortune. "Ever since she recorded 'Let's Stay Together,' which was written by myself and Al Green, people have been calling, wanting to know if I had any more songs like that."

Working with Ann Peebles and Tina Turner in the mid-to-late 1960s, Willie felt like he was on the right track with female singers. What he needed, really wanted more than anything else, was a strong male vocalist who could complement his instrumental sound. Fortune smiled on him in Midland, Texas, in the summer of 1968. He had scored that year with another instrumental hit, "Soul Serenade," and he was touring to promote the record.

"It was real hot that day, like a hundred and twelve degrees," Willie laughs. "We pulled the bus up to the club in Midland. This guy runs up to me. He says his name is Al Green. He said, 'I'm stranded here. Can I work with you tonight so I can get back home?'

"So we went in to rehearse. I heard him sing. I said, 'Hey, man, you've got a neat style.' He was about twenty. I said, 'Why don't you go back to Memphis with me. Let's work on some stuff. You could be a star.'

"'How long would it take to do it?' he says.

"'About eighteen months," I say.

"He said, 'I don't have that long to wait.'

"When the show was over, we got stranded in the lot because a car wouldn't let us out of the driveway. Finally, Al comes and jumps in the bus and we took him back to Memphis. It was eighteen months exactly when 'Tired of Being Alone' was a million seller."

Willie, at long last, had the voice.

■　●　■

On August 19, 1966, the Beatles performed at the Memphis Coliseum. The Ku Klux Klan had pickets outside the coliseum because of comments John Lennon made about the Beatles being more popular than Jesus Christ. The police were asked to keep an eye out for firearms.

Word was out: the Beatles were going to get their asses kicked. By the time they took the stage, John, Paul, George, and Ringo were basket cases. Halfway through the performance, someone threw a firecracker onto the stage. George Harrison nearly fainted.

The Beatles' manager, Brian Epstein, made arrangements for them to visit Stax. T. G. Sheppard was working there then as a record promoter. He remembers looking up one day to see the Beatles walking down the hall. "I kind of freaked out," he says. "They were talking about recording at Stax and the word got out. A mob of people showed up. They were big fans of Otis Redding and people like that. I guess they just wanted to see where all those records were cut."

As usual, there was a lot of confusion about the reason for the visit. Jim and Estelle had learned the music business by the bootstrap method. They learned the hard way that people didn't always do things for the reasons they said they were doing them. "I don't think they ever meant to come [to record]," says Estelle. "They just wanted to get something stirred up for their concert." The debacle left Estelle so distraught she refused to buy Beatles albums for the record shop. "As I look back, it's funny," she said in 1995. "But then I was in tears."

The following year, the entire Stax stable went to Europe as part of the Stax/Volt Revue. While the tour was in London, legend has it the Beatles stopped work on their *Sgt Pepper* album to take in a performance. Carla Thomas heard that, too, but never saw them at the performance. "What pleased me is that I was the only artist out of the bunch of folks on the tour who performed at a club called the Bag of Nails," says Carla. "Booker played for me, but I was the only vocalist. In that little club was Paul McCartney, and the fact that he was there says something about the Memphis sound."

By January 1967 the Memphis sound was on the verge of a major overhaul. The Mar-Keys had broken up as a touring band in 1965. The best-known club band was Ronnie and the Devilles, but after years of getting nowhere, Ronnie ditched the Devilles to start up another group. The three surviving members of the Devilles—Danny Smythe on drums, Gary Talley on guitar, and Bill Cunningham on bass—looked around for a singer and a keyboard player. Smythe brought John Evans into the group to play keyboards, then they looked for a singer.

"Danny said, 'We need somebody who can sing like a nigger,'" says Evans, who then apologizes for using the n-word. "In those days it was not such a derogatory term. Danny admires black music more than any person I know. They asked me if I knew anybody. At that time, it would not have been a viable alternative to have a black member in the band. I called a friend and he said, 'Well, there's this guy who was in a talent show.' I said, 'Is he any good?' He said, 'Yeah, but I don't really know why.'"

Evans found out that his name was Alex Chilton, and he gave him a call. He was surprised to find out that he was only sixteen (the Devilles were all nineteen), but he invited him to an audition. Three years' difference at that age is a lot, and that concerned some of the guys in the band, but they figured they could overlook the age thing if he could really sing. If they had prepared themselves for the age difference, they had not prepared themselves for what they saw when he arrived for the audition. All the members of the band were dressed in the preppy fashions of the day: Gant shirts, Gold Cup socks, and Bass loafers. "There was a dress code without having a dress code in those days," says Evans. "Alex came in wearing a faded black T-shirt, jeans with holes in the knees—and that was not acceptable in those days— and a blue jeans jacket, and no one wore those except farmers, blue-collar workers, you know, trailer park people, for heavens sake. On top of that, he comes in cold weather and he had on a men's dress scarf, like you would wear with an overcoat."

When Alex sang, he seemed older, more experienced, so the Devilles forgave his eccentric dress and asked him to be their singer. Later they discovered that his mother owned an art gallery and his father was a jazz musician. The family lived in the gallery and in the minds of nineteen-year-old musicians, that explained Alex's eccentric dress and personality. They started doing gigs as the Devilles.

As the Devilles regrouped, Chips Moman and Dan Penn, who had jumped to American from Fame studio in Muscle Shoals, Alabama, were hired to play on a session at Fame with a Memphis-born singer named Aretha Franklin. There was a buzz out about Aretha. Chips and Dan were anxious to see if she measured up. She had been signed to Atlantic by Jerry Wexler, who decided to record her in Muscle Shoals after Jim Stewart turned down another one of Wexler's "deals" to record her at Stax. Wexler knew it would piss Jim off if he invited Chips and Dan to the session. For Dan, a hard-core country boy who was seldom without sunglasses and a cigarette dangling from his lips, it was a chance to return home as a conquering hero. For Chips it was just another paying gig: have guitar, will travel. They recorded one complete song, "I Never Loved A Man," and laid down the track for a second song written by Chips and Dan, "Do Right Woman." Then everyone packed up and went home.

With the success of "I Never Loved a Man"—it peaked at No. 9—Wexler sent for Moman's American rhythm section. They went to New York and completed an entire album within one week. Other songs on the album were "Natural Woman" and "Chain of Fools." One of the songs recorded that week, "Respect," had been released earlier by Otis Redding. Aretha liked the song and wanted to record it herself. The Memphis boys were happy to oblige, as was Wexler. What better way to stick it to Stax than by re-recording their work? In June Aretha Franklin's version of "Respect" went to No. 1 on the pop charts, only two weeks after its release. Otis Redding was stunned. None of his records had ever cracked the Top 20.

Spirits soared at American. Aretha hadn't recorded at American, but she had used American players and Memphis songs, so there was a gut feeling they were headed in the right direction. Sometime between the New York session and the success of "Respect," Dan Penn was approached by a deejay about the Devilles. Dan talked to Chips about the group. Sure, he said, bring 'em in. Dan booked them for a 10 A.M. session and notified them the day before, sending word for them to pick up a tape of original songs he had put together. That night, John Evans and another band member stopped by the studio to pick up the tape. "Dan wasn't there, but he had left the tape there with our names on it," says Evans. "So we went back and listened to the tape. There were three tunes on it. 'The Letter' was the only one we could stand to listen to. It was short, very simple."

When they went by the studio the next morning, they got the second jolt of their young careers (Alex's avant-garde appearance had been the first). "Dan was wearing Bermuda shorts that came down to

The Box Tops. L. to r.
Gary Talley, William Cunningham,
John Evans, Alex Chilton,
Danny Smythe.
Photos courtesy of the
Mississippi Valley Collection,
University of Memphis,
University Libraries

the middle of his kneecaps," recalls Evans. "If that weren't nerdy enough, he was wearing a white T-shirt with the sleeve rolled up around a pack of Lucky Strikes. He was the darndest thing to see. He was wearing high-topped tennis shoes with athletic socks rolled up."

Dan told them Chips wouldn't be coming in. He would be their producer. They looked around the studio. Dirty ashtrays and food were piled everywhere. The studio looked dark and foreboding. "We didn't know what to think," says Evans. "Dan was primarily a writer, but he worked as an engineer. Dan thinks, 'Uh-huh, here's my chance to do something.' I think it was the first tune he had ever produced." Evans showed the other guys in the band the chord progression for "The Letter"—Dan suggested to Alex that he pronounce ae-ro-plane in three syllables—and thirty-three takes later they had a record that redefined the Memphis sound.

"The Letter" was released on Mala, a New York-based label that specialized in black music. By then the Devilles had changed their name to the Box Tops. To everyone's surprise, especially the group's sixteen-year-old lead singer, "The Letter" peaked at No. 1 in September 1967, becoming the first No. 1 pop hit ever recorded in Memphis by Memphis artists.

Chips Moman was elated with the success of "The Letter," even if Dan Penn, who had never produced anything in his life, and had never even looked like he wanted to produce anything, had produced the record. But it seemed to confirm his worst fears about what could happen if he didn't stay in the studio twenty-four hours a day. He would never let that happen again. For the next five years he would eat, sleep, work, and play at the studio, working at a fanatical pace, and never, ever, would he again take his eye off the sound board. Creatively, it would pay off. He would produce a string of over 120 hit records at American, one of the most impressive feats in American music history. Physically, it nearly destroyed him.

Chips began his second flowering (the first had been at Stax) with Wilson Pickett, whom Jerry Wexler had brought up from Muscle Shoals, and Bobby Womack, a songwriter and guitarist who had played on some of Pickett's previous sessions. Pickett was first up in the studio. Womack waited his turn. "I gave Wilson Pickett all my songs," says

Womack. "Every time he asked for another one, I gave it to him. I was so happy. He got his whole album down and then they said, 'Bobby, you're next.' [Pickett] walked out of the studio and they said, 'Well, what do you want to cut first?' I didn't have a damn song left. I tried my best to write something. Chips came in and said, 'Hi, Bobby, how's it going?' I didn't tell him I had given Pickett every song I had. I started playing 'Fly Me to the Moon,' and Chips said, 'Speed it up. That's a smash. Let's cut it.' It was about two o'clock in the morning. He never knew that 'Midnight Mover' and the others were on the Pickett album. They'd have really shit in their pants if they had known that."

In those days, everything Chips touched became a hit. He cut another Top 10 hit with the Gentrys ("Cry Like a Baby"), then followed that up with Dusty Springfield's "Son of a Preacher Man," B. J. Thomas's "Hooked on A Feeling," and Neil Diamond's "Sweet Caroline." Then he got word that the King himself, Elvis Presley, wanted a hit.

■   ●   ■

In the summer of 1967 Otis Redding and his band, the Bar-Kays, played the Fillmore in San Francisco. Otis rented a houseboat while they were there. The bay, with its ever-present dock and soothing ocean rhythms, had a mystical attraction to a Southern boy from inland Georgia. That fall Otis took a couple of months off to recuperate from minor throat surgery. Because he was booked on December 8 at Vanderbilt University in Nashville, he stopped off in Memphis before the concert, with the hopes of doing some recording. He told Steve Cropper he had a new song.

"Otis was always writing," recalls Steve. "Every time he came to Memphis to record, he always had fourteen or fifteen ideas. A little piece of this, a little intro there. He played me what he had, and it was only the first verse. I sat there with him and within about half an hour we had written the other two verses and the bridge."

The song, "(Sitting on) the Dock of the Bay," was unfinished when Otis left for Nashville. Otis played acoustic guitar on the track, but Cropper had not dubbed in his own guitar parts. Nor had he added the sea gulls and ocean waves that appeared on the final version. "The day we cut that song, Otis and I looked at each other and said, 'This is a hit,'" says Cropper. "Not everybody in the studio agreed with us, but we knew in our own minds that this would be his biggest record. In this business, you know when you have a winner."

Jim Stewart wasn't so sure about the song, because it deviated from the tried-and-true Stax formula. But if he was less than enthusiastic, he can be forgiven, because he had other, more pressing matters to deal with. Unknown to the musicians, Stax was in the midst of a major crisis. Jim's relationship with Wexler had been deteriorating all year. Wexler was playing up to Chips, slipping him money to help keep his studio afloat, while glad-handing Jim and distributing the records produced at Stax.

In October 1967 Atlantic announced it was being acquired by Warner Brothers. Wexler assured Jim he would be staying on and nothing would change in the Stax/Atlantic relationship, but that was not the case. *Everything* was about to change. The Atlantic/Warner Brothers merger meant Stax and Atlantic would have to renegotiate their contract. It was then that Jim found out his relationship with Atlantic was not what he had thought. Unknown to Jim, the original agreement had transferred ownership of the Stax master tapes to Atlantic. It was spelled out in the fine print, but Jim had not read the fine print. He had taken Wexler at his word. In reality, all that Stax owned was a name and the future work recorded by its artists. Atlantic owned everything Stax had recorded to date. It was the business equivalent of date rape.

That news probably didn't surprise Estelle, who never liked Wexler. If she hadn't been a lady, she probably would have told him off. After "Last Night" was released, she complained to Jim that Wexler was not promoting it the way he should. Jim told her to call him and talk to him about it. "I did, and I told him that it had been a hit in Memphis and a record that could be a hit in Memphis could be a hit anywhere," says Estelle. "Well, he didn't like my attitude at all. He called Jim back. He said, 'Don't let your sister get on the phone anymore to me. I don't want to talk to her.'" Estelle laughs. "Well, I proved him wrong. I knew it was a hit."

After the Nashville performance, Otis flew to Cleveland, Ohio, in his new, twin-engine Beechcraft to appear at Leo's Casino. The next morning, December 10, he called his wife before heading out for a performance in Madison, Wisconsin. He sounded depressed, not himself. Two weeks earlier Atlantic had concluded its deal with Warner Brothers. Did Otis know he had become a pawn in the Stax-Atlantic negotiations? Did he know he was the only bargaining chip Jim had to get a better deal with Atlantic? On board the Beechcraft with Otis were Bar-Kays Ben Cauley, Jimmy King, Phalon Jones, Ronnie Caldwell, and Carl Cunningham, and pilot Richard Frasier, a twenty-six-year-old flight instructor with 1,290 hours of flight time. It was a cold, wintry day when they left Cleveland. At 3:25 that afternoon, moments before they were scheduled to land, Ben Cauley awoke to feel the plane spinning out of control in the rain. The Beechcraft crashed into the frigid waters of Lake Monona three miles from the Madison runway. After impact Cauley grabbed a seat cushion and stayed afloat until help arrived. He looked for Otis and the others. He was the only survivor. "Why me?," he thought.

The timing of the crash was suspicious. The report issued by the National Transportation Safety Board listed the cause of the crash as "undetermined." The left wing and the left propeller were never found. That meant the plane probably broke up in midair and separated from the fuselage. Had the plane been sabotaged? If the plane was spinning, as Cauley reported, that would indicate the possibility of an explosion on the left wing or the possibility that the engine cowlings had been loosened prior to takeoff, causing the engine to drop from the wing, sending the plane into a spin. Unfortunately, federal officials could not make a determination of the cause of the crash without examining the wing fragments.

Three months after the crash "(Sittin' on) The Dock of the Bay" was the No. 1 pop record in America. It was the first No. 1 record Stax ever had, and it could not have come at a better time. Sadly, Otis never heard the finished record. That fact would haunt Cropper for the rest of his life. Despite the success of the record, the future of Stax was in doubt. By May Jim had three options: he could sell out to Atlantic and watch Stax be shut down and absorbed by the larger company; he could try to make it as an independent (against overwhelming odds); or he could find a buyer who would allow Stax to stay in business as a separate label. Jim and Estelle chose the third option. They severed their relationship with Atlantic and accepted an offer made by Gulf & Western. Estelle flew to New York to give the bad news to Wexler personally (oh, what a glorious moment that must have been for her), and Jim and Al Bell flew to Los Angeles to sign the deal with Gulf & Western.

It was Estelle's last act as co-owner of Stax. One result of the Gulf & Western buyout was that Estelle, the heart and soul of Stax Records, stepped out of the picture entirely. "I saw they were going to beat me out of part of mine, so I dealt with them and got my part before they gave up on Stax," says Estelle, who surrendered her interest in the label for four thousand shares of Gulf & Western stock and an annual salary of twenty-five thousand dollars for five years. The agreement also called for her to stay out of the music business for five years. With Estelle out of the picture—and no women around to call them to task—Jim and Al Bell took Stax in a radical new direction. They wanted to play hardball.

■   ●   ■

From the time of Otis's plane crash and Estelle's buyout, events overtook not just Memphis, but the entire nation. On February 1, 1968, Priscilla Presley gave birth to Lisa Marie, giving Elvis his first and only child, but news of the Vietnam War and presidential politics overshadowed Elvis's good fortune. On March 31 President Lyndon Johnson went on television to announce a unilateral halt of bombing above the twentieth parallel in Vietnam. Then he stunned the nation with an announcement that he would "neither seek nor accept" his party's nomination for president.

The Vietnam War made 1968 one of the most convulsive years in American history. Antiwar protests kept the president a virtual prisoner in the White House. His political allies were deserting him because of his war policy. *Press-Scimitar* editor Meeman bucked the prowar editorial policy set by Scripps Howard and came out against the war.

Abe Fortas looked to be at the height of his powers in the beginning of 1968, when Lyndon Johnson nominated him to replace Earl

The National Guard with rioters following
the assassination of Martin Luther King Jr.
Photo courtesy of the Mississippi Valley Collection,
University of Memphis, University Libraries

Warren as chief justice of the Supreme Court. Scandal erupted, however, when it was disclosed that Fortas, while a Supreme Court justice,
had accepted a "consultant's fee" from a Florida businessman. After
the story was reported in the press, Fortas gave the money back, but
it was too late. The businessman already was under investigation by
the Securities and Exchange Commission. Eventually, the businessman
was convicted on stock manipulation charges and sentenced to one
year in federal prison.

Meanwhile, Richard Nixon was elected president. Fortas's accept-
ance of the money was scandalous, and the Senate, charged with

The Civil Rights March that followed King's assassination. The building rear left at the intersection of Third and Linden is the fire station that was later converted to 3-Alarm Studio in 1986.
Photo courtesy of the Mississippi Valley Collection, University of Memphis, University Libraries

approving his appointment as chief justice, stated its intention to hold the nomination in abeyance until after Nixon took office.

Senator Robert Griffin of Michigan, who led the fight to block Fortas's nomination, received death threats. Tennessee Senator Howard Baker spoke out in opposition to Fortas's nomination, as did Hamilton S. Burnett, the chief justice of the Tennessee Supreme Court. Saying Fortas's lack of ethics made him "sick," Burnett called for the justice's impeachment. Fortas had "violated every principle of honesty," he said. In Memphis, Fortas's supporters did everything they could to help (no doubt the death threats against Griffin originated from a 901 area code), but the old anti-Crump coalition, now represented by Baker and Burnett, rose to the challenge and destroyed Fortas's base of support. In May 1969 Fortas was forced to resign from the high court.

On April 4 civil rights leader Martin Luther King was shot to death by an assassin at the Loraine Motel, only two blocks from Abe Fortas's former home. In the wake of King's assassination, blacks rioted in eighty cities, including Memphis. Nationwide, twenty-nine people died and two thousand were injured. It was the most widespread racial unrest in American history. Mobs of angry blacks roamed city streets, looting and setting fires. Memphis officials set a 7 P.M. curfew and called in National Guard troops. If there was ever a turning point in Memphis music, a point beyond which there was no return, it was the King assassination.

Don Nix and Duck Dunn were standing in front of the Stax studio when the rioting began. "There was a lot of activity. People were moving around in the streets," says Nix. But they weren't overly concerned. Stax was located in a black neighborhood, but they knew every shopkeeper on the street. It was inconceivable to them that anyone would hurt them. "We went back inside and Isaac [Hayes] said, 'Man, ya'll better go home.' He said, 'Let me carry you and Duck home.' We said no. By then you could see smoke on the horizon."

Jim and Estelle locked the doors at Stax. They stayed locked for a week. "Jim took all the masters and took them home," says Estelle. "We didn't know what might happen. The building might go up in flames. Out of respect we closed until the riots were over and things settled down. We were protecting ourselves." Estelle smiles, sharing a secret. "I don't think they ever knew we took all the master tapes out of there."

When the riots ended Jim put a chain link fence around the back entrance to the studio. The gates had locks. "I thought that was when the music started dying," says Nix. "After that, you couldn't go back out on the street. That was my neighborhood. We spent more time there than we did at home."

The summer of 1968 was especially bleak for Elvis. He had a brand-new baby girl, and he was still in demand as a movie actor, but his music career was stone cold dead. He had not had a Top 10 hit since June 1965, when "Crying in the Chapel" peaked at No. 3, below "Wooly Bully." If he turned on the radio, he heard songs by the Byrds, the Beatles, the Rolling Stones and, perhaps worst of all, a whole gang of unruly Memphians turning out records at Stax, Hi, and American. Elvis was a relic—and he knew it. If he watched television or read newspapers, all he heard or saw was talk of race riots and antiwar demonstrations. He became a virtual prisoner in Graceland.

"There was a period of time for a few months when it was really tough," says T. G. Sheppard, who spent a great deal of time with Elvis in those years. "There was a big fear of people breaking into Graceland to kidnap him or Lisa Marie. I remember being in the den, then all of a sudden everyone was scrambling because someone had called the house and said someone had climbed over the wall and had something in their hand and they were pointing it toward the house. Everybody was outside and Elvis was freakin'. He grabbed his gun. There was a fear in him that I had never seen before. He started talking about wanting gun turrets on top of the house and it rubbed off on everyone else. Everybody was scared."

In June Elvis recorded an NBC television special for a December broadcast. The show got good reviews, and writers who had not mentioned Elvis in years began talking about his "comeback." Elvis needed a new album to build on the momentum of the television special. Colonel Parker made plans for him to return to Nashville, but at the last minute Elvis decided he wanted to record in Memphis. Parker turned to the man who, at that moment, was the hottest record producer in America: Chips Moman.

In January 1969 Elvis walked into American with his full entourage. He had not recorded in Memphis since 1955. No one was sure exactly what to expect. Chips's studio musicians, known as the 827 Thomas Street band, would lay down the tracks. Elvis hadn't worked with real musicians in years. "He obviously hadn't had any direction in a great

Elvis Presley after attending a luncheon in 1971 at which he was named one of the Jaycees of America's "Ten Outstanding Young Men in America."
Photo by Dave Darnell, © *The Commercial Appeal*

while," says Moman. "If he had, I don't think he would have cut all those junk records he cut. When I told him he was off pitch, his entourage would come up and say, 'Oh, don't tell him that.'

"Well, why not?

"I saw quickly I did not want to go on the speaker, 'Hey, man, dah-dah-dah,'" says Moman, mimicking an exchange. "Every time he did something wrong, I walked out into the studio and into the booth where he was singing and I had a quiet conversation with him. He took direction great, but I'm sure Elvis wouldn't have taken direction over the monitors where fifty people could hear me say he was flat. That would blow things out of proportion. But if you did it quietly, one on one, it was no problem at all.

"When he went at it, he was either on or off. If he was off, it was better to do it another day. A lot of people didn't understand how I could get him to do so many takes. I would have him sing a song twenty or thirty times, over and over. Back up and fix little lines that he would miss. He went through it without a problem.

"He wasn't the world's greatest singer, but he had a sound." Chips laughs, giving the King his due. "I worked with people who were more talented, but nobody bigger."

Chips got the most out of Elvis when they were alone in the studio. "We did the best work before everybody would come in," says Chips. "Some of the time we cut the tracks before he got there and put his voice on it when he got there."

Chips recorded enough material during those sessions for two albums. Most critics consider their work together to have been the most productive since Elvis's early Sun sessions. Among the songs recorded were "In the Ghetto" (which gave Elvis his first Top 10 song since "Crying in the Chapel"), "Kentucky Rain," "Gentle on My Mind," "Any Day Now," and "Suspicious Minds," which peaked at No. 1 in November. It would be Elvis's last No. 1 record.

Elvis's career was given new life. In December 1969 Chips and Al Bell of Stax were honored in Atlanta by one thousand radio and recording executives at the annual Bill Gavan Radio Program Conference. Bell was named Recording Executive of the Year and applauded for his promotional efforts. Chips was named Producer of the Year and cited for his work with Elvis. "It's a wonderful honor for me," Chips told the gathering. "But my staff at the studio should receive most of the credit. They make the music. I just turn the knobs and make a few suggestions."

THE SEVENTIES:
THE DREAM DIES HARD

With the success of "Suspicious Minds," the floodgates opened at American. It's cruel to say, but the consensus was that if Chips Moman could record a hit with a relic like Elvis, he could record a hit with anyone. From 1969 to 1973 the studios at American, Hi, and Stax cranked out hits like there was no tomorrow.

Chips and Tommy Cogbill, who had joined Chips as a producer/partner, actually had to turn people away. Early in 1970 Columbia Records called to book a session for Bob Dylan, but when the record company insisted on Chips being listed as the engineer and not the producer, they were told to hit the road. Not turned away at American were Neil Diamond, whose two albums recorded there, *Brother Love* and *Touching You*, spawned the hit singles "Sweet Caroline" and "Holly Holy"; Dusty Springfield, whose *Dusty in Memphis*, viewed by many as one of her best albums, hit the charts with "Son of a Preacher Man" and "Windmills of Your Mind"; Petula Clark, whose Memphis LP gave us "People Get Ready" and "That Old Time Feeling"; B. J. Thomas, with four albums, which included the singles "Hooked on a Feeling" and "Eyes of a New York Woman"; Paul Revere and the Raiders, with *In Memphis*; Herbie Mann, with *Memphis Underground*; Joe Tex, with "Hold On to What You Got" and "Skinny Legs"; Dionne Warwick, with "Lost That Lovin' Feeling" and *Soulful*; and Brenda Lee, with *Memphis Portrait* and the singles "Sisters in Sorrow" and "I Think I Love You Again."

It was the session with Brenda Lee that had the biggest impact on Chips's personal life. One of the songs chosen for the session was written by a New York songwriter, Toni Wine. Discovered by producer Don Kirshner at the age of fourteen, Toni was a child prodigy who had studied as a classical pianist at the Juilliard School of Music for nine years. By 1970 she had a number of hits both as a songwriter and a vocalist. She wrote "A Groovy Kind of Love" for the Mindbenders, "Black Pearl," "Candida," "Tonight You're Going to Fall in Love with Me" by the Shirelles, and the themes for *To Sir with Love* and Dick Clark's *American Bandstand*. In 1969 Kirshner persuaded Toni to record a duet. He named the group the Archies. Their first single, "Sugar, Sugar," went straight to the top of the charts. The Archies sold over thirteen million records, but the only payment Toni ever received was a dozen roses. It was enough to make her want to quit the business. "I will always be grateful to Donnie [Kirshner] for putting me in the music business," says Toni. "I love him dearly for that. I hate him dearly for not being honest with me. I never signed anything with him because he was the daddy. That was a very bad thing in my life."

One day Toni's publisher got an urgent phone call from Chips. He was in the middle of a session with Brenda Lee and had lost the lyrics to a song written by Toni Wine. How quickly could he get the words? Curious about the Memphis music revolution, and perhaps more interested in meeting the guru than she would admit to herself, Toni caught the next plane. It was a flight that would change her life. "I had no plans for the next few days, so I took the song down personally," says Toni. "When Chips and I first met, I had no idea of what to expect in him or in the city of Memphis."

Toni and Chips could not possibly have been more different. Not only was she Jewish, she was New York Jewish, which, to a tattooed Georgia boy brought up to say "yes ma'am" and "no ma'am," was the ultimate kind of Jewishness, a fact later confirmed, in his mind, by her Yankee-stubborn refusal to embrace without question his opinions, musical or otherwise. Sparks flew. From the street the studio must have looked like a welder's shop. It was love at first sight. Toni had long black hair and a face that would stop any man dead in his tracks. Chips had never met anyone like her. To her, Chips, with his

Gary Cooper looks and mannerisms, was as exotic as anything she had ever imagined in New York.

"She's aggravating, but she knows exactly what she's doing." Chips laughs, then pauses, breaking into a wide grin. "Also what everybody else is doing." Chips and Toni turned that three-day visit into a passionate love affair and eventually into a marriage.

Memphis defined the blues, then reshaped it into rhythm and blues. It invented rock 'n' roll, then refined into it a pop bastardization of jazz through the use of orchestral arrangements. If the genius of the city is that it can create art forms out of thin air, its saving grace is that it can package those creations in reusable containers. Memphis was never a "band" city. The individual was always supreme. That was the drawing card in the 1970s. It was where you went to make records that set you apart from the group. Artists by the hundreds poured into the city with empty cups. When they left their cups were filled to the brim.

Petula Clark had a big hit with "Downtown" before she went to American. When she arrived in Memphis she was astonished by the laid-back atmosphere in the studio. She told reporters that working there was "like having a party." Asked about the songs she was recording, she seemed evasive. Did she intend to keep them a secret? Petula laughed at the reporters. "Yes, it's a secret," she said. "But we're in the dark, too. You see, we won't know until we do them." Petula had discovered what every artist who works with Chips discovers: he withholds songs from artists until he thinks the session has just the right feel.

"In a way, I aggravate a lot of singers," says Chips. "I let my singers learn a song the same time the band does. To me, there is a freshness when they do it together. Great singers get bored quickly. I keep the songs away from them on purpose." Chips also has a strategy for song selection. "Going in, I'm a nervous wreck. The artist is a nervous wreck. The band is worrying about whether an amp is going to blow out. You get things going pretty smoothly, then you pull out your best song. I never use my best songs going in. I'll do a couple of songs before I pull out a song I think is a hit."

Visualize, if you can, a recording session conducted by Gary Cooper in *High Noon*: that gives you a fairly accurate picture of what it is like to work with Chips. If it was frustrating for singers because of the uncertainty, it was comforting in the way everyone worked together to make the best record possible. Dionne Warwick was so impressed by her Memphis experience that she tried to launch a record label there with Marty Lacker, one of Chips's investors at American. They named the label Sonday Records in honor of Dionne's son. Unfortunately, the label fizzled before it could get off the ground, and Dionne never returned to Memphis to record.

■　●　■

Willie Mitchell is one of the most consistent figures in Memphis music. Emotionally, he has maintained a straight line, a middle C, for thirty-five years. As I think of Lil Hardin as one of the grand ladies of American music, I think of Willie Mitchell as one of its true gentlemen. He can be arrogant at times, for sure, but that is more of a defensive weapon than anything else.

Musically, he has a gift for finesse. While his competitors at Stax wrote the book on using horns to accent vocals, he used his more intricate understanding of orchestration to wrap melodies around the vocals. A small handful of musicians were involved with the hits that came out of Memphis during the 1960s and 1970s. Willie shared Al Jackson (on drums) with Stax, and Jim shared the Memphis Horns (Wayne Jackson and Andrew Love) with Chips. Even though he was using some of the same players used by the other studios, two things made Willie's sound unique: first, he pulled the drums up so they were more immediate, more hypnotic; second, in what would appear to be a contradiction, he smothered the tracks with a lushness of sound that oozed sweet soul.

Al Green was the perfect singer to complement Willie's vision. He wasn't a versatile vocalist, but what he did, no one could do better. Willie and Al didn't find each other musically right away. They had a few false starts. One of their first records was a remake of the Beatles's "I Want to Hold Your Hand." It was a terrible record, and sales reflected that, but Willie and Al weren't discouraged. They tried another remake, this time with the Temptations' "I Can't Get Next to You." It wasn't a hit, but it came close. At least they were headed in the right direction.

Willie felt the pressure. The last hit to come out of Hi was his own "Soul Serenade" in 1968. In early 1970 Chips had Elvis's "Don't Cry Daddy" and Neil Diamond's "Holly Holy" on the charts. Willie's mentor, B. B. King, was on the charts with "The Thrill Is Gone." In early 1971 Ike and Tina Turner scored big with "Proud Mary." Willie believed in Al, so he pushed him to write his own material. "It wasn't just Al's voice, it was his attitude," says Willie. "He wanted it so bad. That's what I liked about him. He was going to make it one way or another."

Al brought Willie a song he had written titled "Tired of Being Alone." Willie liked it. They recorded it, and in October 1971 it went to No. 12 on the pop charts. Al brought him another song, "Let's Stay Together." Willie liked the song, but it needed a little work. With Al Jackson's help, they smoothed out the rough edges, getting it perfect, then sat back and watched it climb the charts. In February 1972 it was the No. 1 record in America.

For the next three years Willie and Al enjoyed unparalleled success with their patented pop-R&B formula: "Look What You Done for Me" (No. 16), "I'm Still in Love with You" (No. 6), "You Ought to Be with Me" (No. 3), "Call Me (Come Back Home)" (No. 15), "Here I Am (Come and Take Me)" (No. 13), "Sha-La-La (Make Me Happy)" (No. 9), and "L-O-V-E" (No. 16). That translated into eight gold singles and six gold albums. Success in a recording studio is contagious. As Willie and Al soared, other Hi acts came into their own. Ann Peebles scored with "I Can't Stand the Rain," Sly Johnson with "Take Me to the River," and Otis Clay with "I Die a Little Each Day."

The music at Hi was becoming "blacker," which is to say, fewer white musicians were being asked to participate in the sessions. Among the white wannabe singers who hung out at Hi in the late 1960s, before the color bar was raised, was Rita Coolidge. The Nashville-born daughter of a Baptist minister, she moved to Memphis in 1968 after graduating from Florida State University. "My parents had moved to Memphis while I was in college," says Rita. "When you get out of college and don't have a job, you go wherever your parents live. When I got to Memphis, it was, to me, the recording center of the world. I

Al Green, c. 1970s.
Photo courtesy of *The Commercial Appeal* Collection,
Center for Southern Folklore Archive © 1995

had been to Nashville. I had been to New York. I had not been to California, but the music that was being made in Memphis then was the music I had in my collection, the albums that I value and treasure with my life."

Rita had been offered an assistantship at FSU to work on her master's degree, but while in Memphis she realized that a career in music was what she really wanted. For a while she lived with Don Nix, who by then was one of the hottest producers at Stax. She became a regular at all the studios, but especially at Willie's. That was scandalous in the late 1960s; it wasn't something nice white girls did. The scandal became family-wide when her sister, Priscilla, married Booker T. Jones, giving the city its first interracial Memphis music marriage. Not until Lisa Marie Presley married Michael Jackson, thirty years later, would there be a second.

Willie remembers Rita as a listener. "She used to sit up all night with us," says Willie. "Just sit in the studio and watch what we were doing. I knew she was a singer, but we never did anything she wanted to sing at Hi." For a while Rita did commercial jingles for Pepper-Tanner, then she recorded a couple of singles at American, one of which was written by Memphian Donna Weiss, who later won a Grammy for "Bette Davis Eyes." Those two records opened doors for Rita on the West Coast, enabling her to leave Memphis in 1969 to join the Delaney and Bonnie tour. "Immediately, I was doing sessions because of Delaney and Bonnie and doing television shows because of Pepper Records and just never went back to Memphis." Subsequently, she recorded a string of successful albums for A&M, including *The Lady's Not for Sale*; throughout the 1970s she toured with then-husband Kris Kristofferson and often performed with Leon Russell.

Willie invested a lot of emotional and creative capital in Al Green. But Al was skittish, a cat on a hot tin roof, not someone you'd want to put all your hopes on. Al, who has spent much of his life imitating a deer caught in the headlights of an oncoming car, was a bad investment—not because he was dishonest, but because he was possessed with personal demons only he could understand. In 1974 Al was scalded with boiling grits by a former girlfriend, who then committed suicide using Al's pistol. The incident changed Al. Willie and Al maintained their hit-making relationship in the studio, but it started slipping away, and by 1976 Al wanted a divorce. Al recorded a couple of albums without Willie, then abruptly quit music to devote his life to the ministry.

Willie was devastated.

One of the rules of Memphis music is that once something goes wrong, once *anything* goes wrong, you had better hold on for dear life, because full-blown disaster is just around the corner. Al Green provided a bridge between pop and R&B at a time when the record-buying public was losing interest in R&B. By 1976 the hits were being recorded by artists such as Paul Simon and the Bee Gees, white singers doing white music. With Al gone, the reality of the record business set in with Willie. Those hit records had been great for morale, but they hadn't put much money in the bank. "We had hits with Hi, but they were on London Records," says Willie. "We just leased the masters to London. . . . We got a little bit of the money, but the record companies got most of it." Like everyone else, Willie was zapped hard by the curse of the pyramids.

■   ●   ■

Across town at Stax, the sweet soul on which the label had been founded was reflecting the times—and the times were strident. The King assassination changed everything. Blacks never bought the story that King's assassin acted alone. They had come in enough back doors to know where the trash was piled. James Earl Ray did not kill Martin Luther King. Memphis killed Martin Luther King. Everyone knew that. All roads lead to Memphis.

Fearing the politicization of the music produced at Stax, Jim had the foresight in 1965, long before the assassination, to bring Al Bell aboard to salve the festering black anger that was lapping at the door like waves from an advancing hurricane. The assassination merely accelerated the advance of the storm. If black anger had been the only threat in the late 1960s, the situation would have been manageable, but the music industry itself was changing. In New York and Los Angeles organized crime's infatuation with the music industry was injecting new elements into the formula for success. Jim resembled a Walter Mitty character who had been dropped into a snake pit. When he and Estelle had started Stax, the atmosphere was one of love and dreams of creating something out of nothing. Now Estelle, the ever-present housemother, was gone, and the dreams had turned into nightmares. The music business, as Jim learned, was no place for nice guys.

Bell brought a New York record executive, Johnny Baylor, into the fold in 1968. At the time, he was operating a small label, Koko, which had one artist on its roster: Luther Ingram. Baylor was black, proud, and convinced you never got anything in life you didn't fight for. Luther Ingram gave Stax one of its biggest post–1960s hit, "(If Loving You Is Wrong) I Don't Want to Be Right," but Baylor's role at Stax was

Al Bell and Jim Stewart at Stax Studios, c. 1970s.
Photo courtesy of the Deanie Parker Collection,
Center for Southern Folklore Archive © 1995

as an enforcer, not as a talent scout. Baylor was Jim's muscle, his protection against the barbarians at the gate. They were frightening
times.

Stax underwent radical changes. Booker T. Jones was the first to
leave. In 1969 he took his wife and entire extended family to Los
Angeles. He was fed up. "There were so many doors that were closed
to me here, and at the same time there were doors that were open to
me there," says Jones. "My plan was to take the MGs away from Stax
Records and take them to A&M Records, and of course, that did not
work."

Two of the studio workhorses for Stax during the 1970s were Don
Nix and Bobby Manuel. From his start as a sax player in the Mar-Keys,
Nix branched out as a songwriter and producer. In the late 1960s and
early 1970s he wrote a number of hit songs, including the blues-rock
anthem "Goin' Down." He produced albums for Albert King, Leon

Russell, Joe Cocker, Delaney and Bonnie, Jeff Beck, and Freddie King, and somehow found time to work on the Bangladesh concert with ex-Beatle George Harrison.

Don had his own way of doing things. Recording sessions at Stax were usually done on the spur of the moment. That suited Don just fine. Don is a spur-of-the-moment guy. Albert King's critically acclaimed *Lovejoy* album offers insight into that process. Don walked into the studio one day and was told it was his turn to do Albert King. "Everyone else had produced Albert," says Nix. "I was told to do it—more than asked to do it. But after we started the album, it was a lot of fun."

Don suggested to Albert that he record a cover of the Rolling Stones' "Honky Tonk Woman." Don wrote the other seven songs on the album during the session. "I would get a line, a guitar line—back then they all had one that they repeated—and you just write a song on top of it," says Nix. "When you get that down, you start putting things on top of it. I'd just show the players a couple of simple lines." Some of the songs that emerged from that session were "Lovejoy, Illinois," "Like a Road Leading Home," "Bay Area Blues," and "Everybody Wants to Go to Heaven."

Albert didn't mind working that way, according to Nix, and even if he had, it wouldn't have mattered. That was the system. "Albert was an artist," say Nix. "'Just show me what to do. Show me where to stand. Tell me what you want me to do.' He had done that stuff for so long, his attitude was, 'Get me in, get me out.'"

Despite the politics of racial confrontation outside the studio, the mood inside, among the musicians, was friendly. They were there to make music. "The black guys were a lot easier to work with for some reason," says Nix. "Albert might be hard to get along with sometimes. Leon [Russell] always told me to go in there and whether you know or not, act like you know what you're doing. Like, I'd do string sessions. I'd have an arranger. I'd go in there: 'Hey, Albert, how you doing?' If he'd say, 'That don't sound right,' then I'd say, 'You're right. Who's doing that?' I did fifty-one albums. Nobody ever said, 'Do you know what you're doing?' I'd always say, 'Did anyone make any mistakes?' Then take it from there."

Albert King on a street outside of Stax Records, c. 1971.
Photo by Don Nix

Bobby Manuel was hired in 1968 as an engineer. He was playing guitar with a band at Club Paradise when he heard that Jim Stewart was looking for someone to help out in the studio. The job paid only seventy-five dollars a week, but it was a chance to get his foot in the door. His first month on the job he was told to engineer a Delaney and Bonnie session. "Man, I had no training at that time," says Bobby. "Ronnie [Capone] was cutting someone else. He said, 'Man, you got to do it.' I said, 'I don't know how to do it.' I went in there green. I cut one song out of sync. It was fearsome thinking about trying to get balances. I nearly had a heart attack."

Before Booker left Manuel sometimes replaced Cropper on guitar when the MGs went on the road. That happened once while Cropper was in Atlanta. The MGs played some dates on the road, then went into the studio when they returned to Memphis. "Sometimes it was touch and go," says Bobby. "Cropper was kind of a general, you know, and they were always digging at him. There I was, I hadn't been there hardly any time, and I was sitting there playing with the MGs. That was heavy duty to me. Then in through the doors from Atlanta, with briefcase in hand, came Steve Cropper. I thought, 'Oh, man.' I jumped up. Booker and them didn't say anything. I knew it was going to be horrible. I don't know what they ever did with the tape. I know it was cut."

Before long Manuel was doing a little bit of everything: writing songs, engineering, playing guitar, producing sessions. When Steve Cropper became the second casualty of the "new" Stax and left in 1971, Manuel was even more in demand. "I got to do Albert King, Little Milton, the things Cropper had been doing," says Bobby. "In 1973 I started playing with Isaac [Hayes]. That was the hottest band happening. Our first job was in Detroit. It killed me to be able to be accepted in those circles by black people. I remember getting a standing ovation for a solo. That meant more to me than anything. I'm not so sure the solo was unique. Maybe it was the uniqueness of one white guy in the band. Regardless, it was a great experience."

In 1971 David Porter's writing partner, Isaac Hayes, scored Stax's second No. 1 record with his "Theme from *Shaft*." The song was honored during the 1972 Oscar awards. Isaac set the tone for the remainder of the decade when he rose from the depths of the stage amid whirling clouds of steam, his shirtless, black body bound in glistening chains. The gesture may have been show-biz symbolism, but for all its hokiness, it represented deeper emotions that were changing the face— and the music—of America.

To understand those changes it is helpful to remember that rock 'n' roll and the sweet soul music that emanated from Stax and American were invented by Southern boys barely out of their teens. They weren't card-carrying liberals, but neither were they racists. They didn't go to church every Sunday, but for the most part, they were superstraight guys who didn't drink on the job (Estelle would have kicked their asses) or venture too far from the social norm. They were light years behind the rest of the population when it came to drug use. Don Nix, no stranger to drug use in the 1970s, says drugs weren't a factor at Stax. "I never saw drugs in Stax, never," he says. "In the sixties, I'm sure people took them then, but not in there." Don laughs with the knowing vibrato of someone who has been there. "I would have seen them. I would have been the guy to know. There were never any drugs in Stax. A lot of people said there was, but there never was. People were having too much fun."

In 1970 Jim Stewart and Al Bell borrowed enough money from an overseas lender, Deutsche Grammophon, to repurchase Stax from Gulf & Western. They worked out a new distribution agreement with Columbia Records. For two years Jim and Al operated as equal partners. Then, in a move as mysterious as it was ill advised, Al bought out Jim, who stayed on as the chief executive. By then the work atmosphere was intolerable. Guards were posted at the entrance of the studio and a mood of gangsterism prevailed.

"When Johnny Baylor and those guys came, that's when things got bad," says Bobby Manual. "That's when the ugliness started coming out."

Baylor was known to fire his pistol on occasion inside the studio. Polite conversation gave way to intimidation and threats of violence. Mean-spirited jive talk echoed in the old theater night and day. Stax was burning the candle at both ends. While they were learning to deal with gangsters in New York who wanted kickbacks to distribute their records and others who wanted payola to put the records on the air, they were being threatened by local neighborhood punks who demanded money or they were going to burn the place down. Pistol-whippings in the studio were commonplace. "They pistol-whipped a guy in the room next to me in New York once, and I left," says one Stax insider. "There were guns and gangsters and other little punks following them around wanting to be gangsters. The creative forces were breaking down."

Stax got its third No. 1 record in June 1972 when "I'll Take You

Isaac Hayes in the Stax parking lot, c. 1972.
Photo courtesy of the Mississippi Valley Collection,
University of Memphis, University Libraries

There" by the Staple Singers topped the charts. The success of the Staple Singers proved there was still a market for old-time soul, as did a string of hits by Eddie Floyd and Johnnie Taylor, but by then Stax was on a collision course with disaster.

■　●　■

In the early 1960s John Fry, a preppy, white Memphis high school student, decided to start up a record label in his grandmother's sewing

Jim Dickinson and Alex Chilton while they
were recording the first Big Star album.
Photo courtesy of the Mississippi Valley Collection,
University of Memphis, University Libraries

room. He recruited a couple of high school buddies, John King and
Fred Smith. It turned out to be more difficult than they thought, and
they moved on to other things (Smith later started up an air freight
company and named it Federal Express).

After high school Fry knew he wanted to do something with recording equipment, but he wasn't sure what. He was considering starting
a business to record promos for radio stations when a piano player
named Jim Dickinson (and several others) talked him into getting into
the record business. Dickinson had all the musical talents not possessed by Fry and none of the business acumen.

In 1966 Fry founded Ardent Recording studio. Unlike most people
who open studios, Fry had no ambition to be a star himself (or if he
did, he kept it to himself). It was the business side of music that
appealed to him. He set out to build the most technically advanced
studio in the South. By the early 1970s he had facilities that surpassed
those at Stax, American, and Hi. Stax often used the facilities at
Ardent and became one of its best customers.

In 1972 Fry reactivated his record label. Stax agreed to distribute his product. No one remembers the first album, but the second one was by a group named Big Star. Alex Chilton was recruited to front the group. He had been in musical limbo since 1969, when he had walked offstage during a Box Tops performance and never returned. Chilton had an explosive personality. He hated the media. At times, it seemed he hated his fans.

Big Star's album, called *#1 Record,* was progressive for its time. It had Beatles-like harmonies and a hard-edged attitude. Musically, it seemed on the verge of something. Exactly what, no one knew. Unfortunately for Big Star (the name came from a Memphis supermarket chain), the release of the album coincided with difficulties Stax was having with Columbia Records. It was a good album and should have produced a hit or two, but it slipped between the cracks and died a quick death. Encouraged by good reviews, Fry decided to do a second. Titled *Radio City,* it, too, received favorable reviews but was totally ignored by the public.

Fry decided to do a third album. He had been the engineer/producer for the first two, but he asked Jim Dickinson to do the third—and final—Big Star album. Jim is not the best keyboard man ever to come out of Memphis (he would have competition from Booker T., Memphis Slim, Bobby Woods, and Bobby Emmons), but he is the most versatile and the most passionate about his craft—and he's an excellent producer. By 1974 he had worked as a sideman at Stax and American (he had wanted to engineer but Moman wouldn't let him), had played for six months with the Miami-based Dixie Flyers (but returned to Memphis because he got homesick), and played piano on the Rolling Stones' classic "Wild Horses."

Jim is a walking motion picture. Images flicker on him like old-fashioned drive-in movie theaters. You can see him coming a half block away because of that iridescent glow. Voices emerge from his coat sleeve, his shoes, his hat. I think Jim has probably absorbed every image, every sound, he has ever come in contact with. I'm not sure, but he may have developed that talent while studying drama at Baylor University.

Jim was the perfect person to work with Alex Chilton. Talking to

Alex is a little like talking to a barking dog, only without the barking. Jim, the laid-back hippie, and Alex, the mercurial antichrist, slammed the studio door on the rest of the world and explored the more creative aspects of musical madness. The resulting album, aptly titled *The Third*, was a masterpiece of organized chaos. As you might expect, it was immediately canned and imprisoned in darkness for six years.

When the album was released in 1980, Chilton told a *Press-Scimitar* reporter, "Most people who make records these days don't understand that you can just walk in and start slogging it out, with people playing all bad chords and out of rhythm and everything, and it can sound great." Then he cryptically added, "But I also like to do conceptual, neatly symmetrical things. . . . If you go into the studio with something really disorganized, a lot of the time it's too murky to really hit people right at first as strongly as something that's more arranged." When the album was re-released in 1995 a reviewer for *Pulse* magazine called it "alternative pop's flagship album." By then, Big Star was hailed as one of the great rock bands in American history, even though it never had a hit record or sold enough albums to pay studio expenses.

At about the same time that Big Star was self-destructing, a Texas band, ZZ Top, started recording at Ardent. The band had been together since 1969, but after five years of one-nighters, it had nothing to show for its efforts. In 1974 ZZ Top performed at the Memphis Blues Show, not exactly a high-paying gig. The band was at rock bottom. While in town, they dropped by Ardent to talk to Fry's chief engineer, Terry Manning. Musically, they never left. Almost all of ZZ Top's post-1974 albums have been recorded in Memphis, a fact the group does not like to publicize (if you don't believe me, just ask them and watch them dash for the horizon, their beards blowing in the wind).

Even Fry is hesitant to talk about it. When he does, he downplays Ardent's role in the group's success. "I would like to be able to tell you that what we offer them is so unique they could not get it elsewhere," says Fry. "We offer them good facilities and do a good job for them, but there are other people who could do the same thing. . . . There is a factor of the chemistry of the people working together, but

I cannot paint a picture that would say ZZ Top could not live without Memphis."

ZZ Top has a lot in common with Big Star. Both groups are revered by the critics, but unlike Big Star, ZZ Top is one of the most successful touring bands in history. Like their recording sessions, there is an air of mystery about ZZ Top's success. It's all part of the Memphis *thang*.

■　●　■

By 1973 Memphis music was imploding (and exploding at the same time), disintegrating into jagged-edged fragments that hurled about like debris in a hurricane. Priscilla left Elvis for a karate instructor, and the King was unable to sustain the success of the hits he recorded in 1969 at American. Because his contract with RCA Records called for another album, his longtime producer, Felton Jarvis, put together a new session. But Elvis was tired and depressed. He didn't want to travel to Nashville. He asked if he could record again in Memphis. "Sure," said an associate, "I'll call Chips." But Elvis, who apparently had not taken direction at the 1969 sessions as well as Chips had imagined, said no. He didn't want to work with Chips.

Jarvis said he would come to Memphis. He booked studio time at Stax for July and then hired Chips's studio musicians to play on the session: Reggie Young on guitar, Tommy Cogbill on bass, Bobby Emmons on organ, and Bobby Woods on piano. It was a strange session. Also in the studio that week was Isaac Hayes. Jim Stewart put guards inside and outside the studio. Isaac had his black bodyguards; Elvis had his white bodyguards.

When he got to the studio, Elvis was in a foul mood. So were the musicians. CBS television was in town to do a segment on Isaac Hayes for the *Harry Reasoner Report*. CBS was not interested in talking to Elvis. You can imagine how Elvis felt. He was the King of Rock 'n' Roll, yet he had been emasculated by Priscilla, the love of his life. He was a movie star, but his movies were a joke and he knew it. Isaac Hayes, with his shaved head and menacing black glare, won an Academy Award for *Shaft*. Elvis never came close to winning an Academy Award. By

1973 Isaac had won Grammys for Best Pop Instrumental Performance, Best Instrumental Arrangement, and Best Original Score Written for a Motion Picture. By contrast, Elvis had won two Grammys: one for Best Inspirational Performance and one for Best Sacred Performance.

On top of Elvis's career insecurities, he was deathly afraid of something or someone. It went beyond fears of jealous fans jumping his fence. In 1970 he flew to Washington on impulse to see President Richard Nixon and FBI director J. Edgar Hoover. On the plane he wrote a letter to Nixon in which he pleaded for credentials as a federal agent at large. Drugs were ruining the nation. He wanted to do his part to put a stop to it. He wanted to become an informant against the entertainment community. He would gladly tell the FBI who was using and selling illegal drugs. It was his duty. In his letter he said he would be staying at the Washington Hotel under the name of John Burrows. "I will be here for as long as it takes to get the credentials of a federal agent," he wrote.

Nixon met with Elvis, though Hoover did not. When Elvis left Washington, he had an honorary badge that he thought made him a federal agent. Some analysts have interpreted Elvis's trip as a roundabout means of getting back at the Beatles and other British groups whom he imagined to be advocates of drug use. Others say he was simply on drugs himself and didn't know what the hell he was doing. Still others say organized crime was putting a squeeze play on him, and he thought the federal government would protect him if he were a federal agent. Supporting that theory are a number of photos in which Elvis posed wearing a DEA jacket. He was sending a message to someone.

Jim Kingsley, a reporter for *The Commercial Appeal*, wrote a brief story about Elvis's Stax session, but getting more play in the story was an account of Isaac's session and the Harry Reasoner interview. Elvis was yesterday's news. A newspaper story that gave more space to Isaac Hayes was bad news indeed for an ego as severely bruised as Elvis's. The Stax session fizzled. Elvis returned to Stax in December and tried again, this time without the musicians from American, but that session, too, was a failure.

By this time Chips Moman was fed up. He and his partners at American had produced an incredible string of hits. No studio had ever done more, yet no one was calling him to accept Grammys or Oscars. Even the local music awards shows ignored his efforts. "For me, it just kept getting more and more aggravating," says Chips. "At the time when Memphis was the hottest thing going, the city didn't seem to really care."

In 1973 Chips closed up his studio and left town. He went to Atlanta for a while, then moved to Nashville where he built a new studio. "We had eighty or ninety Top Twenty records that year, and the music business awards came up and a guitar player got nominated and won it who had never played on a hit record. I said, 'You know, this place doesn't seem to like us too much. Why don't we just tear this studio down and leave.'. . . And we left, every one of us. We pulled the kids out of school and left."

I've spent countless hours talking to Chips about his reasons for leaving. My feeling is that he really believes that one incident was the reason. Time has a way of pigeonholing emotions. I think his real reasons for leaving are more complicated. His marriage was falling apart, and he wanted to marry Toni Wine. The business of making records had become dangerous, whereas before it had been merely dirty. There was talk that the Mafia was moving into Memphis. Grand juries were being convened to investigate the music business. The King assassination had made race relations in the city strident. Chips had recorded his share of soul music, but Memphis was more than that to him. It was the birthplace of rock 'n' roll, and he sensed that the city's musical identity was being subverted by racial politics. The final straw must have been Elvis's refusal to return to American and his own band's decision to sign on for Elvis's Stax session. Chips must have felt betrayed, not just by his band, but by the city itself. Chips packed up and left positively overnight. The last record he cut in Memphis was Billy Lee Riley's "I Got a Thing about You, Babe."

■　●　■

In its final three years of operation, Stax Records was a runaway train steaming toward disaster. Under the direction of Al Bell, it engaged in financial speculation and became politicized by the strident demands of black activists who saw the company as a political arm of the black-power movement. Though he had sold his half-interest to Bell, Jim Stewart stayed on as president, providing continuity to its musical direction. Jim and Al had conflicting visions. Jim saw Stax as a musical entity, a record label that celebrated the black experience. Al saw Stax as an economic entity, a company that could be used to further black economic and political interests.

In 1972 Stax invested $176,000 in a Broadway play, an adaptation of Joe McGinnis's best-seller *The Selling of the President*. The plan was to cash in on an album recorded by the cast. But the show closed after five performances, the album was never made, and Stax lost its investment. For two years Stax tried to purchase a Memphis franchise for the American Basketball Association. It signed black comedians Richard Pryor and Moms Mabley to recording contracts, and while Pryor was unmistakably a major talent and record sales soared on his first release, *That Nigger's Crazy*, it was the sort of project that confused the studio staff and did nothing to further the musical direction of the label. Adding to the confusion was an album titled *I Am Somebody* by the Reverend Jesse Jackson. There were even efforts to get into the movie business. For a three-year period beginning in January 1972, Stax scored Top 20 hits on only three occasions, all with the gospel-based Staple Singers.

Stax financed its ventures during those years with loans from Union Planters Bank of Memphis. Some reports put the loans at $18 million. If money was pouring into Stax through loans and record sales, it was pouring out into one bad venture after another.

Rumblings from the avalanche that would eventually crush Stax were first heard in June 1973 when federal prosecutors in Newark, New Jersey, convened a grand jury to hear evidence of possible kickbacks and tax violations in the record industry. The investigation had begun when federal officials linked a CBS Records official to a heroin ring operating between Canada and New Jersey. Subpoenas were issued to officers in eight record companies, including Atlantic, London, and Stax. The Associated Press reported that information obtained at a court hearing indicated Stax "lost $406,000 in 1971 because of an alleged scheme in which two vice presidents were involved in kickbacks with Stax distributors." Stax responded by hiring the prestigious law firm of Edward Bennet Williams in Washington, DC.

The nightmare for Stax grew worse by year's end when a federal grand jury in Memphis was convened to look into its corporate affairs. Jim Stewart and Al Bell were told to turn their records over to the grand jury. That same year, the Internal Revenue Services announced it was reviewing the company's tax returns. As a result, the IRS filed a $1.8 million lien against the holdings of Johnny Baylor. In June of that year CBS Records fired Columbia Records president Clive Davis and announced it was suing him for $94,000 allegedly misappropriated from company funds. CBS denied that his dismissal had anything to do with the grand-jury probe.

Amid the chaos, Johnny Baylor booked a flight from Memphis to Birmingham. At the Memphis airport he was asked, as part of the airport security measures, to open his attaché case before boarding the plane. Inside the briefcase, according to a *Press-Scimitar* reporter, were $130,000 in cash and a check for $500,000. Baylor was allowed to board the plane with the money, but when he arrived in Birmingham federal agents were waiting for him. When the incident was reported, Jim Stewart defended Baylor. He said the money belonged to Baylor and was his to do with as he pleased. No charges were filed, but the IRS kept the money, since it had a lien against Baylor.

The federal probe in New Jersey did not result in indictments against any Stax officials, and the company's legal difficulties eased somewhat in 1974, but by then problems had arisen with CBS over distribution arrangements. The federal grand jury in Memphis was still investigating Stax, but the company was in dire economic straits, and Jim reinvested his money in the company (all of it, by some accounts) in an effort to keep it afloat.

In 1975, as the end was drawing near, a group of businessmen from Chicago came to Memphis to discuss moving Stax to Chicago or Gary, Indiana. As an incentive, the businessmen offered Stax office space in a thirteen-story hotel owned by Holiday Inns of Memphis. While the negotiations were taking place, the Stax family started showing signs of strain. Barbara Jackson, the wife of Al Jackson, allegedly shot her husband during a domestic argument. The police filed assault charges against Barbara, but they were dismissed after she convinced a judge she had shot Al in self-defense. She testified he had beaten her and tossed her into a flower bed. Two weeks after the shooting, Jim Stewart sent a letter to Shelby County sheriff Roy Nixon asking that Jackson be considered for a special commission to carry a pistol. The letter said that Jackson "travels quite extensively and carries large sums of money."

Perhaps spurred by rumors of Stax's relocation plans, Union Planters Bank pushed for payment of $10 million in unpaid loans. That put a stop to any talk of relocation. In September 1975 Al Bell and Joseph Harwell, a loan official at Union Planters, were indicted on charges they conspired to obtain $18 million in fraudulent bank loans. In a separate case, Harwell pled guilty to embezzling $284,000 from the bank and was sentenced to five years in prison. The prospect of going on trial with an admitted embezzler did not paint a rosy picture for Bell. He accused the bank of racism. Two nationwide defense funds were set up for him by civil-rights groups.

On the evening of October 1 Al Jackson went to the Mid-South Coliseum to attend a closed-circuit telecast of the celebrated Muhammed Ali–Joe Frazier fight. He had filed for divorce from Barbara and had rented an apartment at 1350 Walnut Hall Court. He planned to move in at the end of the week. While Al was at the fight, Barbara went to a beauty parlor appointment. When she returned home that night, she was greeted by a young black man who tied her hands behind her back and demanded money. She told him she didn't have any. He ransacked the house.

When Al returned home after the fight, the burglar, described by Barbara as a tall black man with an Afro and a mustache, untied Barbara so she could open the door. Once Al was inside, the intruder tied them both up and again demanded money, according to Barbara. He made Al lie face down on the floor. Then he shot him five times in the back. After the shooter left, Barbara untied herself and dashed from the house to get help. As she ran outside, she later told police, she saw a young white man wearing a white shirt standing near the door. He ran when he saw her. Police attributed the murder to a botched robbery attempt and left it at that. No arrests were made; Al Jackson's killer was never found. When I spoke to police officials in 1995, they were uncharacteristically tight-lipped about the murder and unwilling to discuss details of the crime.

Two months after the shooting, three creditors filed an involuntary bankruptcy petition against Stax. At the hearing Jim Stewart spent three hours on the witness stand. He said he couldn't recall a lot of details of Stax's financial transactions. Irvin Bogatin, the lawyer representing the bank, cited the "miserable exhibition" of business savvy demonstrated by Stewart and said it would do little good for the bankruptcy trustee to keep the record company going. He called Stewart an "artist," not a businessman. Stewart's lawyer protested, saying Bogatin was slandering his client, but Bogatin continued, saying Stax's creditors were endangered by the lack of operating capital in the company. He compared it to a crap game. "It's just like Las Vegas," he said. "If you continue to roll the dice, you may walk away with two million dollars, or you may leave with nothing."

The judge agreed and signed the order to close Stax. Stewart was stunned. Leaving the courtroom, he told a reporter: "I'm at a loss. One minute you're producing records and the next minute you're shut down. I don't know what to say."

When Jim Stewart went to the studio on January 13, 1976, he was greeted by federal marshals and a group of Stax employees standing outside the building. The door was sealed by order of the bankruptcy judge. Jim turned around and went back home. The others stayed for a while, milling around on the street. "We didn't know what we were going to do," says Bobby Manuel. "Nobody said much. There wasn't much conversation. I had thought I would retire there. It was security."

Bobby went home and broke the news to his wife. "We could have made it if they had left us alone," he says. "The majors couldn't deal with us. The local people were running scared. There could have been some racial things involved. Stax was a maverick. It was like a thorn in some people's sides. You know, 'Look at all those black guys with Cadillacs!'"

The Stax family was stunned. Among the artists and musicians there was always a feeling it would be salvaged. "When the crash came, it was a shock," recalls Carla Thomas. "I always figured that someone, somewhere, would bail Stax out. There were a lot of things happening, the IRS thing, and people felt they didn't want to get involved. But the artists felt that as important as Stax was, people would not let it go down. There was a lot of resentment and anger about the final crash, including my own."

Watching from a distance, Estelle Axton shook her head in disgust. Intuitively, she had seen the fall coming. She blames it on Al Bell. "I wanted [Jim] to get rid of him," says Estelle. "I said, 'Jim, he's going to take the company'—and he did. He was going to buy Jim's part after I got out. I think he gave him about five hundred thousand dollars. All he did was make the first payment, and the company was going down. So he coaxed Jim into getting back in, and that's when it went under. Jim lost his house, he lost everything. He trusted Al Bell. I didn't. That was our disagreement."

The crash affected Estelle deeply. To her, it had always been a people business. "It hurt," she says. "I just wondered what was going to happen to all those kids. Would they go with other companies?"

Bobby Manuel was among those asking that very question. Like the others, he kept thinking a white knight would ride up and make everything all right again. For two months he stayed on the phone, talking to the others, exchanging news. Surely, Memphis would not allow Stax to die.

Then reality set in. The defining moment is emblazoned in his memory. His money was gone. He had run out of groceries. There was no immediate hope of finding work. He loaded his shotgun and his wife into his Mercedes. Then he drove to the nearest pawn shop. With his wife waiting in the car, he went inside and pleaded with the pawn shop owner to give him fifty dollars for the shotgun. "Think about that," says Bobby today, shaking his head. "They felt so sorry for me. That killed me."

■　●　■

In the midst of the insanity at Stax, Estelle Axton's buyout clause that prohibited her from reentering the record business expired. Once again she was a free woman (in the business sense). You would think the troubles at Stax—the gangsterism taking place in the studio and the federal grand jury investigations—would have discouraged her from getting in the music business again, but it appeared to have the opposite effect.

In 1974 she decided to start up another label in partnership with her son-in-law, Fred Frederick. They named the label Fretone (again using a hybrid of their names). One of the first acts they signed was Johnny Keyes, a Chicago-born singer who had worked with Packy Axton in the mid-1960s after Packy had left Stax. Unfortunately, shortly after they began their project Packy died of liver disease. Estelle was devastated. She thought about quitting the music business, but decided to continue, partly to honor Packy's memory.

When the Keyes project fizzled, she cut demos with some other artists, but nothing looked very promising. Then in 1976 Rick Dees, a local deejay, came to her with an idea for a record based on the disco craze sweeping the country. He used a duck's voice on his morning radio show with great success, and he thought a disco song done in a duck's voice would be a hit.

"I had to think about that for about three weeks before I agreed to produce it," says Estelle. "I thought, 'This could be a hit for ten years and younger. If they can't buy it, Mama or Grandma would have to buy it for them.'" She paired Dees with Bobby Manuel, who had started working for her after the Stax shutdown. Bobby was already working with another artist for Fretone, Catherine Chase. "I kept putting [Dees] off because I was doing this Catherine Chase thing," says Bobby. "I said I would finish the Catherine Chase thing, then do the other one. That way I knew I would be able to eat another month. I went month to month then."

Memphis was desperate for hits. In 1975 Al Green made the Top 20 with "L-O-V-E" and the Staple Singers grabbed the No. 1 slot with "Let's Do It Again," but the surprise hit of the year came from Chips Moman. After arriving in Nashville, he wrote songs with producer/songwriter Larry Butler. One of the songs was titled "(Hey Won't You Play) Another Somebody Done Somebody Wrong Song." They offered the song to B. J. Thomas. By April they had the No. 1 pop record in the country. To Chips, Memphis music was a state of mind, not a geographic location.

Don Nix left Stax at about the time gunfire was becoming a common occurrence in the studio. He worked with Leon Russell for a while in Los Angeles, then put together a band, the Alabama State Troopers. They recorded an album or two and were successful as a touring band. As an added attraction, Nix asked Furry Lewis to be the opening act.

"The reaction was amazing," says Nix. "We had a three-hour show. I would come out first and introduce Furry, and he would walk out alone, and I would watch the peoples' faces as he walked out. Here was an eighty-seven-year-old black man with a guitar who they had never heard of. From the first sound of his voice until he got through they would sit and listen, and there would be a lot of applause at the end of every song."

In 1974 Nix moved to France. During a trip to England he met George Harrison's American-born secretary. They started dating, and he commuted to England to visit her, often staying at Harrison's 101-room mansion at Henly-on-Thames. "When I first met him, it really intimidated me because he was a Beatle," says Nix. "But he was just a good guy. It was real comfortable." Nix said Harrison spoke about the Beatles in the third person, as if he were not a part of the group.

Nix was in England when Stax shut down. Over there it was page-one news. By the time he returned to America, the dust had settled and most of his friends had fled the city. I asked Don about the last time he saw the Stax studios. "Why, it was with you," he said, reminding me of a trip we made to the studio in 1989. "Remember that day we drove down and the ceiling was all falling in? When I think of Stax now, that's how I remember it."

As Bobby Manuel and Rick Dees put together a disco song about a duck, the drama at Stax was being played out to its conclusion. Between January and July 1975 Union Planters Bank investigated the possibility of operating the company itself. The bank already had purchased the assets of East Memphis Music Corporation, the publishing arm of Stax, at a public auction. When it became obvious that the bank could not operate the label as a viable business, the judge declared Stax bankrupt and ordered the sale of the company assets.

Bobby Manuel remembers the sale with bitterness. He and Jim Stewart went to the courthouse in the hopes of purchasing some of the studio equipment. Atlantic Records told Jim it would back him in the purchase of some of the equipment. What they saw at the courthouse nauseated them. "To see people sitting in the courtroom cutting cocaine and laughing, taking hits in the courtroom—I will never forget that," says Bobby. "They were like wolves." The entire lot of equipment was sold for fifty thousand dollars to one buyer. Bobby and Jim left empty-handed.

A jury acquitted Al Bell of all the charges against him, but convicted the bank officer, Joseph Harwell. Two years later, Johnny Baylor was convicted of fraud after being charged with diverting $2.5 million from Stax's creditors. Isaac Hayes filed for bankruptcy. Jim Stewart sat in his kitchen and calmly drank a cup of coffee as his home and possessions were auctioned off by the bank.

When Bobby and Rick had "Disco Duck" nailed down, they went into the studio. "We used the same band I was cutting Catherine Chase with," says Bobby. "Everyone's line was, 'Well, it's gonna be the worst record ever made or it will sell a million.'

"I don't think it was the worst record ever made. It had a great Memphis groove. It was that old MG thing I learned. It hooked and was in tune with the times. If we were going to be artsy about it, we would say, 'Well it was a parody of disco.' But really and truly it wasn't. Some of the guys who worked on it like to say that to people. It was just a fun record."

"Disco Duck" broke the Top 20 in September 1976 and went to No. 1 in October. Estelle had struck again. "She felt vindicated, and I think that meant a lot to her," says Bobby. "I'm not sure she was happy the way she left [Stax] . . . but she has an ear for records. I tell you, everyone loves that woman."

In some respects, Estelle Axton is the forgotten woman of American music. No woman has ever had more success. No woman has ever had to fight so hard to carve a niche for herself in a male-dominated business. She was responsible for the first major hit to come out of Memphis ("Last Night") and she was responsible for the last No. 1 hit ("Disco Duck"). There is no shortage of people willing to take responsibility for the hit records and soulful sounds that came out of

Stax during its glory years, but in my opinion, it was Estelle Axton who gave the label its most enduring identity. Those teenage musicians and songwriters who found a home at Stax viewed Miz Axton as a mother figure. They worked hard to please her. Otis Redding may have sung "Try a Little Tenderness," but it was Estelle Axton who kept the tenderness in the music.

■　●　■

On August 16, 1977, I was driving along a Greenville, Mississippi, boulevard on my way home from the *Delta Democrat-Times,* where I was employed as a newspaper reporter, when I heard on the radio that Elvis Presley was dead. The deejay cracked a couple of "King is dead" jokes, then played an Elvis song in tribute. Typical radio schlock. The next morning I picked up a copy of *The Commercial Appeal.* Four-fifths of the front page was devoted to coverage of his death. DEATH CAPTURES CROWN OF ROCK AND ROLL, read the banner headline. Inside was another full page of news stories and photographs. Elvis's personal physician, Dr. George Nicholoulos, told reporters that a heart attack was the possible cause of death. Elvis had been found face down in his upstairs bathroom at 2:30 P.M. Fire department medical technicians tried to resuscitate him on the way to the hospital, but got no response. At 3:30 P.M. hospital emergency resuscitation teams pronounced him dead. By 4 P.M. a crowd of 150 people had gathered at the hospital. They all had the same question: "Are you sure there's no mistake?"

T. G. Sheppard was at Graceland the night before. Elvis was scheduled to leave Memphis the day of his death on his private jet to kick off a tour in Portland, Oregon. Everyone had gathered at Graceland to get ready for the tour. "I went by and spent about an hour," says Sheppard. "Elvis was playing racquetball, and I didn't get a chance to say anything to him."

The next day Sheppard left for Nashville. He was on the road when Elvis's body was found. As he drove up to his house, the telephone was ringing. It was J .D. Sumner. "He said, 'Are you sitting down?'" recalls T. G. "I knew then what had happened. I said, 'It's Elvis, isn't it?'

Beale Street looked bleak in the mid-1970s.
Photo courtesy of the Mississippi Valley Collection,
University of Memphis, University Libraries

"He said, 'Yes.'

"I wasn't surprised. He was huge. I knew something had to give. I could see him deteriorating, with his weight and all that. I knew something was going on inside, but I hadn't spent much time around him in the past few years because of my own career. It was scary [to see him go down], especially when you were there in the lean years and saw him lean, mean, and sharp-looking. Then, to see him change, it was very depressing."

10

THE EIGHTIES: RISING OUT OF THE ASHES

y 1980 the Memphis music industry was fending off extinction. There were a handful of studios still in operation, but with the exception of Ardent Recording, most were subsisting on a meager and musically incestuous diet of nickel-and-dime demo sessions. Ardent flourished because it diversified into corporate video and attracted a handful of out-of-town recording groups such as ZZ Top by offering them special incentives to record in Memphis.

There were several popular club bands in town, including Fever, Good Question, Beauty and the Beats, Larry Raspberry and the Highsteppers (a carryover from the Gentrys), and the Breaks, which broke out of the club scene long enough to record two albums for RCA Records, though neither album hit and the group's hopes for success were short-lived. Susanne Jerome Taylor, the striking, dark-haired lead singer for the Breaks, emerged from the band's flirtation with success with a cynical attitude toward the business. "I would like to see the record companies get behind the artists they sign," she says. "It's so political. They may not like your manager or something and then you get squashed like a bug."

Taylor's mood was indicative of the despair felt by the entire music community. Despite the musicians' best efforts, failure was their constant companion. The record companies wouldn't look once, much less twice, at the talent in Memphis, and local opportunities were confined to the club scene. Incredibly, the pay scale in the early 1980s was the same as it was in the mid-1960s; bands could expect paychecks of two hundred to four hundred dollars a night, which for a band of four or five members barely stretched beyond minimum wage.

By 1984 the only Memphian headed for the national charts was Jimi Jamison, who that year became the lead singer for the Chicago-based band Survivor. Two years earlier the band had scored with "Eye of the Tiger," a song Sylvester Stallone used as the theme to *Rocky III*. Prior to joining Survivor, Jamison had been a member of two Memphis bands, Target and Cobra. Jamison toured with Survivor eight months of the year but maintained a home with a big, grassy backyard in Memphis, where his wife, Debbie, and their son lived while he was on the road. Jamison joined Survivor with no fanfare. His escape from the Memphis doldrums into mainstream music may have encouraged—or depressed—other Memphis musicians, but for the general public, his departure was a non-event that passed without notice.

■　●　■

Three months after I arrived at *The Commercial Appeal* in 1982, the wire services carried a story that Abe Fortas had died of a heart attack. We ran an obituary editorial that praised Fortas for his liberalism in defending the rights of criminals. No mention was made that he died in disgrace. Or even that he was born in Memphis. He had become a nonentity.

That year a committee from the National Academy of Recording Arts and Sciences came to Memphis to consider the city for the site of a music hall of fame. NARAS had been talking about building the museum for eight years. Sam Phillips got behind the project, as well as John Fry and all the other music survivors left in the city. I wrote editorials putting the support of the newspaper behind the project. After a brief look at the city, NARAS announced it would build the museum in Atlanta. I wrote an editorial that said the obvious: "Memphis didn't depend on NARAS to carve its music niche in the world, and it can't depend on that, or any other, organization to help the city carry on its music tradition. Memphians must do that themselves."

I was baffled by NARAS's decision. Why Atlanta? It didn't make sense. By the time the Rock and Roll Hall of Fame was formed, NARAS scrapped the Atlanta project. Gregg Geller, the former head of A&R for RCA Records, was at the Hall of Fame dinner when Cleveland, Ohio, was chosen as the site for the museum. He watched with sympathy as Sam Phillips argued that Memphis was where any rock 'n' roll hall of fame belonged. "There were a great many people, myself among them, who felt that if it could not be built in New York, Memphis was the logical place," says Geller. "There's one major reason why it went to Cleveland. That's because the people there wanted it desperately and they organized themselves to attract it."

In December 1983 *The Commercial Appeal*'s Sunday magazine, *Mid-South,* ran a feature on Beale Street. A Memphis deejay was quoted as saying, "The new is gonna be better than the old. It's gonna be three times as good." That quote caught the skeptical eye of editor Michael Grehl, who asked me to spend some time sampling the nightlife on Beale. The city was spearheading a project to revitalize the street, and the newspaper had mixed feelings about it.

After spending an evening at Club Handy—the club had just re-opened on the east end of the street—I wrote an editorial that urged the city to get behind the "second chance" history was offering the street. But if Beale Street is going to be "three times as good," I wrote, "it's going to take some second-look thinking among the city's music agnostics, particularly in the financial community." In the months that followed, Grehl, whose office overlooked Beale Street, allowed me to write editorials on a regular basis in support of the street's revitalization.

Shortly after Christmas 1984 *The Commercial Appeal*'s editorial board met to discuss ways to focus attention on Memphis's vanishing music industry. There was a consensus that the newspaper should do what it could to help. It was decided that I would do a series of interviews that would run on the editorial pages. It was an unprecedented gesture from a newspaper that, over the years, had kept itself at arm's length from the music industry.

The interviews ran from January 12 to March 17, 1985, and solicited the advice of twenty-seven individuals closely tied to the Memphis or national musical scene. They were asked why Memphis had become a music wasteland and what could be done to resurrect it. The interview that was to prove pivotal was the one I did with Chips Moman. For that interview, I flew to Nashville on a bitterly cold day in January. Moman's studio was located in southeast Nashville, a respectful distance from Music Row, the heart of the country music industry. The studio was unpretentious, and there was no sign outside to even indicate it was a studio.

I wasn't sure what to expect. Moman loathed the press and had done no interviews since leaving Memphis. Two other record producers were scheduled to meet me at the studio for a joint interview, but they didn't show up. A man wearing jeans, a pullover shirt, and a Greek sailor's cap greeted me at the door. He looked like he might be the janitor. I asked him for directions to Mr. Moman's office. He laughed and said that, well, he was afraid he was Mr. Moman.

We conducted the interview in the dimly lit control room. The console dials blinked and stared with space-age complexity from the shadows. Moman was eager to talk about Memphis. He said he left because of the backbiting and the nit-picking. I asked if he had ever regretted that decision. Moman's eyes glistened. "Let me tell you, that was a mistake," he said. "But when you work as much as we did, you sit there in that little building and you get paranoid. We didn't know what we had. I've always considered that a mistake. Not in the sense that we didn't all do better when we left. We did. But if we had done the right thing, and stayed there and tried to help all these people who were doing it wrong and tried to make people understand that Memphis was more than Soul City, who knows, we might have done more there than we did away from there. I think we would have. Every record I've cut since then, I've said, 'Yeah, I cut it in Nashville, but my music is still in Memphis,' because that's there I got it. That's where I learned it, that's where I felt it."

To my surprise, Moman said he would return to Memphis under the right circumstances. "Memphis needs someone to get all those guys there together," he said. "When you pull great songwriters to a place, you're doing more than getting a hit song, you're teaching the would-be songwriters there to do better. If you're around people who are in a rut, you will write in a rut because you don't have to do much to be

**Chips Moman shortly after he moved
back to Memphis in 1985.**
Photo by Dave Darnell

good. You need competitiveness. Unless you have it, you'll just lie
around. What's that old saying? The young fighter fights all the best
fighters to learn. It's no different for songwriters. You have to fight
all those best songwriters to write great or play great. Something has
to set the lead. There has to be a competitive spirit in the city."

Just talking about Memphis had a rejuvenating effect on Moman.
The longer we talked, the more energetic he became. At the end of
the interview, he invited me to stay for a recording session with
Johnny Cash. Moman's wife, Toni Wine, came into the room, and we
talked more about Memphis. While we were talking, Cash's wife, June
Carter, arrived at the studio. She had come to sing background. She

bubbled with enthusiasm. As she spoke to Moman and Toni, her bright eyes danced about the studio. Moman told her I was from Memphis. With that, June smiled broadly and talked about what a wonderful city Memphis had been in the early days of John's career.

While we were talking Waylon Jennings, wearing a long coat and a black hat, appeared in the doorway. He smiled when he saw June, but when he saw me, he paused, hesitant to encounter a journalist. June nudged him into the room. Within minutes, the sound of heavy footsteps echoed outside in the hallway. Dressed in black, a winter coat falling past his knees, Johnny Cash stuck his head into the control room. He seemed uncomfortable when he spotted me, but June quickly introduced us, and he relaxed and fell into an easy banter with Waylon and Moman. They got into a discussion about health food diets and vitamins. Johnny looked at me, his eyes dancing: "See, those are the kinds of drugs you talk about when you get our age." Everyone laughed. All of them had had some rough years in the pre-health food days.

Jack Clement's name came up. Clement was expected to show up for that day's session. "Jack Clement was the silent type, you know," says Johnny. "When he first started he was really shy. A lot of things went on around Sun Records, and later people would sit around and you'd hear people say, 'Who did what, when was that, and what happened at that session?' People would argue about it, and then they would finally get around to asking Jack Clement. He'd tell them exactly because he was there, all day long, every day."

Later Johnny, June, Waylon, and Toni left the control room to do voiceovers. As they stood at the microphone, Moman communicated with them over the speaker system. He asked Waylon to recite the lyrics of a song about Memphis that had been written by Clement. Before he recited the lyrics, Waylon leaned over, his head bobbing, peering into the darkened control room. He looked for me in the shadows. When he saw me, he said, "Be sure you say they are Jack Clement's lyrics." I nodded. Waylon smiled and recited a verse from a song that characterized Memphis as a place "lost between right and wrong."

When he finished, everyone, including Moman, suddenly got warm and toasty about Memphis. The feeling continued throughout the session and into the night, when Clement showed up with a bag of food. As Cash sang and Moman gave directions, and as the engineer, David Cherry, pushed sliders and turned dials. Clement and I sat in the back of the control room and put away an astonishing number of Krystal burgers and icebox lemon pies.

As I flew back to Memphis the next morning, I felt that something important had happened in Nashville. It was still cold, but the sky was a brilliant blue and the clouds were a fluffy white. About halfway between Nashville and Memphis the jetliner jerked, lurching back and forth several times. The passengers looked wide-eyed about the cabin. We awaited the bad news. Several minutes went by, then we heard the pilot's voice. He advised the passengers that those ticket holders who had planned to continue past Memphis would be put on another plane for their "convenience." The pilot never told us we had lost an engine. Was someone trying to tell me something?

■　●　■

My interview with Moman ran on January 31. When I arrived at the newspaper that morning, the phone was ringing off the hook. Moman's comments that he would consider returning to Memphis had energized the music community. At the editorial board meeting that day, Grehl suggested I interview Ron Terry, the chairman of First Tennessee Bank. He felt it would be a good idea if the business community had an input into the series.

I interviewed Terry in his plush offices in the First Tennessee Bank building. Terry had read the interview with Moman. He recalled with fondness the first time he saw Johnny Cash. Fresh out of the navy in 1956, he had taken a job as a trainee at a bank frequented by Cash. He recalled the day Johnny and June came in to tell everyone goodbye because they were moving to California. Terry acknowledged the impact music had had on Memphis's social and economic development, and he expressed a hope that music would make a comeback in Memphis.

"If you could talk Chips Moman into coming back to Memphis, that would be a major first step," he says. "Maybe Chips Moman would be followed by someone else. But you put a half dozen Chips Momans together with what they do in the music industry, then you have a music industry. . . . It's something the banks would love to see. It means good business for us."

After the interview we chatted some more. Terry suggested I interview Memphis mayor Dick Hackett for the series. As he walked me to the door, he told me to let him know if there was anything he could do personally to help the music industry. Back at the newsroom, I asked Grehl what he thought about my doing an interview with Hackett. He thought it was a good idea. Within days, the interview with Hackett was scheduled.

Hackett had been mayor for little more than one year. At the age of forty-one, he had shocked everyone by winning the election with 60 percent of the vote. No one knew much about him. His only other elected position had been as county clerk. As a leader he was a total unknown. We sat in the sitting area away from his massive desk. Hackett said he was willing to put the same emphasis on the development of the music industry that he had put on the development of other areas of the city's economy. Then, out of the blue, he said something that astonished me.

"For the right producer or studio, listen, I can make them a bargain on some land—and I'm talking about like one dollar—if they will contribute toward creating that atmosphere or climate in the city," said Hackett. "The city has a lot of land scattered around. There is some land on and around Beale Street, and if I can make a contribution on behalf of this community to entice that recording studio to come to Memphis—and, I understand from the professionals in the field, that is what we need to get the ball rolling—I will make a substantial contribution by coming up with the land or the buildings we have available. But it will have to be someone with a track record, someone who can produce."

I asked if he would be willing to go to Nashville to talk to Moman. Sure, he said. Whatever it takes. After the interview, as we stood at the door and talked, Hackett said he would make arrangements to go to Nashville as soon as possible. "Should I take someone with me?" he asked. "Someone in the business?"

"Yes," I said.

"Who should I take?"

"Take Ron Terry," I answered, recalling Terry's commitment.

"But I don't know Terry that well," Hackett said, looking slightly embarrassed. "He wasn't really one of my supporters. Do you think he would go?"

Yes, I was positive. "Tell him I gave you his name."

"I'll do that," he said, excited. "I'll call him today."

■　●　■

On a cold, windy day in mid-February, with the temperature in the low thirties, Mayor Dick Hackett and Ron Terry walked into Nashville's Berry Field Airport terminal on a secret mission. Hackett carried a red carnation, a signal for a clandestine contact. He had been asked jokingly to carry it in his mouth. For a brief moment, he considered doing just that, but his mayoral dignity prevailed over his flair for the dramatic and he carried the carnation at his side, as any other suitor courting a music industry legend would have done.

Neither Hackett nor Terry had ever seen the man and woman they had come to Nashville to meet. They had seen a picture of the man, but knew nothing about the woman except that she was younger than the man. In the picture, the man wore a Greek sailor's hat and a striped knit shirt. Across the room they spotted a man wearing such a cap and shirt. With the man was a younger woman. Hackett and Terry approached the couple, the red carnation extended as a greeting. "I wasn't about to put this [it] in my mouth," said the mayor, handing the flower to the young woman. He smiled broadly. "My name is Dick Hackett."

The woman looked startled. "Who?" she said, unsettled by the sudden attention. The woman's companion glared at the two men.

"Aren't you Chips Moman, the record producer?" Hackett asked.

The man and the woman exchanged glances, then informed the mayor of the state's largest city and the chairman of the state's largest bank that they had made a terrible mistake. Hackett wilted along with the flower. They then apologized to the couple and quickly blended into the crowd. After what seemed like an eternity, they heard their names on the public address system. They were instructed to go to a car rental booth.

At the booth they met Toni Wine, who promptly packed them into a four-wheel-drive Blazer and headed out of town, south toward Nolansville. The roads were covered with ice, and Toni, driving the new vehicle for only the second time, drove fast, probably a little too fast. The wheels barely touched the road. Once the Blazer skidded across the ice under a red light in heavy traffic, eliciting a three-part harmony of *shittt!* as Dick, Ron, and Toni held on for dear life. By the time they reached the Momans' farm, the mayor and the banker, slightly unnerved by the ride, had loosened their corporate neckties to breathe a little easier. "Within five minutes, I felt like I had known Chips and Toni for years," says Hackett. Meeting them, he says, "took a lot of anxiety out of my heart and mind."

As Hackett and Terry got comfortable at the farm, Memphians perused that day's edition of *The Commercial Appeal*. In a front-page story, Hackett offered city-owned land or buildings for one dollar to any successful record producer who would move to the city and help rejuvenate the music industry. On their visit to the farm, Hackett and Terry offered Moman an abandoned fire station just off Beale Street. They also offered him financing to renovate the fire station into a state-of-the art recording studio. They parted company that day convinced that something could be worked out. After they left, Moman called me at the newspaper. "Everyone showing the interest they did got me fired up," he said. "I'm ready to pack up and go."

Negotiations continued for several weeks. On several occasions, just when an agreement seemed possible, problems arose. Finally, Hackett and Moman reached a verbal understanding. To my surprise, Hackett came by my office so I could interview him for a news story for the next morning's edition. The sight of the mayor sitting in my office as I worked at my computer had curious reporters backed up in the hallway outside. Probably never in the newspaper's history had a mayor dropped by after hours to chat with an editorial writer. Boss Crump would not have been caught dead in this newsroom. Certainly he would not have been seen talking to an opinion writer—and at night! The irony was not lost on me at the time. "Dick Hackett is either a genius or a damned fool," I thought.

Finally, on April 5, 1985, Chips and Toni came to Memphis to tour the fire station. At a press conference the next day, with Hackett and Terry at their sides, Chips and Toni signed an agreement to relocate in Memphis. After the signing, Hackett handed me the pen and thanked me for my efforts on behalf of Memphis music. Looking tired and a little bit embarrassed by the publicity, Chips, who had only given a handful of interviews in his life, told a room packed with television cameras and reporters that he was happy about returning to Memphis.

"Chips Moman is going to be the Fred Smith of the music industry," Hackett told the reporters, referring to the founder of Memphis-based Federal Express. "Right now I don't think anyone realizes what the positive impact of his arrival may be. You are dealing not only with dollars but with an excitement."

Shortly after that, Grehl asked me to invite Chips to the newspaper to meet the editorial board. Because Grehl liked the idea of government and private enterprise working together, he supported Hackett's efforts to rekindle the music industry. Chips showed up at the newspaper shortly before noon and was escorted into Grehl's office, where the editorial staff was gathered. With Chips was Herb O'Mell, who had worked with him in the early days. Since then O'Mell had been in and out of the music business. It was my first time to meet him. Chips talked about his dreams for Memphis music and thanked the newspaper for its support. By the time the meeting was over, Grehl was satisfied that Chips was a good investment of the newspaper's time.

A final agreement with the city was still months away, but Chips, along with Toni and their eight-year-old son, Casey, packed up and moved to Memphis. They were offered a suite at the Peabody by Gary Belz, at that time the general manager of the hotel. Belz, whose father, Jack, and grandfather, Philip, owned the hotel, had long dreamed of becoming a player in the music industry. Aside from a business partnership with a Memphis music promoter, his efforts had been stalled.

Working out of the hotel, Moman wasted no time putting together his first recording project. He had no home, no studio, no office, but he had a telephone and that was enough. He also had a hit album on the charts, *The Highwaymen,* which he had recorded in Nashville with Johnny Cash, Waylon Jennings, Willie Nelson, and Kris Kristofferson. Chips decided that his first project would be a homecoming album. He would bring the surviving stars of Sun Records back to Memphis to record a reunion album.

By the end of the summer, Chips had office space at the Peabody. He had been unable to find a house in Memphis, partly because of his notoriety. Toni complained that they would see a house advertised at one price, but by the time they arrived to view the house, it would experience a sudden jump in price. On August 26, 1985, Chips opened his office on the third floor of the hotel, a floor used mainly for hotel business operations. The office was tucked away behind a labyrinth of doors. To get there, you had to pass through a double door marked EMPLOYEES ONLY, then proceed down a long corridor with unpainted walls and dangling electrical wires. Inside the office were three desks, a sitting area with leatherlike couches, and a wet bar. "That hall suits me," Chips said, laughing. "It's my style."

Soon every wannabe and used-to-be musician in the mid-South made a beeline to the hotel. Lines formed outside the door, and the telephone rang constantly. In keeping with his theory that songs were the key to success, Chips signed two Memphis songwriters to contracts on the first day.

With the announcement of the Sun Records reunion, the music industry—and the national media—worked themselves into a frenzy. The session was scheduled to begin on September 15. The next day, Chips staged a press conference in the lobby of the Peabody. CNN carried it live. Every major television network was there, as were reporters from most national magazines and newspapers. As the Four Horsemen—Johnny Cash, Jerry Lee Lewis, Roy Orbison, and Carl Perkins—walked out into the lobby to sit at the table with Chips and Sam Phillips, the crowd in the packed lobby applauded wildly. People hung over the balcony, clung to the massive pillars in the lobby, and stood on chairs to get a glimpse of the four music legends.

For about thirty minutes the Four Horsemen fielded questions from the press. Carl Perkins probably spoke for everyone when he said the opportunity to make music history left him with an "emotional high." The stage was set.

Memphis was ready to roll the dice.

■　●　■

Also catching the reunion virus in 1985 were Willie Mitchell and Al Green. Although they had remained friends and kept in touch since recording their last album in 1976, their careers had taken separate directions. Out of the blue, Al called Willie in April 1985 and asked if he would be interested in doing another album. Willie was ecstatic. For eight years Al had devoted his life to the ministry and gospel music. Willie had given up ever hearing from him again.

In August Willie invited me to attend one of the recording sessions. His studio is located in a residential area of southwest Memphis, not far from downtown. The neighborhood is predominantly black and offers a curious mix of safety-barred windows and screened porches. When I arrived at the studio, the same building Hi Records had used for its headquarters, I had to pound on the steel-reinforced door for several minutes before anyone inside could hear me knocking.

Willie and Al were animated that day, laughing and joking like kids on school recess. Willie told me he had not slept a day since receiving the telephone call from Al. "Day and night I hear the album over and over," he said.

Willie played one of the songs they were working on. He cranked the music up loud. With his hands clapping, Al danced back and forth behind the console, singing along with the music. Willie raised his arms, punctuating the air as he kept time with the driving beat of the music. For Al and Willie, it was the good old days all over again. The album, *He Is the Light,* was released in October by A&M records.

When the song ended, Al marveled at the clarity of the tape. "The album is so clear you can hear every single instrument," he said. He looked at Willie. "I guess that goes to good producing."

Willie laughed, displaying the good humor that characterizes their relationship. "That goes to paying me to be the engineer," he said, grinning. "The more money you've got, the more clearer I can make it."

Willie Mitchell at his desk.
Photo by Greg Campbell

Al doubled over with laughter. When he regained his composure, he told me making the album had nothing to do with money. "This is like Chips Moman, Johnny Cash, Carl Perkins, Jerry Lee Lewis, and Roy Orbison getting together," he says.

What he liked about working with Willie, he says, was his level of professionalism and his willingness to take charge of the project. "It takes a producer to come up with the right sound, the right voice quality," he says. "It takes a producer with some nerve to tell me to go home to sleep for two days because I've lost the midrange in my voice."

Al looked at Willie, the admiration glowing in his face. "I said, 'Come on, let's give it another shot,'" Al said.

"He said, 'You don't have a bottom to your voice. You have only tops.'"

"I said, 'Well, whatever you're talking about, I'm gone.'"

Al and Willie exploded into loud, raucous laughter.

"Willie to me is like a counselor," said Al. "But mostly he's a friend. And I take his advice very seriously. I think we're basically trying to prove something to ourselves. I know I am."

I asked Al what he wanted to prove.

"To see if the quality is really there," he said, his voice growing somber. "We want to see if we really got it. At this age now—I'm in my upper thirties—I want to see if I've really got it."

Willie nodded. Amen.

■　●　■

In the weeks following the Four Horsemen session, Chips worked feverishly to get the tapes mastered and ready for presentation to major record labels. By the time Chips finished performing his magic, he had ten songs recorded by the pioneers of rock 'n' roll that were unlike anything else on the market.

Because the album was unique, it became apparent that the miracle Chips had performed in recording it would have to be duplicated in the business arena if the album was ever to see the light of day. To Chips's surprise—and almost everyone else's—the major labels did not jump at the chance to purchase the album. One by one, the rejections mounted. The feeling among most of the record executives was that the album was too out of the ordinary and would be difficult to market. Ironically, that was the same thing they said back in 1954 when Sam Phillips first took a chance on rock 'n' roll.

The strain of working out of a hotel, and the uncertainty of the album's future, began to show on Chips's face. He looked tired on most days, and he grew more and more irritable. What he needed was a studio to work out of, not a hotel office. He pushed for finalization of the deal Hackett had been working on since spring. Meanwhile, he took O'Mell on as his chief assistant, hired a secretary, and purchased a house at 191 Waring with money he borrowed from First Tennessee. The Nashville farm was paid for and appraised at over a million dollars. The loan, which would return to haunt him, was an attempt to get settled and working as quickly as possible.

By the end of November 1985 Hackett was ready to present his proposal to the city council. He announced he was backing down from an earlier proposal to sell city property to successful record producers willing to relocate in Memphis. He didn't admit it publicly, but the reason for the turnabout was that he had been bombarded with complaints from some of the other studios. Their arguments were emotional: you're doing something for Chips Moman, so why aren't you doing something for us? Hackett wasn't about to turn city property over to the motley crew of musical misfits demanding favors from him, so he opted to back away from his commitment. It was yet another example of how prone the Memphis music community is to self-destruction.

Under the terms of the agreement Chips would be allowed to use an abandoned fire station at Third and Linden for a lease payment of one dollar a year. He would have the option to purchase the property at appraised value at the end of five years. In addition, he would receive a loan for $750,000 arranged by the Center City Commission, which would issue bonds for that amount that would be purchased by First Tennessee Bank. Chips would be required to make his loan payments to First Tennessee Bank. "There's no way we can say we've given Chips a deal," Hackett said in response to critics. "He's given us a deal."

The internal bickering that had driven Chips from the city in 1970 resurfaced, but in all the excitement no one seemed to notice—or if they did, they didn't think it was very important. By February 1986 it was apparent the major labels were going to pass on the album. At the urging of Belz and others—who saw not just dollar signs but stars in their future (show business can be intoxicating)—Chips decided to form his own record label to distribute the album. Starting a record label had been on his list of things to do from the beginning, but initially it wasn't his plan to use the homecoming album as the label's first product.

O'Mell and Belz, with their extensive contacts in the financial community, targeted potential investors. The list they put together, with a few exceptions, read like a who's who of business in the South: Philip and Jack Belz of Belz Investments; financial consultant John Tigrett of Memphis, whose son, Isaac, founded the Hard Rock Café chain; Fred Smith, chairman of Federal Express; Bernard Blasingame, president of

Aqua Glass Corporation; and Buddy Lazar, president of Star Distributors. In all, there were eighteen investors. They never publicly disclosed how much they invested, but it was somewhere between $1 million and $2 million. They christened the new label America Records.

"One of the things we see in the label is the possibility of making Memphis a major music center," Belz told a reporter on the day the announcement was made. "We see more labels, more studios, more live music in Memphis as a result of America Records."

A date was set for the release of the homecoming album. Reaction was enthusiastic. The very thought of having a label in the city again gave hope to a generation of musicians and singers who had only dreamed of the opportunities enjoyed by previous generations of Memphis musicians. No one was more enthusiastic than Chips. For the first time since the initial discussions about relocating in Memphis had begun, he was able to visualize the musical pot of gold at the end of the rainbow.

Given the domination enjoyed by the major labels, the biggest obstacle facing any independent label is its ability to secure a strong distribution system. Chips's solution was to launch a two-pronged attack: first, to secure a distribution agreement with a major label; second, to use television to directly market the album to consumers. "We're trying to set trends, not follow them," he explained. "We're trying to be different. We don't want to use the old-fashioned ways used by the record companies."

Chips contacted Steve Popovich, then the head of PolyGram Records in Nashville. Popovich had made his mark on the music industry with the rock act Meat Loaf. In 1977 Popovich, then with Epic Records, had joined with Stan Snyder and Sam Lederman of Columbia Records to form an independent label, Cleveland International. Their first release was Meat Loaf's *Bat Out of Hell*, an enormously successful album. Unfortunately, Marvin Aday, the 260-pound lead singer, couldn't handle the demands of success. As Meat Loaf's career fizzled, so did Popovich's dreams.

By the mid-1980s Popovich had relocated in Nashville and taken over the reins of PolyGram's country division. A big, burly man with an aggressive approach to music, he was just the kind of player Chips wanted on his team. Popovich knew the ropes. With PolyGram taking on retail distribution, Chips was confident he could launch a tele-marketing effort that would make the album a multimillion seller. To have a successful telemarketing effort Chips knew he had to have more than just an album. He needed a package.

One evening I got a telephone call. "Busy?" asked Chips. "I got something to talk to you about."

Chips picked me up at my apartment, and we drove to an all-night waffle house. We ordered eggs and waffles and downed a few cups of coffee, then Chips told me what was on his mind. If I would write a booklet to accompany the album for its telemarketing sales, I could retain the copyright and use the booklet to launch my own magazine. American Records would not pay me to write it. My compensation would be an opportunity to spin off a business venture from the pro-ject. If the album was successful—everyone just knew it would be— so would the magazine. I told him I would think about it. It would mean resigning from *The Commercial Appeal,* with no certainty of an income. It would be the biggest risk of my life. But it hardly seemed possible that the homecoming album would not be successful. Besides, I knew that a national music magazine based in Memphis would play a critical role in the revival of the city's music industry.

Meanwhile, cracks were forming in America Records. Almost immediately after getting involved in the project Fred Smith decided he wanted out. The other investors did not think that would be fair, and they balked at releasing him from his commitment. Smith asked John Fry to represent his interest in the label. Fry would attend the meetings and report back to Smith. That didn't go over too well with Chips. Fry owned a studio that would compete for attention and business with the studio Chips was going to build. The comfort level was not high, but to the credit of both men, they tried to make the most of the situation.

One day I was at the hotel office when Fry and some of the other investors showed up for a meeting. They talked about the album and about plans for new projects. Fry's eyes darted during the discussion. Something was bothering him. Finally, he spoke up. Nothing personal, but he didn't think I should be present. "Why?" Chips asked.

"He might tell people what we're doing," Fry said.

"We've got nothing to hide," Chips said. And I stayed at the meeting.

During that same meeting concerns were expressed about the label's options if the majors decided to play hardball and block distribution of the album. Without missing a beat Chips said that wouldn't be a problem because the Hell's Angels would be available as enforcers. Chips was joking—at least I hoped he was joking—but his comment had the desired effect: the yuppie investors swooned like schoolgirls at the thought of the Hells Angels becoming their partners. Did they envision themselves in a Harley motorcade, with biker chicks at their side and rock music blaring from heavenly speakers? Who could blame them if they did?

Chips's hotel office was always busy. Songwriters, musicians, and music publishers showed up at all hours of the day and night. Also finding their way to the hotel office were young girls seeking autographs. Because Jerry Lee Lewis and Carl Perkins were often at the office, the girls pursued them for their autographs—and to pitch songs to Chips.

One day a group of five or six young women in their late teens or early twenties came into the office, saw Perkins, and fluttered about the room, taking turns getting his autograph. After they left Perkins gave one of the most sensual descriptions of a twenty-year-old woman I have ever heard. "There's just something about those twenty-year-old bodies," he said, shaking his head with admiration. His voice got low, dropping down to a purr. "They're so firm—so perfect." He moved his hands through the air, caressing the figure of an imaginary woman.

Once I was sitting in the hotel lobby with Chips when a former Miss America contestant came up and sat next to him. Between frequent trips to the restroom, from which she always returned with a white powder on her nose, she held Chips's hand and sang to him above the chatter of the busy lobby. "Is this really happening?" I thought. The poor girl sang her heart out. Chips took the audition in stride, never once grimacing, not even when her voice ventured into the outer regions of caterwauling. It was the first and only time I ever felt sorry for a beautiful woman.

America Records wasted no time getting *Class of '55* on the market. The album cover was designed by a Memphis artist. Photos of the session, taken by Dave Darnell, *The Commercial Appeal* photographer who accompanied me on the interviews, were used on the album. When it was released in mid-May, sales were brisk at local stores. WMC FM-100 program director Robert John aired the album immediately. "The reaction has been phenomenal," he said. "There was not one negative call."

By then work was progressing on Chips's new studio, which he planned to name Three Alarm Studio. It would be a state-of-the art facility with the best digital equipment money could buy. In May 1986 I handed in my resignation to David Wayne Brown, who had become acting editor after Grehl's retirement. The week I left the newspaper Grehl called me at home to say he had heard about my resignation. He said he was sorry to see me leave the newspaper and wished me luck with the magazine. Sadly, that would be our last conversation.

The summer of 1986 was pivotal for Memphis music. The first major record in over a decade had been released. The national media had rediscovered the city after years of neglect. Other producers were talking about moving to the city. A national music magazine was in the works. For the first time in decades, the banks were talking about making loans to music entrepreneurs. Each day brought more good news.

Anxious to try out his new studio, Chips made plans to record an album with Bobby Womack for MCA Records. Perhaps mindful of their first collaboration, he felt the "magic" that would flow from a reunion would make that project as special as *Class of '55*. Of course, that wasn't what the music community wanted him to do. They wanted him to focus on local talent. Chips had signed a local group, Reba and the Portables, to a recording contract, but his efforts to place them with a major label had been unsuccessful. He needed someone with a track record to help him launch his new studio. Womack had been reduced to playing hotel lounges in recent years, but the talent was still there, and Chips was convinced he could get a hit record out of him.

Reba and the Portables, c. 1980s.
Photo by James Dickerson

Leaving the newspaper enabled me to get more involved in the music community. I called Michael Barrickman, A&R executive at EMI Records in New York, and he flew down to Memphis to sample the talent. I took him by Three Alarm, where Chips played him the demos he had recorded on Reba and the Portables. I took him to a club to hear a group called Vienna. It featured a female singer, Klaudia Kroboth, who had emigrated to Memphis from Austria and married a Memphis building contractor. Reba, with her powerful pipes, and Klaudia, with her exotic stage presence, were the best the city had to offer. Barrickman passed on both groups. I took another A&R executive from Los Angeles by to hear them. "Hmmm," he said. "Interesting." I invited Rick Blackburn, head of CBS Records in Nashville, to Memphis to listen to a half dozen acts. He was impressed with Reba but didn't like the band. I took him by several studios, including Ardent. Not since Jerry Wexler's visits in the 1960s had a label head visited Memphis studios. Blackburn asked the studio personnel lots of questions, but they squirmed and seemed ill at ease. They had never met the head of a record label and didn't know what to say. I had arranged for him to listen to the best country act in the city, but when we arrived, the club was empty. The singer had changed venues without telling me. Blackburn's visit was not a success.

By May 1986 America Records had moved its offices from the Peabody to an office complex off Beale Street. The building offered a nice view of the Mississippi River, but Chips seldom used his office there. "If you ever need an office, use mine," Chips told me. "I don't like offices."

■　●　■

By summer the marketing of *Class of '55* hit full stride. "The Birth of Rock 'n' Roll," Carl Perkins's solo effort, was the first single released. Reviews of the album were good. Unfortunately, sales were slow. Television sales especially were disappointing. On a trip to Nashville during that time, I stopped by PolyGram to visit Popovich. To my surprise and amusement, I found him behind a massive desk, shuffling papers, barking orders to staffers—and wearing a jogging suit. He was optimistic about the album. Talking to him, I kept thinking, "Why is this man wearing a jogging suit, and what does he know I don't know?"

The investors in America Records voiced concern. Sometimes, on my visits to the office, I would run into some of the investors who had dropped by to help with strategy planning, telephone calls, or packaging mail-outs. Most of their investment had been spent on up-front payments to Chips, Cash, Orbison, Lewis, and Perkins, with each person receiving advances against royalties in the neighborhood of $250,000. They began to wonder how they could tap into Chips's post-*Class of '55* career. It wasn't money they feared losing (they all had plenty), it was the loss of prestige and—perhaps most important—the loss of their dreams that bothered them the most.

Popovich decided to do a video for "The Birth of Rock 'n' Roll." He called Arnold Levine, who had done videos for Bruce Springsteen, Billy Joel, and Neil Diamond. Levine flew into Memphis and hired a local film crew. For the video, Levine got a vintage 1955 blue Cadillac. "Basically what I did was take a vintage car and use it as a time machine," says Levine. "I have two kids out on a joyride in the early morning. The two kids happen to be fifty-year-olds doing what kids do."

Included to be in the video were Jerry Lee Lewis and Rolling Stone guitarist Ron Wood, who made the trip to Memphis to hand out with his heroes, Perkins and Lewis. I had never seen a video being made, so I stopped by to watch. When I arrived everyone was on edge. Lewis had not showed up. They were scheduled to shoot a scene in which Lewis sat in the backseat of a car and danced his feet across the top of the front seat. The director asked if I would mind being Lewis's stand-in. Why not, I thought. As the crew impatiently swatted flies and complained about the heat, I changed into Lewis's pants and shoes and proceeded to dance my way into video history. Later, when Lewis failed to show up for a second scene, I was again asked to impersonate the Killer. For a brief minute in the video my face is visible. Several weeks later I viewed the finished video with Perkins at the offices of America Records. During the dancing-feet scene he cut his head around and grinned at me: "You don't keep bad time for a writer." Perkins seemed to like the video, but I could tell he was hurt that Lewis had failed to show up for all the scenes.

Sales was never Chips's strong point, though he will swear to you that he is a natural-born salesman. P. T. Barnum was one of his childhood heroes. But if the truth be known, Chips is an artist, and he has an artist's temperament. As the weeks went by, and dreams of the album's being a major success faded, he realized he needed to return to what he does best, make music. He put his salesman's hat aside and prepared for his session with Womack. They had worked magic together once before. Surely they could do it again.

"I'm nervous at the start of every session, but I was extraordinarily nervous about Bobby this time because I didn't know whether the studio was going to go up in smoke," Moman says, referring to the fact that the equipment was untested. "But you know, I couldn't think of anyone I would rather try to get a hit with than Bobby. He's got a distinct style. He's a great singer, writer, and guitar player. That's about all you could ask for."

For Womack, the decision to return to Memphis was a tough one.

Bobby Womack at Three Alarm Studio.
Photo by James Dickerson

It had been eighteen years since he had recorded in the city, and he had built a new life in Los Angeles. His friends warned him not to go. "I had all the people on my end saying, 'What do you want to go to Memphis for?'" he says. "I told them my music is what Memphis is all about. It's very peaceful, it's loving and caring, and the people there, the musicians, are like that. It's a magical place."

While in Memphis Womack stayed at the Peabody. One day he ran into Stevie Wonder in the lobby. Wonder was in town to attend an awards show for black recording artists. Wonder asked why he was in Memphis. "I said, 'Stevie, this is where it's happening.'"

Stevie looked puzzled. "Memphis. You sure?" Womack knew he had planted a seed. The next night he called Stevie at the hotel to check up on him. "They said Stevie had gone to a studio to do some recording," Womack laughs.

For Womack, the Memphis magic was partly cultural. "I go where the soul people are—not just for the people in the studio, but for the people who walk the streets," he says. "This is where you get the raw soul. In L.A. you have to lock the door to get inside your soul, and even then you can get caught up in the electronic slickness of what everyone else is doing." Memphis has an energy of its own, he says. "This is the capital. You can't cut no bigger than Elvis and Al Green."

Womack's album, *Womagic,* was released in November 1986. The reviews were excellent, but the album stalled on the charts. By the end of the year, nerves were on edge at America Records. Tempers flared. The most frequent question was "When are we going to do another album?" Chips stopped going to the office. Pressure was the last thing in the world he needed.

One night Chips was sitting in his den when he got a telephone call from Gary Belz. One thing led to another, and Belz called Chips a motherfucker. Chips calmly hung up the phone, got in his car, and drove to Ardent, where Belz was waiting.

Chips strode into the studio and slapped Belz hard across the face.

"You call me a name, you do it to my face," he said, and left. Belz was stunned.

With that gesture, more symbolic than anything else, Memphis music entered a new era. All-out war erupted in the Memphis music community—and Memphis's dark side, alluded to by Jim Dickinson in such graphic terms, rose to bay at the moon.

THE EIGHTIES:
THE EMPIRE STRIKES BACK

n October 1987 Gary Hardy, the new owner of Sun Studios (Sam had sold the historic studio several years back), received a telephone call from A&M Records. They wanted to book a full day in the studio. They wanted an "authentic" rockabilly sound. They didn't say who they were booking the studio for, but that was fine with Hardy.

About a week later, Hardy got a call from Jack Clement, who wanted to know if he had heard from U2 yet. Hardy was stunned. That was the first indication Hardy had that he had booked the studio for a U2 session. At that time U2 was considered the best rock 'n' roll band in the world. Most of Hardy's clients were wannabes who booked time at the studio because it was cheap and had a recognizable name. U2 was the big time.

Clement arrived in Memphis the day before the session to check out the studio. He was surprised to learn that the studio was even in operation, but not surprised to hear from U2, because he had worked with them on a Woody Guthrie tribute album. "We did a song called 'Jesus Christ,'" Jack recalls. "We had a big time and got along real good. A couple of months later they called me back. They said they would only do it [come to Memphis] if I could be there."

U2 had two reasons for recording in Memphis. The first was to capture that old slapback sound for which Sun is famous. The second was to cut a track for B. B. King. U2 met King the year before in Dublin during King's Ireland tour. "They came backstage after the show, like artists sometimes do," recalls King. "When they were getting ready to go, I said, 'Sometimes when you're writing a song, why don't you write one for me.' Bono smiled. I didn't hear from him for over a year and then one day my manager called and said he had just heard from Bono. He said he'd written a song for me." U2 was kicking off its U.S. tour in Fort Worth, Texas, and wanted to know if King would open for them. King jumped at the chance.

"I discovered Bono had written a song, not just for me, but for us to sing together," says King. "I was real excited about it. But I'm not good with chords. I was teasing him about it. I was surprised about some of the lines being done by a young man. They were so strong. That night, according to the Forth Worth papers, when we did the song as a finale, forty thousand people came to their feet. I was really happy."

When Bono, the Edge, Adam Clayton, and Larry Mullen Jr. arrived at the Sun studio, they did what every tourist does: they gawked at the photos of Elvis and the Four Horsemen. They did overdubs on "Jesus Christ," then laid down tracks on three other songs. For "Angel of Harlem," Clement brought in the Memphis Horns to give the track a taste of the old Stax sound. What emerged, though, was more a reflection of Chip Momans's American sound. New York had a wall of sound; Memphis had a briar patch of sound. It was layered more intricately and hit you just above the knees instead of in the face. The second song was "Love Rescue Me," a folk-gospel tune written by Bono and Bob Dylan. The third song was "When Love Comes to Town," the one Bono wrote for B. B. King. It was a perfect, back-of-the-beat choice for a duet with King. All three songs ended up on U2's *Rattle and Hum* LP.

For Jack Clement, U2 was no different than any other four-piece band he had ever worked with in the studio. "Of course, they were a lot louder than the bands I worked with in there," he laughs. "But I put the instruments in the same spots in the room—except I used baffles this time. It does seem to be a magic room. I think that is because there is so much leakage. It sounds better when you play it back than when you hear it in the room. It's magic.

"All they wanted me to do was be a clown and just be what I used to be. So I danced around so they'd pay attention to me and forget the songs. That's what I do. I perform for my artists. I dance for them. It keeps their minds off the songs. People sing their best when they don't know what they're doing. They're not thinking about anything, just watching the dancing figure.

"They seemed to love it, you know. I danced around with a beer bottle on my head. I try to keep artists distracted. Sometimes they get too intense. Sometimes if you cut a song more than once you can never go back and cut it like you did. There's times when you have to slow it down so you can start over. I go out and say something to the artists totally out of left field. It shatters their concentration and they get totally out of what they were doing. Then they're ready to start over."

■　●　■

That year the floodgates opened. Everyone, it seemed, wanted to record an album in Memphis. Between 1987 and 1989 R.E.M. recorded its *Green* album at Ardent, Jim Dickinson produced an album with the Replacements, Stevie Ray Vaughan recorded his last two albums, the Fabulous Thunderbirds recorded two albums, ZZ Top did another album, and ex-Beatle Ringo Starr recorded an album with Chips Moman.

Sadly, the talent indigenous to Memphis languished on the vine. Becky Russell sang backup on the U2 album, but her own band, Reba and the Portables, was going nowhere fast. One of the best singer/songwriters in the city, Klaudia Kroboth, seemed close at times to getting a deal, but success wriggled just out of her grasp. Two Memphians got deals with major labels, Rob Jungklas and John Kilzer, but their records slammed into a brick wall when they got to the charts.

One of the most encouraging things to happen for Memphis artists occurred when Bob Pittman, the former head of MTV, created his own record label, QMI Music. The first two acts he signed were from Memphis: Ella Brooks, a black R&B singer, and Jimmy Davis, a twenty-three-year-old roots rocker in the John Mellencamp tradition. Pittman made a big deal of the signings and held a party at the Rum Boogie Café on Beale Street to celebrate his entry into Memphis music.

Pittman had just left MTV and was eager to make a splash as a

Jimmy Davis shortly after he signed with QMI Music.
Photo by James Dickerson

record executive. As one of the creators of MTV, he certainly had the
track record to do great things in music. Whether he was a genius
when it came to music remained to be seen, but no one could doubt
his genius as a media guru. I met Pittman for the first time at the
party and then later talked to him about the signings. "What I liked
about Ella and Jimmy was that they both have a very real sound," he
said. "Originally we cut a deal with Ella. I went to Memphis to work
out the deal. While I was there, Jimmy performed for us. He was just
a natural. He could say stuff that if I said it, they'd say, 'Jeez, what's
that guy talking about?' But Jimmy says it and you say, 'Yeah, that's
right.' Springsteen has that quality."

Pittman was determined to do for QMI what he had done for MTV, though he acknowledged that making a success of an independent label was tough. To date, only David Geffen had managed to pull it off. "Probably most independent labels that fail are underfinanced and don't have strong relationships in the business," said Pittman. "They're trying to build their relationships through the label. They also probably get the last look at every piece of music. We have what David Geffen had—key relationships with the players. And we have plenty of money."

Would QMI become the Sun Records of the 1980s? Would Memphis talent, yet again, rise from the ashes of ignoble defeat? The city held its breath.

■　●　■

With the *Class of '55* and Bobby Womack projects foundering on the charts, Chips Moman returned to his pop music roots. That was one area where American had been unrivaled in the late 1960s. Ironically, Chips turned to a member of the very group that had helped bring about the demise of the Memphis sound: the Beatles.

When Ringo Starr arrived in February 1987 to record at Three Alarm Studio, the city displayed all the poise of a giddy teenager. There was a Ringo buzz on the streets. TV newscasts shared news of Ringo sightings. Callers to radio programs swapped Ringo stories. It had been twenty years since a Beatle had been in Memphis. This time there were no Ku Klux Klan protests and no cherry bombs. Not yet, anyway.

The Beatles had been one of my favorite groups, so I was delighted when Chips asked me to drop by the studio. Chips had booked the 827 Thomas Street Band for the session, so I knew everyone there except Ringo and his actress-wife, Barbara Bach. When we were introduced, Ringo offered a hearty handshake; Barbara offered a smile that made my knees buckle. The sessions lasted into April, with Ringo and Barbara frequently commuting to Los Angeles.

Two things impressed me about the Ringo session. First, I was surprised at how strong his chops were in their natural, unadulterated state. I had been lead to believe Ringo's voice required extensive

Ringo Starr and Chips Moman at Three Alarm Studio during a break in their recording session.
Photo by James Dickerson

rehabilitation in the studio. Not so. Between takes Toni Wine spent time with him at the piano, coaching him on specific lines, but his chops were rock solid. Second, I was surprised at how cozy he was with Barbara. Throughout the session, he was extraordinarily relaxed and playful, snuggling with Barbara, who often sat on his lap with her arms around his neck: very lovey-dovey. Never once did I see any indication Ringo was drinking or using drugs.

The session went really well until Ringo and Barbara left town for a few days. While they were gone, Rheta Grimsley Johnson, a nationally syndicated columnist for *The Commercial Appeal*, wrote a piece about the session. She called Ringo an "aging Beatle," who was yesterday's news. I read the column but thought nothing about it. I passed her Ringo piece off with a "there she goes again" comment and forgot about it. Later that day I stopped by Three Alarm. Chips was livid. He was afraid the column was going to sabotage the session. In his mind, it was the cherry-bomb incident all over again.

"We've got to do something," he said.

Chips wanted to picket the newspaper. I tried to talk him out of it. I reminded him that *The Commercial Appeal* had brought him to Memphis. "They've turned against me," he said.

I explained that Rheta's column was not the newspaper's opinion. He didn't buy that. It must be the newspaper's opinion, he reasoned, or it would not have been printed. It was just one person's opinion, I argued. Newspapers print all sorts of opinions. No deal. I was totally unable to reason with him. He called for a picket the next day on the sidewalk in front of the newspaper.

"You with me or against me?" he asks. What could I say? The next morning I walked the picket line with Chips, Toni, Casey, and about two dozen placard-carrying marchers. From the massive glass wall of the third-floor newsroom, former colleagues peered down at me, some with amused smiles. Chips was wrong to picket the newspaper, but it did offer comic relief to a tense situation. Chips really did believe the column would sabotage everything he had worked so hard to build. If carrying a picket sign made him feel better, so be it.

When Ringo returned to Memphis a reporter asked him about the controversy. "Haven't read it," he said. "Why would I?" Toward the end of the session, Ringo and Barbara gave a party aboard the riverboat *Island Queen* to show they had no hard feelings toward Memphis. I attended the party, along with Charlie Rich, David Porter, and 251 other invited guests. No one was sure what to expect when the *Island Queen* churned out into the Mississippi River. There was lots of barbecue and lots to drink. Reba and the Portables provided the music. It was a typical Memphis party, with one exception—there was a Beatle on board.

The highlight of the party occurred late in the evening. Everyone gathered downstairs in the main room where the band was playing. The hot, smoke-filled room must have taken Ringo back to the days when the Beatles were playing tiny, people-infested pubs throughout Europe. With a cigarette dangling from his lips, he made his way behind a maze of amps and electrical equipment and made himself comfortable on the drum stool. As the band played on, he demonstrated why he is the most celebrated drummer in the world. Within minutes he had the guests mesmerized with his Beatles-like flimming and flamming. "I can't believe it," says a girl standing next to me. "I'm really seeing him play."

The girl's amazement was justified. Except for a handful of studio personnel, who had ever actually heard the ex-Beatle play a live set? Not the hundreds of thousand of fans who packed the stadiums when the Beatles toured. They would have been too overwhelmed by the hysteria of the moment actually to hear the music.

A couple of days after the party I saw Ringo again in the studio. "That was the first time I ever played a riverboat," he said, laughing. He said he was afraid to sample the barbecue. "It's my stomach," he says plaintively, referring to an incident several years ago that almost cost him his life. "Most of the things I eat now have to be broiled. I can't eat spicy food."

When work on the album drew to a close, the musicians and crew had sixteen completed songs. Ringo and Barbara said their goodbyes and flew back to Los Angeles. After the album was mixed, Chips sent Ringo a cassette. Ringo phoned and told him he had rented a limo so he and a couple of friends could listen to the tape in style. Unfortunately, there was a problem. "Wouldn't you know I'd get the only fucking limo in town without a tape deck," he said.

I'm not sure how it happened (I'm not sure *anyone* knows how it happened), but during the next few months the project fell apart. Chips wanted to shop the album. Ringo did not want him to shop the album. John Hartman, a spokesman for Ringo, told reporters Ringo wanted to record tracks with another producer (he tossed out Elton John's name) and wanted to combine the two sessions into one album. The disaster that Chips feared was becoming a reality.

Ringo's attorneys filed a lawsuit in Atlanta to stop Chips from selling the album. In the lawsuit Ringo said he recorded the album while on alcohol and drugs and considered it an embarrassment. Ringo testified at the trial that he had not signed a formal agreement with Moman. In response, Moman's attorney said his client would never have agreed to work with Ringo without an agreement. In a light moment, Ringo took the stand and delighted courtroom spectators by hamming it up into the microphone: "Is it on? Are we rolling, Bob?"

During the trial Toni phoned and asked if I would come to Atlanta to testify. I had never seen Ringo drink or use drugs in the studio, so I told her I would be happy to testify. I rushed to the airport, but a sudden thunderstorm delayed the taxi and made me miss my flight. I phoned Toni and told her I had rescheduled the flight, but she said they had obtained a continuance and it would not be necessary for me to testify.

In the end, the court permanently barred the release of the album and ordered Ringo to pay Chips for the studio time. The old Memphis curse, hoodoo or otherwise, was again afoot. How many sessions could Chips lose and still keep the dream afloat?

■　●　■

In the summer of 1986 my Memphis music magazine, *Nine-O-One Network*, went on sale on newsstands in Memphis and northern Mississippi and was included in the *Class of '55* package that was offered in the telemarketing campaign for the album. The first subscriber was Johnny Cash. The check came in the mail and was signed by John R. Cash himself. Rosanne Cash, his Memphis-born daughter, later told me that Johnny liked the magazine so much he kept a copy on his nightstand table. Soon a subscription check arrived in the mail from Jerry Lee Lewis. With supporters like that, how could I go wrong?

Circulation expanded to fourteen states by the end of the first year. By the end of 1987 the magazine was sold on newsstands in all fifty states, throughout Canada, and in selected cities in Portugal and Japan. Letters arrived daily from Europe, especially from Sweden and West Germany. Word filtered in from the Soviet Union that articles from the magazine were being read on the air by the state-owned radio network. Occasionally, tourists from abroad showed up on the doorsteps to pose for pictures with the staff. *Nine-O-One* was one of the first glossy, four-color magazines to do feature articles on country artists. It was the first to target a baby boomer audience with a mixture of musical styles. We ran articles on the O'Kanes and Robert Cray alongside articles on Cinderella and Europe.

The second issue featured Ron Wood on the cover. Wood had come to Memphis to be in the Carl Perkins video. I interviewed him in a bus

Deborah Allen, c. 1986.
Photo by James Dickerson

during a break in the shooting. We sat in the rear of the bus, along with his wife, Jo. He said Memphis music had had a profound impact on his career. "It was precious to get good stuff from America," he says. "It was a rare commodity to get ahold of that stuff in England. It was treasured as soon as you got ahold of it, so you did the best with it you could. Whereas the guys over here that were making it and the people who were listening to it, it was right under their nose, so they probably didn't realize it was that precious."

Deborah Allen, the Memphis-born singer/songwriter who scored a big hit with "Baby, I Lied," was the cover story for the third issue. I had met her before leaving *The Commercial Appeal*, when I wrote about her efforts to stage a rally in Memphis's Liberty Bowl stadium in support of South African Bishop Desmond Tutu. The rally never took place (stadium officials said it would damage the playing field), but I called Bishop Tutu at his home in South Africa and spoke to him about Deborah. Tutu said he had received a "heartwarming" call from Deborah at a time when he was under severe harassment. The call meant a lot to him. To my surprise, at the end of our conversation Tutu uttered the words "bless you," which from someone else would have been mere conversational filler. From Bishop Tutu, those words resounded with thunder that could have parted the Red Sea.

Other *Nine-O-One* cover stories focused on Aimee Mann; Robert Cray; Gregg Allman, who called me from a studio in Miami, trashed his former wife, Cher, then asked me not to use his comments (he just wanted to get it off his chest); David Bowie; Ann and Nancy Wilson, who gave me one of my favorite interviews; the Bangles, who gave me one of my most playful interviews; and Dan Fogelberg, who, despite a reputation for press bashing, called to do an interview after he saw the magazine on a New England newsstand.

We were the first music publication to take a look at sexual harassment. We ran a cover story on the subject in 1988 after a tearful female employee of a local studio came into our office complaining of treatment she had received by her employer. One evening after work, the studio owner held her down on the floor and ejaculated on her clothing. The next day she confronted the man, only to have her outrage rejected as hysterics. After the confrontation, as if to prove his point, the studio owner walked around the studio with his penis hanging out of his pants: "Penis? What penis? I don't see a penis." When the woman rejected subsequent advances, she was fired. She filed a complaint with the Equal Employment Opportunity Commission. An official there told her they had received similar complaints from fourteen other women, but there was nothing the agency could do because the studio was too small to qualify for intervention.

■ ● ■

Stevie Ray Vaughan stood at the rear entrance of the Peabody Hotel, Memphis's last surviving link to a genteel era that never existed. He shyly backpedaled into the shadows as fashionably dressed yuppie couples brushed past. Wearing a brightly colored parka with Mexican designs and a black, western-style hat, he did anything but blend into his surroundings. Incredibly, no one seemed to notice him.

Stevie was in town to record his *In Step* album. It would be his last solo effort. A second album, *Family Style*, was recorded in Memphis with his brother Jimmie. I was at the Peabody to take Stevie to an interview for *Pulsebeat: The Voice of the Heartland*, the radio syndication I had begun in 1988. I produced two weekly programs, a thirty-minute country show and a sixty-minute blues show in partnership with radio station KFFA in Helena.

Before he went to Memphis, Stevie made his publicist, Charles Comer of New York, promise he would arrange no interviews while he was recording the album; but Comer fudged on that promise and urged him to do the *Pulsebeat* interview as a favor to me. Stevie was registered at the hotel under the name Ben T. Fender; it would be the only interview he granted while recording the album. We set the interview up for the afternoon so he could sleep late after the previous night's session and have time to attend an Alcoholics Anonymous meeting. Stevie had been drug and alcohol free for four years. It was a daily battle.

On the way to the studio Stevie asked if he could smoke. I am a nonsmoker but told him I didn't mind. He seemed to enjoy the cigarette until he pulled out the ashtray and saw that it had never been used. After that he lost interest in the cigarette, holding it at arm's length as if it were a sparkler someone had handed him at a Fourth of July picnic.

Onstage, Stevie had a power-charged presence that made him seem larger than life. Attending a Stevie Ray Vaughan concert was like

Stevie Ray Vaughn at a Memphis hotel.
Photo by James Dickerson

strapping yourself into a rollercoaster: it was not a ride during which you chatted and exchanged pleasantries. It was a foot-stomping, arm-waving, screaming-at-the-top-of-your-voice descent into hellfire. In person Stevie was just the opposite. He was soft-spoken and unpretentious. He was polite and laughed easily, often flashing a down-home grin that betrayed his rural Texas roots. Older women would have called him a sweet boy.

Stevie marveled at the spiritual energy that radiated from Memphis. He gazed out at the streets. In his eyes they were the yellow brick road to Oz. "This is where it all started," he said, looking in the direction of a shopping mall but seeing, instead, some sweltering primeval pool of raw-edged music history. Memphis was a mystery to him. He asked lots of questions. He felt the power, but he couldn't help but wonder what it would be like to be of the blood. That was why he recorded in Memphis: to tap into the bloodline.

At the studio this notion of feeling the music came up often. That was the greatest lesson he had learned from listening to the old masters: "Feel what you play before you play it and then feel it while you play it. I learned early on that if I didn't really care about what I played, it would sound that way. Money pays the bills, but it's not the best thing in life. What we go through inside, that's really it."

Stevie was pleased with the way the album was going. "It's the first record we've ever done sober," he said. "A lot of us [in music] are alcoholics and addicts. But that condition is not just art-related. It's rampant through all parts of society. A lot of artists are under pressure to be larger than life. Thank God some of us have the chance to live through it. Some of us haven't. I'm glad to be among the fortunate ones."

One of Stevie's favorite songs on the album happened by accident. Stevie and his band were at a rehearsal trying to decide what to put on the album. They had run out of ideas. A quietness fell over the room. Stevie drifted over to a corner, his guitar strapped around his neck. Suddenly, there was an explosion in the far corner: a case of spontaneous combustion. "I just felt I had to play this thing," said Stevie. The song, an instrumental he named "Travis Walk," bubbled up from nowhere. "I had never heard it before or thought of it before. It just sort of exploded. It's one of those 'get it' songs."

**Kim Wilson, Jimmie Vaughn, and Dave Edmunds of the
Fabulous Thunderbirds. Photographed at Ardent Studios
during a break in their *Hot Number* sessions.**
Photo by James Dickerson

Like his brother, Jimmie Vaughan was a lifelong fan of Memphis
music. In fact, it was his idea for the Fabulous Thunderbirds to record
in Memphis. "I had never recorded here, and we had done it in London,
in Los Angeles, in New York, and in Austin and Dallas, so we just
decided to do it here," explained Jimmie. Dave Edmunds, who produced
the T-Birds' *Hot Number* album, said he wanted to work in Memphis
because of the players. Jimmie said amen to that. "It's magic here,"
he said.

While they were recording *Hot Number*, I dropped by Ardent studio several times. Once, during a break, Jimmie, lead singer Kim Wilson, Dave Edmunds, their manager, Mark Proctor, and I piled into a minivan for a trip to Beale Street. The other two T-Birds, Fran Christina and Preston Hubbard, had returned to Austin. As the heavy-footed driver sped downtown, tossing us about like loose cabbages, Kim peered out the window. "Man, the people in this town drive like crazy," he said. I responded that Memphis, according to insurance company statistics, was the traffic-light accident capital of the country. With that, Kim eyed the traffic signals with new interest. Was there no limit to the world records held by Memphis?

We went to a restaurant where Joe Savarin, founder of the Blues Foundation, presented them with an award, after which a lady in a white dress strolled up to Kim and cooed, "Sing for me." Seconds later, Kim waved goodbye and dashed out the kitchen into the night air. A few days before that he was walking on the street when a woman shouted out that she just loved his music. "Thank you," he said. Then the woman added: "And I just love the way you play guitar."

Back at the studio, Dave said he had been looking forward to solving the mystery of the Memphis Horns. "I always thought the horns on the old Stax records sounded so unique, and I wondered how they did it," he said. "Now I've worked with them, and I still don't know."

"With a horn player, you can't settle for anything less than the best, and those guys just blew me away," said Kim. "It was entertaining to watch them work. I just sat there, drank beer, and watched them play. I told myself, 'You'd better keep your mouth shut; anything you can think of, they probably thought of years ago.'"

■ ● ■

Ever since the Moman-Belz confrontation, the music community had taken sides. Everyone had a bone to pick. A local music magazine, the *Memphis Star*, published a readers poll in 1987 that gave Moman and Belz its "Captain Oblivion Space Cadet Award" for "stupidity." Backbiting and dirty tricks once again became a way of life for local musicians.

Chips Moman had good days and bad days. By 1988 the entire city had turned against him. Projects were sabotaged. Enemies—and there were plenty—plotted to drive him from town. His son, Casey, came home from school wiping tears from his eyes, upset that friends that used to like him now ridiculed him. Chips made regular sweeps at the studio to eradicate hidden microphones. The only secure room in the studio, he felt, was the control room. Three Alarm was under siege.

The atmosphere was so tense that, emulating Chips, I took steps to protect myself whenever I visited the studio. I never told Chips. That would have made him even more jumpy. There was this feeling at the studio that at any given moment mob gorillas might burst in the door, guns blazing. Chips made lots of deals when he returned to Memphis: deals for a studio; deals for equipment; deals for a record label; deals for a restaurant; deals for just about anything you could think of. I learned early on that once Chips left the familiar circle of the music industry, he was a babe in the woods. Blindly, he made one deal too many. He had absolutely no idea what he was walking into when he returned to Memphis.

Chips had recorded three albums in Memphis. All three were solid creative efforts, but none had torn up the charts. One of the constant criticisms he received from local musicians was that he was doing nothing for Reba and the Portables. They accused him of sitting on the group. Even Becky, the lead singer, expressed doubts to me about Chips's commitment to her career. Nothing could have been further from the truth. Chips tried hard to get Becky a deal with a major label. So did I. He probably didn't tell her about all the rejections (and there were plenty) for the same reason I didn't: it would have destroyed her morale. Plus, for Chips, there was some pride involved. It was hard to admit to Becky that he couldn't get her a record deal.

Somehow Chips kept making music. In 1988 he went to Texas to record an album with Willie Nelson. He liked working with Willie. The sessions were fast (Willie usually nailed a song on the first take), relatively painless (Willie's ego didn't need massaging), and usually profitable (Chip's *Always on My Mind* album with Willie was one of the most successful in country music history). Chips brought the album back to Memphis and mixed it at Three Alarm.

One day I got a call from Chips. He was at a summer house on Horseshoe Lake, across the river in Arkansas, and he and Toni were having a cookout for a few friends. A free meal sounded good to me. By that point I was subsisting largely on a diet of beans and rice. It was hot that day, pushing a hundred degrees, and we spent most of the day on the lake. Toni and Chips bickered constantly, for them an indication that they were still close. If they ever stopped bickering, it would mean the relationship was in trouble.

After the other friends left Chips played Willie's album. In a moment of supreme irony someone had titled it *What a Wonderful World*. In addition to the title song, the album consisted of old standards such as "Spanish Eyes" and "Blue Moon." The music had a healing quality to it. Had he recorded it with an unconscious wish to remake the world around him? When "What A Wonderful World" came up, Toni went into the kitchen (was the irony too painful for her to bear?). Chips and I sat in silence and listened as Willie extolled the colors of the rainbow and the cries of newborn babes. The last song on the album was "Ac-cent-tchu-ate the Positive." When the album ended, there was not a dry eye in the house.

Despite all the craziness, there were plenty of good times. Early one evening I got a call from Chips. Did I want to go on a boat ride? "Tonight?" I said, looking at my watch. Well, why not? I drove over to Chips's house at Waring and we hooked up a massive pontoon boat to his Blazer. Going with us were songwriter David Porter, whose hits "Soul Man," "Hold On, I'm Coming," and "When Something Is Wrong with My Baby" had influenced an entire generation, and another black gentleman, whose name I don't recall. I do remember he owned one of the local Wendy's franchises.

The lake was just across the state line in Mississippi. By the time we got there it was past midnight. The boat ramp was deserted, but among the four of us we were able to lower the pontoon boat into the water and get underway. For several hours we churned up and down the lake, talking about nothing in particular. There were no lights on the boat, but there was a partial moon and we could see where we were going.

Things were going great until I decided to tell my snake story. When I was growing up in Mississippi, I went fishing every week with my grandfather during the summer months. The lake was famous for its bream and its plentiful supply of poisonous cottonmouths. One day a girl was water skiing on the lake when the boat hit a massive bed of cottonmouths. The boat stalled in the water and the girl sank down into the snake swarm. She died before she reached the hospital. After I told the story, no one said a word. The water lapped at the pontoons.

"Speaking of the devil," said Chips, pointing out across the water. In the moonlight was the black triangular head of a cottonmouth slithering across the surface.

"That's it," says David. "I want to go home."

One of the first things Chips did when he moved back to Memphis was to put together a joint venture with Chappell and Intersong Music Group, an international song publisher that owned more than two hundred thousand song titles. It had been twenty years since Memphis had had a major song publisher. If Memphis music was to recapture the glory of its past, it was mandatory that the city jumpstart its publishing community. Ira Jaffe, a senior vice president with Chappell's office in Los Angeles, said the venture would enable his company to tap into the Memphis talent pool. "Chips Moman is a winner," said Jaffe. "When I first discussed it with him, we both said the Otis Reddings, the Elvises, the Box Tops—they couldn't all have just disappeared."

That was in 1985. Two years later Chips was forced to release all the Memphis songwriters he had signed to the publishing company. No sooner did that happen than he was hit with a phalanx of lawsuits over the construction of the studio. Contractors said he hadn't paid his bills. Chips countersued. He'd pay his bills when they finished the work. Then, when he thought nothing else possibly could go wrong, the songwriters filed lawsuits against him.

One day we were sitting in the control room drinking hot chocolate when the phone rang. Chips grimaced as he spoke on the phone. His responses were short: "Oh, no. No." The conversation was brief. He hung up the phone and hurried out of the room. I followed him out into the kitchen. His hands were shaking. He tried to pour himself another cup of hot chocolate.

"What's wrong?" I asked.

"My ex-wife is in the hospital." His eyes were glistening. "She's dying."

Chips looked desperate. Panic set in. He looked like he was going to jump out of his skin. "I'm going to the hospital," he said.

"You don't need to drive in your condition," I said. "I'll take you."

With Chips still clutching the cup of hot chocolate, we drove to the hospital a few blocks west of the old Sun Records studios. Chips's daughter, Monique, was in the waiting room with other family members when we arrived. A few minutes later Toni showed up. The waiting room quickly filled with family members. Chips left to visit his ex-wife. The prognosis was bleak. She had had several heart attacks and had to be resuscitated after the last one.

We stayed at the hospital for a few hours, then I took Chips back to the studio. He kept shaking his head the way people do when bad things happen. Life was closing in on him from every direction. His ex-wife lingered for a while longer, then gave up the fight. Her body was cremated and her ashes strewn along the banks of the Mississippi River.

I wondered how much more Chips could take.

■ ● ■

By 1989 *Nine-O-One Network* had suspended publication for lack of advertising revenues. The radio syndication *Pulsebeat: The Voice of the Heartland* was holding on by a slender thread. The death of a publication is always a sad affair, but it was especially so in this instance because with the demise of the magazine went any hopes of a reborn music industry.

Don Nix and I decided to start our own record label. We named it Pulsebeat Records, a spin-off from the radio syndication. We didn't have any money (I cashed in my life insurance policy to put up my share), but we had plenty of good ideas. By working on "spec" with studios and session players who believed in Memphis music, we hoped to record albums we could place with the majors for distribution. Stax had done it nearly thirty years ago. Maybe it could happen again. We also looked at producing specially packaged cassettes that could be sold on the radio syndication.

"The vast majority of the music heard on radio today can trace its roots back to Memphis," I told a newspaper reporter, then brashly added: "That makes Memphis an ideal place for an independent label. Simply put, we're going to pick up where Stax Records left off." Don's enthusiasm equaled my own. He told a reporter, "When someone sees a record label with the word Pulsebeat on it, I want them to know they have a quality product."

For our first artist we chose Don McMinn, a talented Beale Street bluesman. He was a fixture on the street, where his four-piece group appeared nightly as the house band at the Rum Boogie Café, a popular restaurant and bar. Over the years he had recorded with an impressive assortment of artists, including John Mayall, Memphis Slim, and Jerry Lee Lewis. He had recorded a couple of blues albums that had gone nowhere, so we thought we would point him in a different direction. In 1989 there was a "roots" mentality in country music. We decided to do a country album.

We put together a solid group of musicians, including Tommy McClure, then playing bass with Kris Kristofferson's band, drummer Greg Morrow, who played on the road with Amy Grant, keyboardist Doyle Newmyer, and an unknown steel guitarist named Robby Turner. Chips gave us spec time at Three Alarm, and his daughter, Monique, and Becky Russell came in to sing background. Nix and I assembled a solid list of songs, one of which, "Black Like Me," I thought would be a hit. Still do.

Unfortunately, the record executives in Nashville didn't agree. Something about a forty-something blues singer doing country music didn't sit right with them. I met with executives from all the labels. None would pick the album up for distribution. The only thing good that came from the McMinn session was that Chips dropped by to listen to what we were doing. He was so impressed with Robby Turner he hired him to play on the *Highwaymen 2* album. That opened other doors for Robby. Today he is regarded as one of the best steel guitar players in country music.

THE NINETIES
SOMEBODY GET THE LIGHTS,
PLEASE

n the spring of 1990 Shelby County Sheriff Jack Owens's face was blown away by a shotgun blast in the parking lot of a service station. There were no witnesses. Owens was the first law enforcement officer in Memphis and Shelby County ever to attempt a real war on drugs. He made the apprehension of drug dealers his first priority. A song was written about him; he was on his way to becoming a folk hero. Then, suddenly and without warning, his face was erased. Oddly, he seemed to know it was coming. In the months preceding his death he expressed fears of assassination. He started his car each morning with a remote-control device. After an investigation, his death was ruled a suicide.

By any measure 1990 was one of the worst years in Memphis music history. Chips Moman packed up and left town, again. Stevie Ray Vaughan was killed in a helicopter crash. My magazine, *Nine-O-One Network*, was thrown into bankruptcy, and the radio series *Pulsebeat: The Voice of the Heartland* went out of business. It was as if a bulldozer leveled the last vestiges of creativity, civility, and respect for the law.

No one was surprised when Chips left town. First Tennessee Bank sued him for defaulting on $2 million in bank loans. In the latter part of 1989 Chips sold Three Alarm to a used-car dealer to raise money for his mounting legal problems, but by 1990 Chips was suing the car dealer to recover missed payments. The dealer countersued Chips for removing equipment from the studio. First Tennessee Bank foreclosed on Chips's home at 191 Waring. Chips filed for Chapter 11 bankruptcy.

The insanity climaxed in November when Chips wound up in court with the used-car dealer in a dispute over ownership of the studio. During a hearing to determine ownership of certain equipment that Chips had removed from the studio, Chips jumped to his feet when the presiding judge, Chancellor D. J. Alissandratos, ordered him to return the equipment until a final ruling could be made. Chips protested. Alissandratos ordered Chips jailed for contempt of court. Said the judge, referring to a 1960s hit, "Since we're talking rock music, Mr. Moman, I might borrow from the song to remind you, as you go to jail—'I fought the law and the law won.'"

After forty-eight hours in jail Chips returned to the courtroom in handcuffs. He apologized to he court, saying, "I had a bad day . . . . I'm trying to learn. I do admit I sometimes lose my temper and I apologize." There were newspaper reports, never proved, that Chips grabbed the used-car dealer by the throat in the hallway. By then, public opinion had turned against Chips with a vengeance. *The Commercial Appeal* continued coverage of events—fair coverage, I thought—but reporters never looked below the surface to report why Chips was fighting for his life. Not so fair, I thought, was a story in the *Memphis Flyer*, a weekly tabloid. The front page, under the headline "GOODBYE, MR. CHIPS," read in part: "The city fathers brought him back to save Memphis music. But will Chips Moman just take the money and run?"

"What money?" Chips kept saying to me. His bafflement over what was happening to him was exceeded only by his frustration at his inability to do anything about it. He was under siege, but couldn't fight back, couldn't even defend his good name, because of fears he would endanger his family's safety. He was fighting a losing battle against an enemy that demanded anonymity.

Finally, by mid-year, worn to a frazzle, with no studio to work in, no house to live in, no friends, a son coming home from school each day in tears, a hostile media, and lawsuits at every turn, his health deteriorating (he had crippling episodes of arthritis), Chips, arguably one of the most successful record producers in American history,

packed up his family and returned to his farm in Nashville. Contacted by a reporter from *The Commercial Appeal*, Chips's Atlanta lawyer
said that Chips was tired of being a whipping boy: "He's had about all
the fun he can take here." Chips left town without a word to me. I
got a telephone call from him several months later. He was driving
around Atlanta, and he called me on his car phone. He just wanted to
say hello. He didn't know what he was going to do. He was a refugee.
I wanted to tell him I was sorry I had ever encouraged him to move
back to Memphis, but some things are better left unsaid.

■   ●   ■

When I heard the news that Stevie Ray Vaughan had been killed in a
helicopter crash, I called Charles Comer. As a publicist, Comer was a
heavyweight, working with the Rolling Stones, even the Beatles, but
all those years of press savvy were inadequate to deflect the emotion
he felt over the loss of Stevie. There was anguish in his voice when
he spoke of the death, or rather when he spoke of a life marked by a
constant struggle for sobriety. The tragedy of Vaughan's death was
that it came at the moment he had just put his life together. He was
sober, in love with the girl of his dreams, and enjoying the first
commercial success of his career. He told Comer: "I've been given a
second chance in life, and not many people get a second chance." After
the accident *Billboard* called Comer to tell him Vaughan's *In Step* album
was going to No. 14 with a bullet. "We've never been higher than
thirty-one in our lives," Comer told me. "It's selling fantastically."

Driving home that night, I pulled out the ashtray in my car. There
it was: Stevie's cigarette butt, just as he had left it, unfinished, a
burned-out reminder of life's short fuse.

■   ●   ■

Although *Nine-O-One* and *Pulsebeat*, the radio syndication, were no
longer in business, I kept the office open to focus on Pulsebeat, the
record label. There was a staff of one. Through an unlikely series of
events, I was approached by a delegation of Russians who had come

to the United States from Moscow to network with music executives.

They wanted to know if I would represent a Russian rockabilly band named Mister Twister. They had talked to a Los Angeles producer, Richard Podolor, best known for his work with Three Dog Night, Alice Cooper, and Black Oak Arkansas, about working with a hard rock group, Galaxy. I spoke to Podolor, who said he had heard Galaxy perform in Los Angeles and was interested in working with them. I was intrigued, so I asked the Russians to send tapes and photos. Visually, Mister Twister was a throwback to the 1950s: black leather, tattoos, rebel flags, lots of attitude. Musically, they were right on target. They sent me a videotape of "Blue Suede Shoes." Valery Lysenko, the drummer, played standing up, rockabilly style, and bassist Oleg Usamov, a former English student at Moscow University, sang in decent enough English. I thought they were salable to an American audience.

Their spokesman was Erkin Touzmuhammad, a Moscow-based music journalist. Based on a long series of telephone conversations, Erkin and I became friends. For a communist turned capitalist, he possessed just the right mix of cynicism and idealism. There was no middle ground for him. By the time the delegation made it back to their American base in Brighton Beach, New York, I agreed to represent them, and contracts were signed before they returned to Moscow.

Politically, the situation appealed to me very much. This was before the fall of the Soviet Union. Mister Twister and a number of other groups were under the direction of Ovanes Melik-Pashayev, one of the top record producers in the Soviet Union. His production company, Moscow Rock Organization, had created controversy in 1989 when they held a "Rock Fest" at the nuclear test site at Semipolatsinsk to protest nuclear testing. Not only were they playing Memphis music in Moscow nightclubs, but they were also duplicating American peace marches. Valery, who was nicknamed Hedgehog, was enrolled in KGB Special College when he was given an ultimatum by school officials: he could be a rock 'n' roll drummer or a KGB agent, but not both. Valery chose rock 'n' roll. That took guts in 1989. These were my kind of people.

The *Nashville Tennessean* ran an item about Mister Twister in June 1990 that credited me with becoming "the first American music mogul to bring a Russian band to the U.S. to record." While the Russians worked on their English, I put together a "girls" group made up of Becky Russell; Pamela Byrd, a former Miss Memphis who had a girlish upper range; and Michelle Necaise, a tall, twenty-year-old, blue-eyed vocal ringer for Donna Summer. I named the group Heat Wave.

At the time, I was helping Jim Stewart and Bobby Manuel with a fabulous R&B group, the Coolers. They had been around for several years, and Duck Dunn had been one of the group's charter members. When I told them about Heat Wave, they expressed an interest in coproducing the group, using musicians from the Coolers as needed. We used their studio, the Daily Planet, an analog-equipped music factory tucked away on a side street in a black neighborhood. Working with Jim was an experience unto itself. Bobby did the guitar work on the tracks, proving that he is still the best guitarist in Memphis, but he and Jim alternated on the board. Jim has a terrific ear for vocals, and I was amazed at how precise he was at giving direction to the women.

By 1990 Jim's full beard had grayed and he had a professorial look. He resembled Sigmund Freud, a stark contrast to his high-rolling, bell-bottomed look in the 1970s. Watching him work was a treat. When the music played, his foot tapped and his head bobbed with the beat. It had been fourteen years since the rug had been pulled out from beneath him at Stax and he was still trying, giving it his best shot.

Nancy Hart, a feature reporter for WMC-TV, the local NBC affiliate, asked if she could do a story on the group. Jim didn't want to do it at first. He had done few interviews over the years; I don't think he had ever done a TV interview. He agreed to do the interview as a favor to me, I suspect, and I arranged for Nancy to bring a camera crew into the studio. "These guys are great, they can really sing," Jim said during the interview, giving Memphis its first small-screen look, ever, at one of the giants of American music. "Nothing like this has ever come out of Memphis." Jim said music was a "now" kind of business: "You can't live in the past if you want to stay in the business. You have to be mainstream, rather than recreate a Memphis sound."

Nancy left knowing she had something, not just for the evening news, but for the archives. The story ran in two parts. We were all optimistic about the group. The time seemed right for another girl group, but when I shopped the demos in New York and L.A., I ran into a brick wall. Girl groups are a thing of the past, they told me. Nine months later Wilson Phillips, a group very similar to Heat Wave, had the No. 1 record in the nation.

Undeterred, I went to Nashville to pitch Mister Twister. Russians singing rockabilly! The boys on Music Row, even the ones I had known for years, just didn't get it. Let me get this straight, one label head said: You want me to put out a record of Commies singing rockabilly? No, they're not Communists, I explained, they're just the opposite. In spirit, at least, they're as American as apple pie. "Interesting," he said. "Commies, huh? Very interesting!"

I kept in touch with Erkin by fax and that Christmas he phoned from Moscow to wish me happy holidays. Muscovites didn't have a long history of phoning Christmas greetings to American friends, so I appreciated the call. I told Erkin the prospects didn't look good for Mister Twister, but I promised to stay on the case.

■ ● ■

Can anyone doubt that a curse lurks in the pyramids of the Memphis music pharaohs? Bob Pittman's QMI label ran into trouble before it ever got off the ground. Ella Brooks, its first signee, did not record an album for reasons that were never explained. Rumors attributed it to creative differences or personal problems. Whatever the reasons, she simply vanished from the local music scene. Shortly after the release of Jimmy Davis's first single, "Kick the Wall," QMI had a falling out with MCA, their distributor. Davis's album was left dangling in the wind, even as his video was played every three hours on MTV. With no promotion and distribution, sales were zilch. Then Pittman affiliated with Chrysalis Records. Davis recorded a second album for QMI, but Pittman was unable to reach an agreement with Chrysalis on international distribution arrangements, and Davis's second album was never released.

"We had spent a year making the [first] record and then went through the process of getting it out—and all of a sudden it was over," says Davis. The only money he realized from the two albums, he says, was from the advances, which he describes as small. "Part of me says that's the business, and I know it is, but, yeah, I got a raw deal. Some powerful men over money and pride sacrificed me and my music."

Jimmy Davis wasn't the only one having problems. After years of wrangling with Jerry Lee Lewis over payment of more than $3.7 million in back taxes, the Internal Revenue Service seized his possessions from his Nesbit, Mississippi, home while the singer was touring in Europe. After the seizure, Jerry Lee, his wife, Kerrie, and their six-year-old son, Lee, stopped off in Dublin, Ireland. While Jerry Lee worked on his autobiography, Kerrie sang at a tavern named Bad Bob's.

When the IRS announced plans to sell Jerry Lee's possessions at auction, Kerrie returned to Memphis. She hired a lawyer, who claimed that many of the possessions taken by the IRS belonged to Kerrie and were not subject to seizure. The lawyer got an injunction to prevent the agency from selling the items until Kerrie could inspect them.

A videotape of the seized items was shown in court. When images of Disney videos and Mickey Mouse bed sheets came into view, Kerrie brushed tears from her eyes. "Jerry doesn't sleep on Mickey Mouse sheets," she said, her voice breaking. In addition to items belonging to Lee, Kerrie asked for a collection of photographs and trophies. Kerrie told the court the trophies belonged to a park commission team she had organized and named the Killers. The baseball team, she told the court in a halting voice, was organized to counteract negative publicity about her husband: "I wanted something good since all you ever hear is bad." The judge ruled Kerrie was entitled to keep anything she could prove she had purchased.

Jerry Lee's possessions, about 350 items in all, were piled up in the main room of the auction house. I was there when Kerrie arrived to inspect them. "This is my life," she said, motioning to the enormous pile of household items, all numbered and neatly boxed. There was a look of disbelief on her face. "These are the things I've bought and collected in ten years of marriage. It's everything I've got." A female IRS agent looking through a box picked up a tiny automobile. "Oh," gasped Kerrie. "Could I have that for Lee to play with on the plane?" The IRS agent relinquished the toy, but not before contacting IRS headquarters in Washington, DC, to have a release form faxed to the auction house.

In March 1994 lawyers representing Jerry Lee reached an agreement with the IRS. The Killer ended his exile in Ireland and came home. Kerrie had accepted an award from Irish officials before leaving. They had never received anything like that in America, she said, adding that if they ever did, the IRS would probably impound it. Jerry Lee still owed the IRS money, but the government agreed to return some of his possessions and give him an opportunity to pay off the tab. The IRS was probably influenced by a recording contract offered from Sire/Elektra Records. The resulting album, titled *Young Blood*, was released in May 1995.

The Killer, the most relentless Horseman in the pack, was back, strong as ever. I was glad. For all his excesses, for all his problems and self-inflicted wounds, for all his bravado and arrogance and demonic eyes, he is the best rock 'n' roll piano player the world has ever seen.

■　●　■

"Memphis in May" is the city's showcase festival, a monthlong affair that celebrates a different country each year. Toward the end of the month the festival culminates with a concert that features dozens of big-name blues and rock artists. The honored country for 1993 was Russia. Not all Memphians were happy with the choice—there were rumblings of displeasure from the political right—but most Memphians were eager to learn more about Russia.

"Memphis in May" officials asked if I could book a Russian band for the festival. I considered Mister Twister until I learned from Erkin that Galaxy was recording in New York under a new name, Red Rage. In Moscow the band had sold an unprecedented 1.2 million albums. Erkin said the earlier deal with Podolor had fallen through and they were working with a New York production company. The band did not have a work visa and could not be compensated for their performance, but they agreed to perform in exchange for transportation and expenses. Erkin told me the band members were getting stir crazy in Brighton Beach and were eager to get the hell out of town.

When they arrived at the Memphis airport, I was there to greet them, along with van drivers for "Memphis in May." After two years of telephone conversations, it was my first face-to-face meeting with Erkin. Physically, he was the opposite of what I had envisioned. He had dark hair and a full beard. He didn't look like the Russians you saw in James Bond movies. It was nice to finally match a face to a voice. With him, to my delight, was Ovanes, who had flown in from Moscow to attend the festival. Five band members and a brooding delegation from Ovanes's Brighton Beach organization rounded out the group.

Ovanes fascinated me. He was heavyset, with his dark, thinning hair pulled back into a ponytail; he was probably in his mid-forties. He had begun as a record producer, at a time when it was a rarity, and through the years had developed a Quincy Jones type of reputation. After the walls of communism toppled, Ovanes became an entrepreneur. He took advantage of the changing economics of Russia to become a world-class trader of consumer goods. Erkin told me Ovanes was a millionaire many times over.

Moscow Rock Organization had several bands and solo artists on its roster; I was told I could represent any of them I wished. I considered the possibility of using Memphis as a headquarters for new Russian talent. Red Rage performed on both days of the festival. The weather was hot and the band members were miserable, but they gave a solid performance and the crowd loved their high-energy act. Because none of the band members spoke English, all communications with the sound crew had to go through Ovanes or Erkin. That created some interesting moments when problems arose and Russian words flew thick as Mississippi mud over the heads of the American crew. I particularly liked Slava Sintchouk, the lead vocalist. He had given up a career as a boxer for rock 'n' roll. He was well over six-feet tall, weighed about 220 pounds, and, onstage, displayed the aggressive posturing of a boxer. Before joining Red Rage, Oleg Hovrin, the drummer, had played drums in a folk group while serving in the Red Army in East Germany. Guitarist Dmitri Sharayev was a top-ranked session player in Moscow. All the band members had long, shoulder-length hair, like their American counterparts, and they constantly asked me the same question: "Where's the women?"

Everyone in the group was outgoing, with the exception of the Brighton Beach delegation, who stayed in the background and complained about the heat. I stayed with the group when they performed and traveled with them in the "Memphis in May" van from the hotel to the festival grounds. All the van drivers were volunteers, and as the trips back and forth increased, I noticed that more of the drivers were female. One perky young driver sent a hormonal tremor through the van when she turned around and asked, in that syrupy voice indigenous to Southern womanhood, "Honey, how do you say 'fuck' in Russian?"

■   ●   ■

During the early 1990s a number of hard rock groups, including Tora Tora and Roxy Blue, were signed in Memphis by major labels. For a while, they benefited from the same level of hype that Jimmy Davis had enjoyed a few years earlier. "There are a lot of people in Memphis getting record deals right now—and that's great they are—but that doesn't mean anything," Jimmy said. "It took us six months to get a deal, and two and a half years to get out of it."

The excitement generated in the early 1990s was short-lived. By 1995 Tora Tora and Roxy Blue had faded into obscurity, with neither group ever scoring a hit. When I called Tora Tora's label in 1995 to inquire about new product, they said, "Who's Tora Tora?" Roxy Blue, signed in 1992 by Geffen Records, received the biggest sendup of any band in recent memory. With Motley Crue's management and Guns 'N Roses's producer, Mike Clink, backing them, Roxy Blue was on its way to the "big time," or so the music critics said. When I called Geffen in 1995 for an update, they said the group was no longer on their roster.

As the century draws to a close, the proud and musically explosive Memphis music dynasty seems in the final stages of rigor mortis. Thankfully, three heavyweights—Jim Stewart, Bobby Manuel, and Jim Dickinson—are still there, still trying to breathe new life into the city's music scene. Dickinson almost threw in the towel in 1992, after going to New York to produce the Spin Doctors' second album, *Turn It Upside Down*. He completed the project, returned to Memphis, then

Jim Dickinson on Beale Street today.
Photo by James Dickerson

learned that the group's label remixed the entire album, erasing all of his work. Jim's reaction was understandable: he went into his room, closed the door, and didn't come out for two years. But Jim has it in his blood. By 1995 he was again poking and prodding Memphis's musical crevices, looking for lost knowledge.

Bobby Manuel is the last Memphis producer to score a No. 1 record, and the passing of two decades since that hit has not discouraged him from trying for another. My guess is that if he stays healthy, he'll eventually get it. Music is not a part-time job for him. He's at it seven days a week. Same situation with Jim Stewart. On any given day, you can find him working in the studio, usually with a black artist, recording new material for the R&B charts. He produced an album for Shirley Brown, *Fire & Ice*, that did well on the R&B charts in 1989, and more recently he has been experimenting with soulful rap variations.

"I have to believe I can make something happen," he says. "This town has been operating on finding a deal for the last ten years. I'm so sick of that word. It's talent . . . it's music. It's not a get-rich-quick business. It's a get-poor business. You can get poor quicker than you can get rich."

Jim doesn't like to look back. When he talks about Stax he does so as if peering through the reverse end of a telescope. He likes to keep his distance. When he assesses blame he spreads it around. Still, you get the feeling all is not forgiven. "Everyone ran for cover and got in some blows of their own to help push it under," he says. "Then they realized later, 'Wait a minute, we've lost something.' But it was too late then."

Today the two largest music-related industries in Memphis are Graceland and a dozen or so topless nightclubs. Graceland has become one of the most popular tourist attractions in America, so it's not surprising the biggest music event of the decade was the mammoth Elvis Tribute Concert held at the Pyramid in 1994. Sponsored by Graceland, it attracted scores of artists, from Michael Bolton to Cheap Trick to Tony Bennett. The highlight of the evening was an appearance by Lisa Marie Presley and Michael Jackson, an event so bizarre and appropriate that it seemed symbolic not only of the current state of Memphis music but of its tortured past as well.

Tax receipts show that the topless clubs are second only to Graceland in tourism dollars generated. Though the clubs do not offer live music, as the clubs did on Beale Street in the early days, they have assumed the same roles. When out-of-town recording artists visit Memphis, they sometimes go by Graceland, but they always go by the topless clubs. They hang out there after their shows, and they date the women who work in the clubs. It is one of the main reasons women work in the clubs. Sometimes the bands party at the clubs. Sometimes they invite the girls to parties at their hotels. It's the Beale Street of old, all over again.

Nikki, a striking twenty-year-old brunette from Little Rock, admits that is why she became a dancer. It enables her to meet her rock heroes. Why not just be a fan and hang out at the concerts? Her answer is blunt: "If you're a regular fan, a groupie, you have to suck their dicks. If you're a dancer, they'll let you dance for them and you don't have to suck their dicks."

Tiffany's is a favorite hangout. Guns 'N Roses went by after a concert one night, but Axl Rose left in a huff when a dancer walking down a crowded aisle brushed against him. He had given strict orders that no one could touch him. The other band members stayed. Metallica is another band that frequents the club, as does ZZ Top. One night former Black Oak Arkansas lead singer Jim "Dandy" Mangrum celebrated his birthday on the main stage at Tiffany's.

The clubs are the main drawing card for musicians who come to Memphis, just as the clubs on Beale Street were the main drawing cards in years past. They are the closest thing left to a music scene. The most significant change over the years is that while the female entertainers in the old days were exclusively black, today they are almost exclusively white. For every black woman competing for work as a singer or stripper, there are a hundred white women.

City officials understand the importance of the clubs to tourism, says Tiffany's owner Steve Cooper, but they won't admit it for fear of voters' wrath. "It's a good ole dog for the politicians to pick on," he says. "I don't blame them from the standpoint it keeps them in office. It helps bring in the votes of the fifty- to sixty-year-olds. The closer you get to meeting God, the closer you come to voting to put [the clubs] out of business."

■　●　■

When the blues were hot the performers were young and vibrant. With time, they aged—and their music aged—and eventually their music was replaced by rock 'n' roll. Today we are seeing the same phenomenon with rock. The Rolling Stones are in the same situation Louis Armstrong was in the late 1950s: old men playing a young man's music. Nothing new in rock 'n' roll has been created since the early days at Sun Records. Of course, youth will find a replacement for rock 'n' roll, just as it did for blues and jazz. Maybe they'll find it in Memphis; maybe not. There are those who say Memphis's legacy may be its past. I'm not sure I agree. What happened in Memphis was less an accident of nature as it was a product of the Beast . . . and the Beast lives.

As the century draws to a close Memphis has spun full circle. Once again, it has one of the highest murder rates in the country. Tourists are routinely shot and robbed on Beale Street, as they were at the turn of the century. Drug addiction is soaring. The Hoodoo cartel is stronger than ever. The crime rate, at times, seems overwhelming. Within the past few years a FBI and a DEA agent based in Memphis have been convicted of drug trafficking. A 1995 investigation by *The Commercial Appeal* found sixty-eight convicted felons working in the city school system, along with fifteen hundred other workers with convictions ranging from patronizing prostitution to drug possession.

In July 1995 seven members of a Colombian drug cartel's hit team were arrested in Memphis on charges they conspired to murder several of the city's major drug dealers. Federal authorities said the men had been sent via New York by the Cali cartel to collect up to $5 million in unpaid debts. William Renton, the agent in charge of the DEA office in Memphis, said the arrests proved Memphis had become a market of choice for the Cali cartel. Three years earlier DEA agent Tom Fekete, Renton's predecessor, had organized an eleven-agency task force to combat drug cartel activity in Memphis. The same geographic facts that had made the city America's distribution center, Fekete told a reporter for *The Commercial Appeal*, also made it a hub for drug sales.

All that's missing in Memphis today is another Boss Crump.

In 1994, as so many had done before me, I loaded up a truck with my possessions and headed east to Nashville. I left behind a handful of friends, a pair of burned-out dreams, and the grave of a woman whose spirit hovers over the city . . . . Looking in my rear-view mirror, I surveyed the skyline one last time. Yes, I now understood, even the Four Horsemen knew when to ride with the wind.

Once I got settled in Nashville I gave Chips a call. We talked about getting together, but it was a year before I actually made it out to his farm. I called again in the spring of 1995. Toni answered the phone and said Chips didn't live at the house anymore. They were getting a divorce. He had built a studio out on the farm and was living at the studio. She gave me his number.

Chips told me to come on out. He'd like to see me. He wasn't there when I arrived, but Monique and her boyfriend, Kim, were at the studio, along with Rivers, a talented singer/songwriter Chips had discovered in Memphis. I had only been there a few minutes when Chips drove up. It was good to see him again. Though I had talked to him several times over the years, I had only seen him once since he left Memphis. He looked older, somewhat tired, but he still had the old Moman magic about him.

Chips played me the material he had been recording on Rivers, plus some things he had recorded with Monique. Other than working with family and friends, he didn't want to make any more records. Music wasn't fun anymore.

Monique went to the store and came back with a bag of hamburger. We cooked out on the grill, talked about the weather and some of the good times we had in Memphis, but we danced around the nightmare part of it. He couldn't look at me without thinking about the pain, and I couldn't look at him without thinking about the pain. It was a standoff.

"I took everything they threw at me," Chips said, shaking his head.

Indeed he had. Chips was as surely a victim of the Hoodoo cartel as Elvis could have been and Stax might have been—and Lord knows how many innocent passersby. But he was just as much a victim of his own fierce attraction to the cauldron of creativity known as Memphis music. For it is that witches brew that has made the city unique. You cannot understand Memphis music without understanding the political, social, and criminal forces at work in the city. They are intrinsically linked. Let others speak of the "mysteries" of Memphis music, as they have done for decades in popular magazines and scholarly books. For Chips and myself, at least, the mystery has been solved. Chips was lucky to escape with his life, and he knows that.

Before I left Chips and I went for a drive in my Miata. Chips had owned a Triumph in the early days in Memphis. He wanted to see if the Miata drove like his Triumph. We sped up and down the hilly countryside with the top down, Chips pushing the car to the max, zipping past the farms and dirt roads, making the gearbox whine, skating around the curves. The cool spring wind whipped against our faces. The sun shone brightly. Time stood still. It was a good way to end a day.

Toni Wine, James Dickerson (the author), and Chips Moman at the Moman farm in Nashville, 1985.
Photo courtesy of Dave Darnell

Chart Information

No. 1 Pop Records Recorded in Memphis by Memphis Artists
or for Memphis Labels

SONG	ARTIST	PRODUCER	LABEL	DATE
1. The Letter	The Box Tops	Dan Penn	Mala	1967
2. Dock of the Bay	Otis Redding	Steve Cropper	Volt	1968
3. Suspicious Minds	Elvis Presley	Chips Moman	RCA	1969
4. Theme from *Shaft*	Isaac Hayes	Isaac Hayes	Enterprise	1971
5. Let's Stay Together	Al Green	Willie Mitchell	Hi	1972
6. I'll Take You There	Staple Singers	Al Bell	Stax	1972
7. Disco Duck	Rick Dees	Bobby Manuel	Fretone	1976

Top 20 Pop Hits Recorded in Memphis or by Memphis Artists or Labels

SONG	ARTIST	DATE
1. Heartbreak Hotel	Elvis Presley	1956
2. Blue Suede Shoes	Carl Perkins	1956
3. I Want You, I Need You, I Love You	Elvis Presley	1956
4. Hound Dog/Don't Be Cruel	Elvis Presley	1956
5. Love Me Tender	Elvis Presley	1956
6. I Walk the Line	Johnny Cash	1956
7. Love Me	Elvis Presley	1956
8. Too Much	Elvis Presley	1957
9. All Shook Up	Elvis Presley	1957
10. Teddy Bear	Elvis Presley	1957
11. Whole Lot of Shakin' Going On	Jerry Lee Lewis	1957
12. Jailhouse Rock	Elvis Presley	1957
13. Raunchy	Bill Justis	1957
14. Great Balls of Fire	Jerry Lee Lewis	1957
15. Don't/I Beg of You	Elvis Presley	1958
16. Breathless	Jerry Lee Lewis	1958
17. Wear My Ring	Elvis Presley	1958

18.	Hard Headed Woman	Elvis Presley	1958
19.	Guess Things Happen That Way	Johnny Cash	1958
20.	Tragedy	Thomas Wayne	1958
21.	One Night	Elvis Presley	1958
22.	I Got Stung	Elvis Presley	1958
23.	A Fool Such as I	Elvis Presley	1959
24.	I Need Your Love Tonight	Elvis Presley	1959
25.	Big Hunk o' Love	Elvis Presley	1959
26.	My Wish Came True	Elvis Presley	1959
27.	Smokie, Part 2	Bill Black Combo	1960
28.	Stuck on You	Elvis Presley	1960
29.	White Silver Sands	Bill Black Combo	1960
30.	Only the Lonely	Roy Orbison	1960
31.	It's Now or Never	Elvis Presley	1960
32.	Don't Be Cruel	Bill Black Combo	1960
33.	Blue Angel	Roy Orbison	1960
34.	Are You Lonesome Tonight?	Elvis Presley	1960
35.	Surrender	Elvis Presley	1961
36.	Gee Whiz	Carla Thomas	1961
37.	Running Scared	Roy Orbison	1961
38.	I Feel So Bad	Elvis Presley	1961
39.	Last Night	Mar-Keys	1961
40.	Cryin'	Roy Orbison	1961
41.	Little Sister	Elvis Presley	1961
42.	His Latest Flame	Elvis Presley	1961
43.	Can't Help Falling in Love	Elvis Presley	1962
44.	Dream Baby	Roy Orbison	1962
45.	Good Luck Charm	Elvis Presley	1962
46.	She's Not You	Elvis Presley	1962
47.	Green Onions	Booker T. & the MGs	1962
48.	Return to Sender	Elvis Presley	1962
49.	In Dreams	Roy Orbison	1963
50.	One Broken Heart for Sale	Elvis Presley	1963
51.	Devil in Disguise	Elvis Presley	1963

52.	Mean Woman Blues	Roy Orbison	1963
53.	Bossa Nova Baby	Elvis Presley	1963
54.	Walking the Dog	Rufus Thomas	1963
55.	Kissin' Cousins	Elvis Presley	1964
56.	It's Over	Roy Orbison	1964
57.	Oh Pretty Woman	Roy Orbison	1964
58.	Ask Me	Elvis Presley	1964
59.	Wooly Bully	Sam the Sham & the Pharaohs	1965
60.	Crying in the Chapel	Elvis Presley	1965
61.	Hold What You've Got	Joe Tex	1965
62.	I'm Yours	Elvis Presley	1965
63.	Keep on Dancing	Gentrys	1965
64.	Lil' Red Riding Hood	Sam the Sham & the Pharaohs	1966
65.	Land of 1000 Dances	Wilson Pickett	1966
66.	Born a Woman	Sandy Posey	1966
67.	Single Girl	Sandy Posey	1967
68.	Respect	Aretha Franklin	1967
69.	Baby I Love You	Aretha Franklin	1967
70.	Funky Broadway	Wilson Pickett	1967
71.	Soul Man	Sam & Dave	1967
72.	A Natural Woman	Aretha Franklin	1967
73.	Chain of Fools	Aretha Franklin	1968
74.	I Thank You	Sam & Dave	1968
75.	Cry Like a Baby	Box Tops	1968
76.	Think	Aretha Franklin	1968
77.	Hooked on a Feelin'	B. J. Thomas	1969
78.	If I Can Dream	Elvis Presley	1969
79.	Hang 'Em High	Booker T. & The MGs	1969
80.	Time Is Tight	Booker T. & The MGs	1969
81.	In the Ghetto	Elvis Presley	1969
82.	Sweet Caroline	Neil Diamond	1969
83.	A Boy Named Sue	Johnny Cash	1969

84. Sugar Sugar*	The Archies	1969
85. Suspicious Minds	Elvis Presley	1969
86. Holly Holy	Neil Diamond	1969
87. The Thrill Is Gone	B. B. King	1970
88. Don't Cry Daddy	Elvis Presley	1970
89. The Wonder of You	Elvis Presley	1970
90. I Just Can't Help Believing	B. J. Thomas	1970
91. You Don't Have to Say	Elvis Presley	1970
92. Proud Mary	Ike & Tina Turner	1971
93. Tired of Being Alone	Al Green	1971
94. Respect Yourself	Staple Singers	1971
95. Look What You Done for Me	Al Green	1972
96. I'm Still in Love with You	Al Green	1972
97. Burning Love	Elvis Presley	1972
98. You Ought to Be with Me	Al Green	1972
99. Here I Am (Come and Take Me)	Al Green	1973
100. If You're Ready Come Go with Me	Staple Singers	1973
101. The Most Beautiful Girl	Charlie Rich	1974
102. Sha-La-La (Make Me Happy)	Al Green	1974
103. L-0-V-E	Al Green	1975
104. Another Somebody Done	B. J. Thomas	1975
105. Let's Do It Again	Staple Singers	1975
106. Higher and Higher	Rita Coolidge	1977
107. Bette Davis Eyes**	Kim Carnes	1981
108. Always On My Mind***	Willie Nelson	1982
109. Legs	ZZ Top	1984
110. Sleeping Bag	ZZ Top	1985
111. Burning Heart	Survivor	1985
112. In This Love	Survivor	1986
113. Angel of Harlem	U2	1989
114. Stand	R.E.M.	1989
115. You Got It	Roy Orbison	1989

* written by Toni Wine Moman
** written by Memphian Donna Weiss
*** produced by Chips Moman after he left Memphis

notes

1. Four Horsemen in Search of an Apocalypse

I was present for the entire *Class of '55* session and conducted extensive interviews with the participants on a daily basis. All quotes used in this section are taken from those interviews. Some portions of this chapter are reprinted with permission of *The Commercial Appeal*.

The account of Rick Nelson's flight from Memphis is derived from an interview the author did with Marty Stuart in 1986.

2. In the Beginning, the Blues Were King

Additional information about Memphis's status as the murder capital of the United States can be found in the studies conducted by the Prudential Insurance Company throughout the 1910s, 1920s, and 1930s. Information about the city's problems with cocaine and the booming sex industry can be found in daily news accounts published by *The Commercial Appeal* and from accounts of the era published by the Memphis Police Association. I penned the name "Hoodoo cartel"; information about the cartel is based on my study of the families involved for a period that spans seventy years. I also drew on information of a general nature from George Lee's *Beale Street* and John Harkins's *Metropolis of the American Nile*.

I have used *Press-Scimitar* in keeping with the newspaper's own policy of using the abbreviated version on second reference and on bylines.

The comments by Miles Davis about sex and jazz were made in a taped interview I conducted in 1985.

The account of the William Latura incident was obtained from Memphis Police Department records.

The account of Lil Hardin's death is taken from a United Press International dispatch on August 28, 1971.

3. The Twenties: Furry, Minnie, Sleepy, and Abe

The musical accomplishments of Abe Fortas and the Blue Melody Boys were well documented by *The Commercial Appeal* and the *Press-Scimi-*

tar throughout the 1920s and early 1930s. Both newspapers followed Fortas's career closely until his resignation from the Supreme Court.

Information about the influx of young women into Memphis and the Woman's Protective Bureau can be found in information published by the Memphis Police Association. A 1973 publication by the association offers a case breakdown for the bureau's activities for 1923.

The account of how Furry Lewis made his bottlenecks was provided by Don Nix, who watched him do it on more than one occasion.

Hammie Nixon told various interviewers over the years about Memphis Minnie's sexual exploits. One of the best source books I have found about Memphis Minnie is Beth and Paul Garon's *Woman with Guitar: Memphis Minnie's Blues*. They examine Memphis Minnie's sexuality with fairness and more than a little compassion.

Bonnie Raitt's comments are from an interview I conducted in 1985.

Memphis Minnie's "last" party in 1968 was reported on by *The Commercial Appeal* and the *Press-Scimitar*.

4. The Thirties: Slip-Sliding Away

I was able to reconstruct the methods the Hoodoo cartel used to build their empire by comparing public records of known crime families with newspaper accounts of their business exploits.

The interview with Thomas Pinkston was conducted by Jim Dickinson for his Delta Experimental Projects Compilation album, *Down Home*.

The quotes from Memphis Slim are drawn from interviews contained in the Special Collections room of the University of Memphis library.

Details of the Saddle and Spur Club incident were obtained from stories published by *The Commercial Appeal*.

W. C. Handy's return to Memphis in December 1939 was reported on by both *The Commercial Appeal* and the *Press-Scimitar*.

5. The Forties: The Door Slams Shut

Quotes from Sunshine Sonny Payne about Sonny Boy Williamson 2 are taken from my interviews with him in 1989.

All quotes from B. B. King in this book are taken from interviews I conducted in 1985, 1986, 1989, and 1995.

6. The Fifties: Sowing the Seeds of Revolution

Bobby "Blue" Bland's comments are from an interview I conducted in 1989.

Sam Phillips's comments about "Uncle Silas" are taken from material in the Special Collections room of the University of Memphis library.

All comments from Rufus Thomas in this book are taken from interviews I conducted with him.

Information about the televised Kefauver hearings was obtained from *Facts On File* and Harvey Swados's *Standing Up for the People: The Life and Work of Estes Kefauver*.

The best source of information about Abe Fortas's career can be found in Bruce Allen Murphy's excellent biography, *Fortas: The Rise and Ruin of a Supreme Court Justice*. Much of the source material about Fortas used in this book was obtained from news stories in *The Commercial Appeal* and the *Press-Scimitar*.

This account of Scotty Moore's first meeting with Elvis Presley was based on my interviews with Moore in 1994.

Jack Clement's recollections of his first meeting with Elvis are taken from my interviews with him in 1995. I also interviewed Clement in 1985 and 1986.

Sam Phillips's comments about selling the Elvis contract were taken from material from the Special Collections room of the University of Memphis library. I conducted additional interviews with Phillips in 1985 and 1986.

All Carl Perkins quotes in this book, unless otherwise identified, are drawn from my interviews with him in 1986, 1987, and 1988.

All Johnny Cash quotes in this book are taken from my interviews with him in 1985, 1986, and 1987.

7. The Sixties: From Sweet Soul to Southern Rock

All quotes from Estelle Axton in this book are taken from an interview I conducted with her in 1995.

All quotes from Chips Moman in this book are taken from interviews I conducted with him in 1985, 1986, 1987, 1988, 1989, and 1995.

The quote from Chips Moman's father was taken from an interview I conducted with him in 1986.

Jim Stewart's comments are taken from interviews in the Special Collections room at the University of Memphis library.

All quotes from Carla Thomas in this book were taken from interviews I conducted with her in 1989.

All quotes from Booker T. Jones in this book are taken from interviews I conducted with him in 1986.

All quotes from Don Nix in this book are taken from interviews I conducted with him in 1989, 1990, and 1995.

All quotes from Donald "Duck" Dunn and Steve Cropper in this book are taken from interviews I conducted with them in 1985 and 1986.

8. The Sixties: Stax, American, and Hi Spin Hits Galore

Jim Stewart's comments are from an interviews in *Nine-O-One Network*.

David Porter's comments are from an interview in *Nine-O-One Network*.

Willie Mitchell's comments are from interviews I conducted with him in 1986 and 1989.

T. G. Sheppard's comments are from interviews I conducted with him in 1988, 1989, and 1995.

John Evans's comments are from an interview I conducted with him in 1995.

Details of Otis Redding's plane crash were obtained from the National Transportation Safety Board. Ben Cauley's recollections of the crash were taken from an article by Bill Stuart that was published in *Nine-O-One Network*.

The death threats against Senator Robert Griffin of Michigan were reported by the Associated Press. The comments by Hamilton S. Burnett about Abe Fortas were also reported by the Associated Press.

This account of Elvis Presley's Memphis session was told to the author by Chips Moman.

9. The Seventies: The Dream Dies Hard

The attempted Bob Dylan booking was reported by *The Commercial Appeal*.

All quotes from Toni Wine Moman in this book are derived from interviews I conducted with her in 1985, 1986, 1987, 1988, and 1995.

All quotes from Rita Coolidge in this book are derived from interviews I conducted with her in 1985.

All quotes from Bobby Manuel in this book are derived from interviews I conducted with him in 1985, 1986, 1990, and 1995.

All quotes from Jim Dickinson in this book are derived from interviews I conducted with him in 1985, 1986, and 1995.

All quotes from John Fry in this book are derived from interviews I conducted with him in 1985 and 1986.

The source for Elvis's Stax session was stories written by Jim Kingsley, a reporter with *The Commercial Appeal*. Kingsley died in 1995.

Both *The Commercial Appeal* and the *Press-Scimitar* provided extensive coverage of the legal difficulties experienced by Stax.

Jim Stewart's letter to the sheriff requesting a gun permit for Al Jackson was reported in *The Commercial Appeal*.

Details of the murder of Al Jackson were obtained from the Memphis Police Department, *The Commercial Appeal*, and the *Press-Scimitar*.

10. The Eighties: Rising Out of the Ashes

All quotes from Susane Jerome Taylor are taken from my interviews with her.

All quotes from Gregg Geller are taken from my interviews with him. An extensive interview with Geller was published in the March/April 1987 issue of *Nine-O-One Network*.

All quotes from June Carter Cash are taken from my interviews with her in 1985 and 1986.

The account of the trip to Nashville was provided to me by Ron Terry, Dick Hackett, and Toni Wine Moman.

All quotes from Al Green are taken from my interviews with him in 1986.

All quotes from Gary Belz are taken from my interviews with him in 1986.

The $250,000 advance against royalties is the figure I recall being used at the time discussions were taking place at America Records, but I was not privy to the final contracts.

All quotes from Bobby Womack are taken from my interviews with him.

I was sitting in the living room with Moman when he received the telephone call, then waited at Moman's home while he left the house and returned a short time later and discussed the incident.

Jim Dickinson's comment about Memphis being the center of all evil in the known universe was first made to *Rolling Stone,* then subsequently repeated to me.

11. The Eighties: The Empire Strikes Back

The description of the U2 session at Sun Records was provided to the author by Jack Clement. Additional information about the session can be found in an article by Dawn Baldwin published in the *Memphis Star.*

All quotes from Bob Pittman are taken from my interviews with him.

All quotes from Ron Wood are taken from my interviews with him.

Additional information about the sexual harassment incident can be found in the February 1988 issue of *Nine-O-One Network.* The article was written by Nancy Randall.

All quotes from Stevie Ray Vaughan are taken from my interviews with him.

All quotes from Kim Wilson are taken from my interviews with him in 1986 and 1987.

12. The Nineties: Someone Get the Lights, Please

Sheriff Jack Owens's death was reported extensively by the Memphis media.

The account of Chips Moman's court appearance was gleaned from stories published in *The Commercial Appeal.*

All quotes from Jimmy Davis are taken from my interviews with him.

I attended the court proceedings involving Jerry Lee Lewis's difficulties with the IRS. I have used interviews with Lewis conducted in 1985 and 1986 as source material throughout the book.

All quotes from Jim Stewart are taken from my interviews with him. I obtained some source material in informal conversation with Stewart, other material from formal interviews and from an article I commissioned for *Nine-O-One Network*.

I took the quote from the twenty-year-old stripper named Nikki from interviews done with nearly one hundred Memphis dancers. They provided an invaluable source of information about the music industry, and the social, political, and economic substructure of the city. The story about Guns 'N Roses was told to me by several dancers. I was in Tiffany's and Platinum Plus when Jim "Dandy" Mangrum celebrated his birthday, and when members of ZZ Top and Metallica dropped by.

All quotes from nightclub owner Steve Cooper are taken from my interview with him in 1991.

The arrests of the hitmen from the Cali cartel were reported by *The Commercial Appeal*.

The arrests of FBI and DEA agents on drug-trafficking charges were not reported in the Memphis media, but were provided to me by former members of the agencies involved.

selected bibliography

Books

Booth, Stanley. *Rhythm Oil*. New York: Pantheon, 1991.

Bronson, Fred. *The Billboard Book of Number One Hits*. New York: Billboard, 1985.

Brown, Peter, and Steven Gaines. *The Love You Make: An Insider's Story of the Beatles*. New York: McGraw-Hill, 1983.

Carlin, Richard. *Rock and Roll: 1955–1970*. New York: Facts On File, 1988.

Chase, Gilbert. *America's Music: From the Pilgrims to the Present*. New York: McGraw-Hill, 1955.

Collier, James Lincoln. *Louis Armstrong: An American Genius*. New York: Oxford University Press, 1983.

Dickerson, Jim. *Coming Home: 21 Conversations about Memphis Music*. Memphis: Scripps Howard, 1985.

Garon, Beth and Paul. *Woman with Guitar: Memphis Minnie's Blues*. New York: Da Capo, 1992.

Gruber, J. Richard. *Memphis 1948–1958*. Memphis: Memphis Brooks Museum of Art, 1986.

Guralnick, Peter. *Sweet Soul Music: Rhythm and Blues and the Southern Dream of Freedom*. New York: Harper & Row, 1986.

———. *Last Train to Memphis: The Rise of Elvis Presley*. Boston: Little Brown, 1994.

Handy, W. C. *Father of the Blues: An Autobiography*. New York: Da Capo, 1941.

Harkins, John E. *Metropolis of the American Nile*. Oxford, MS: Guild Bindery, 1991.

Haskins, James. *Voodoo & Hoodoo: Their Tradition and Craft as Revealed by Actual Practitioners.* Chelsea, MI: Scarborough House, 1990.

Herzhaft, Gerard. *Encyclopedia of the Blues.* Fayetteville: The University of Arkansas Press, 1992.

Key, V. O., Jr., *Southern Politics.* New York: Random House, 1949.

Lee, George W. *Beale Street: Where the Blues Began.* College Park, MD: McGrath, 1969.

McAleer, Dave. *Hit Singles: Top Twenty Charts from 1954 to the Present Day.* San Francisco, CA: Miller Freeman, 1994.

Miller, William D. *Memphis During the Progressive Era.* Memphis: Memphis State University Press, 1957.

Muirhead, Bert. *The Record Producers File.* Dorset, UK: Blandford, 1984.

Murphy, Bruce Allen. *Fortas: The Rise and Ruin of a Supreme Court Justice.* New York: Morrow, 1988.

Panassie, Hugues. *Louis Armstrong.* New York: Da Capo, 1979.

Parker, John. *Elvis: The Secret Files.* London: Anaya, 1993.

President's Commission on Organized Crime. *Organized Crime and Cocaine Trafficking: Record of Hearing IV.* Washington, DC: U.S. Government Printing Office, 1994.

Schuller, Gunther. *Early Jazz: Its Roots and Musical Development.* New York: Oxford University Press, n.d.

Shaw, Arnold. *Dictionary of American Pop/Rock.* New York: Schirmer Books, 1982.

Swados, Harvey. *Standing Up for the People: The Life and Work of Estes Kefauver.* New York: Dutton, 1972.

Taylor, Frank. C. *Alberta Hunter: A Celebration in Blues.* New York: McGraw-Hill, 1987.

Tucker, David M. *Memphis Since Crump: Bossism, Blacks and Civic Reformers.* Knoxville: University of Tennessee Press, 1980.

Whitburn, Joel. *Billboard Top 1000 Singles (1955–1992)*. Milwaukee, WI: Hal Leonard, 1993.

Wilson, Charles Reagan, and William Ferris. *Encyclopedia of Southern Culture*. Chapel Hill: University of North Carolina Press, 1989.

Articles

Baldwin, Dawn. "Memphis Rocker: A Soft Touch for Romance." *Nine-O-One Network* (July/August 1987).

———. "The Main Attraction." *Nine-O-One Network* (November/December 1986).

———. "Inside the U2/Sun Studio Sessions." *Memphis Star*, December 1987.

Dickerson, James. "901 Interview with Robert Pittman." *Nine-O-One Network* (July/August 1987).

———. "B. B. King." *Nine-O-One Network* (December 1987).

———. "Memphis Women Rockers." *Nine-O-One Network* (January/February 1987).

———. "Perkins & Friends." *Nine-O-One Network* (July/August 1986).

———. "Portraits/Don Nix." *Nine-O-One Network* (December 1987).

———. "The Lady Wants to Rock & Roll, Now!" *Nine-O-One Network* (November/December 1986).

———. "The Fabulous Thunderbirds Get a Memphis Groove." *Nine-O-One Network* (May/June 1987).

———. "Together Again." *Nine-O-One Network* (November/December 1986).

———. "901 Interview with Gregg Geller." *Nine-O-One Network* (March/April 1987).

———. "901 Interview with Ron Wood." *Nine-O-One Network* (September/October 1986).

————. "901 Interview with Michael Barrickman and Dick Williams." *Nine-O-One Network* (November/December 1986).

————. "Fabulous Thunderbirds: Texas Band Toughs it Out to the Top." *Nine-O-One Network* (September/October 1986).

King, Larry L. "Everybody's Louie." *Harper's* (November 1967).

Landers, A. L. "Latest Styles, Fall and Winter, 1913–1914." *Ell Jay Garments*, Shelbyville, TN, n.d.

Randall, Nancy. "The Men Who Shot Elvis." *Nine-O-One Network* (July/August 1987).

————. "Elvis." *Nine-O-One Network* (July/August 1987).

————. "Where Are They Now?" *Nine-O-One Network* (October 1987).

————. "Survivor's Jimi Jamison." *Nine-O-One Network* (October 1987).

————. "Sexual Harassment." *Nine-O-One Network* (February 1988).

————. "John Kilzer." *Nine-O-One Network* (February 1988).

————. "Elvis—The Memory Lives . . ." *Nine-O-One Network* (December 1987).

Stuart, Bill. "Otis Redding." *Nine-O-One Network* (February 1988).

————. "Wearing the Label." *Nine-O-One Network* (October 1987).

White, Owen P. "Sinners in Dixie." *Collier's* (January 26, 1935).

index